FOUR DECADES OF CHORAL TRAINING

by

Gerald F. Darrow

The Scarecrow Press, Inc.
Metuchen, N. J.   1975

Library of Congress Cataloging in Publication Data

Darrow, Gerald F   1931-
    Four decades of choral training.

    Bibliography: p.
    1. Choral singing. 2. Choirs (Music) I. Title.
MT875.D23   784.9'62   74-31205
ISBN 0-8108-0791-2

PREFACE

This book describes the nature of choral training as it is evidenced in the writings on the subject published in the English language between 1930 and 1970.

Discussions with choral conductors, observations of choral rehearsals and concerts, and a preliminary review of the published writings indicated that there were basic patterns of agreement concerning choral training as well as significant differences of opinion. However, no study could be found which had attempted to determine systematically the patterns which do exist. There is no source to which the choral conductor can go to compare his methods with a compilation of opinions on a particular problem. There is no source which clarifies for the inexperienced conductor the inherently vague terminology which one must use when describing an aural art. Nor is there a source to which conductors can go to find procedures which have been endorsed by a significant sampling of the profession. Further, there is no comprehensive bibliography which lists writings on choral training by John Finley Williamson, F. Melius Christiansen, Robert Shaw, Fred Waring, Father William Finn and others who have made significant contributions to the field of choral teaching and have expressed some of their ideas in published form. The lack of such information led to the undertaking of this study.

Because of the many different kinds of choral ensembles and the varied aspects of the choral conductor's work, it was necessary to limit the present study to certain phases of the choral art in order that the area of coverage be kept to a reasonable size. Therefore, the phases of choral teaching which are considered are: 1) tone quality; 2) breathing; 3) posture; 4) intonation; 5) range; 6) dynamics; and 7) diction. Some phases which are not included are conducting technique, musical style and interpretation, music learning, vocal auditions, and rehearsal planning. In short, the study deals with the concepts and techniques of choral voice training.

There are various sources of evidence which may be considered in studying the nature of any discipline. For example, a study of choral training might be approached through interviews with conductors and teachers, a questionnaire study, observations of rehearsals, or a study of significant conductors and their choirs. However, this study is an analysis of the writings on choral training published in books and periodicals. The publications analyzed were those concerned with the mixed chorus of changed voices; writings on the adolescent voice and the problems of changing voices are not included. No further attempt is made to delineate the level of maturity of the choral voices to which the writings are addressed. In other words, it is assumed that the high school choir may be approached with methods and concepts analogous to the adult or professional choir. An important delimitation of this study is that publications concerned with individual voice training are not included. The sources of data are restricted to writings which are explicitly addressed to choral singing.

This study does not attempt to present various schools of thought in choral training such as those which have developed around certain conductors (e.g., Fred Waring) or educational institutions (e.g., Westminster Choir College). Other writers have focused their attention upon these specific influences. In contrast, the present analysis seeks to establish general patterns of agreement or disagreement among the authors in order that a more comprehensive view of the art may be achieved. In so doing, this study sacrificed the relative importance which each individual author gave to a specific aspect of choral training. However, the value of the annotated bibliography is that the reader may be led to the writings of the authors and thereby study their statements within the appropriate context.

The procedure which was employed in this study consisted of the following steps: 1) compiling a working bibliography of over 950 sources covering the forty-year period, 1930 to 1970; 2) formulating basic questions to be used as criteria for analyzing the sources (e.g., What are the characteristics of good choral tone quality? What are the recommendations for developing good choral tone quality?); 3) reading the sources and extracting the statements; 4) analyzing the statements, developing chapter outlines; and 5) reporting the findings.

Chapters two through eight contain the description of choral training as determined by this study. The Author-Coverage Tables which are placed at the beginning of each chapter show the outlines which were evolved from the collected statements, the number of authors who discussed each sub-topic of the outline, and the page number of this study's presentation of that discussion. Within each chapter, representative statements by the authors are quoted. The number of the writing as it is listed in the bibliography is given in parentheses. If the source is a book, the page number is included.

The author wishes to gratefully acknowledge the generous contribution which the following people have made to this book: Dr. Jack Watson, for his guidance during the study's formative stages; Dr. Thurber Madison and Dr. Hugh Johnson, for their helpful suggestions and criticisms concerning the reporting of the study and the Board of Regents of the University of Wisconsin for their grant of a leave of absence and stipend.

Most deeply, the author is indebted to his wife, Sarah, without whose understanding and support the study could not have been completed.

ACKNOWLEDGMENTS

The author wishes to thank the many writers and publishers whose copyrighted material is reprinted in this book. Although it was impractical to request permission for each of the selections which are quoted, the following sources are gratefully acknowledged:

Amateur Choir Trainer by Henry Coleman. Copyright 1932, Oxford University Press. Used by permission.

Artistic Choral Singing by Harry Robert Wilson. Copyright 1959, G. Schirmer, Inc. Used by permission.

The Art of A Cappella Singing by Smallman and Wilcox. Copyright 1933, Oliver Ditson Company.

The Art of the Choral Conductor by William Finn. Copyright 1939, 1960, Summy-Birchard Company. Used by permission.

Choral Conducting by Archibald Davison. Copyright 1940, Harvard University Press. Used by permission.

"Choral Cultism" by Maynard Klein. Copyright 1947, Theodore Presser Company. Used by permission.

Choral Directing by Wilhelm Ehmann. Translated by G. D. Wiebe. Copyright 1968, Augsburg Publishing House. Used by permission.

"Choral Director as Voice Teacher" by Arnold Jones. Copyright 1960, Allyn and Bacon, Inc. Used by permission.

The Choral Director's Handbook by Walter Ehret. Copyright 1959, Edward E. Marks Music Corporation.

Choral Music and Its Practice by Noble Cain. Copyright 1932, M. Witmark and Sons.

The Chorus and Its Conductor by Max Krone. Copyright 1945, Neil A. Kjos Music Company. Used by permission.

Chorus Master by L. Woodgate. Copyright 1949, Ascherburg, Hopwood and Crew.

A Comprehensive Program of Church Music by Federal Lee Whittlesey. Copyright 1957, by W. L. Jenkins. Used by permission of The Westminster Press.

Conducting Choral Music by Robert Garretson. First Edition. Copyright 1961, Allyn and Bacon, Inc. Used by permission.

Fundamentals of Choral Expression by Hayes Fuhr. Copyright 1944, University of Nebraska Press. Used by permission.

Glee Club and Chorus by Van. A. Christy. Copyright 1940, G. Schirmer, Inc. Used by permission.

Natural Singing and Expressive Conducting by Paul Peterson. Copyright 1955, 1966, John F. Blair. Used by permission.

"Radio: A Teacher of Music" by Fred Waring. Copyright 1944, Music Educators National Conference. Used by permission.

Some Techniques for Choral Success by Lloyd Sunderman. Copyright 1952, Belwin-Mills Publishing Corporation. Used by permission.

Technique and Style in Choral Singing by George Howerton (Catalogue number 0 3867). Copyright © MCMLVII by Carl Fischer, Inc., New York. International Copyright Secured. All rights reserved. Used by permission.

"The Technique of Choral Procedure" by John Finley Wil-

TABLE OF CONTENTS

x

LIST OF TABLES

CHAPTER 1

THE SEARCH FOR PATTERN AND PERSPECTIVE

The forty-year period from 1930 to 1970 represents a grand era in the development of choral technique. Viewed from a more distant perspective, it may indeed prove to be an historical period which had a coherency of purpose and a realization of fulfillment.

The early years of this period were characterized by a search for methods to develop the performance abilities of choral ensembles. A rapid increase in choral activities in high schools and colleges fostered this attention to teaching methods. Earlier choirs had been composed of adult singers in oratorio or other singing societies or, if they included young voices, had been developed by a choir school affiliated with a large church. However, with a new emphasis on education, hundreds of directors flocked to the summer Christiansen Choir Schools, the Westminster Choir School, or clinics and workshops in search of methods which would make their choirs sound like the fine choirs which were touring the country. The issues discussed and demonstrated were usually centered around some aspect of technique such as the distinctive sound of certain choirs, the elements and techniques of ensemble blend, the development of vowel tone, or problems of diction and intonation. However, as this forty-year period came to a close there was evidence that this search for basic techniques had been at least somewhat concluded. No longer was our attention centered upon the distinctive sounds and techniques of our great choirs, but rather upon the performance of the literature which is our rich heritage and the performance practices which are appropriate for that literature. There was a movement away from interest in choral technique for its own sake to the matters of musical style, interpretation and performance practice.

1

SOME HISTORICAL PERSPECTIVES

The choral singing which flourished in the middle decades of the twentieth century was nurtured by basic emphases of our culture. Most notably, the vigorous growth and increased importance of our high schools and colleges provided a favorable environment for the development of ensemble singing by ambitious and inspiring conductor-teachers. A heightened public awareness of the arts and a prolific professional and educational concert life provided the stimulus for ensembles and performances of highest quality. Finally, a wide dissemination of performance practices and literature was made possible through the many concerts and through new developments in mass communication, particularly in the recording industry.

Historically, the forty-year period beginning 1930 was preceded by an era of pioneering efforts with repeated arrivals on the scene of new organizations and conductor-teachers whose work would nourish the full flowering of the choral epoch which was to follow. Indeed, the period from 1900 to 1930 may be referred to as the "Significant Beginnings. " The developments of this era have been described by Kegerreis[1] and it will suffice here to mention only the names: Peter Lutkin, as founder of the Northwestern University A Cappella Choir in 1906, F. Melius Christiansen as founder of the St. Olaf College Choir in 1911 with his extensive American tours beginning in 1920, and John Finley Williamson as founder of the Westminster Choir in 1919 and the subsequent tours which he began in the 1920's. To these one might add the Schola Cantorum of New York, organized by Kurt Schlindler just before World War I, and conducted by Hugh Ross beginning in 1926. Finally, the new interest in choral singing was dramatically demonstrated by the formation of the First National High School Chorus, 300 singers from twenty-four states under the direction of Hollis Dann for the 1928 Chicago Convention of the Music Supervisors National Conference.

The second perceivable historical pattern in our century was the decade of the 1930's. This period was clearly the culmination of the A Cappella Era in American

1.   Richard Kegerreis, "History of the High School A Cappella Choir" (unpublished Ph. D. dissertation, University of Michigan, 1964).

choral singing. F. Melius Christiansen and John Finley
Williamson and their respective choirs reigned as the supreme masters. Williamson developed an avid following
through his Choir School at Dayton, Ithaca and later at
Princeton. Christiansen taught his choral methods to hundreds of followers in his summer choral schools. Both
men toured extensively with their choirs, as did many other
choirs which were influenced by their methods and styles
of singing. Howard Swan describes this era:

> And then along came the 30's and all of a sudden
> things exploded. And all of a sudden we had the
> opportunity to study with master teachers: John
> Smallman, Father Finn, F. Melius Christiansen,
> John Finley Williamson, and Clarence Dickinson.
> And as we became excited and as we developed
> organizations to perform these works, the pub-
> lishers (seeing an extra dollar here and there)
> began to bring out some literature that was worth-
> while. And then the next question: How do you
> practice? How do you rehearse? How do you
> prepare a group to sing this literature? And this
> involved all of the development of choral and vocal
> techniques. And then we found there were differ-
> ences of opinion as far as (capital letters, if you
> please) the KIND OF TONE ... with which these
> pieces should be sung. And so we had workshop
> after workshop and demonstration after demonstra-
> tion on the subject of Choral Tone. But it was
> exciting, particularly when we, for the first time
> perhaps, began to sing pieces of music unaccom-
> panied. Oh, we had to learn how to spell 'a
> cappella, ' but still it was worthwhile. (378)

    At the height of the A Cappella Era there were
striking varieties of choral sound and techniques. Indeed,
there was great interest in choral technique and the methods
used to develop a sound such as the "St. Olaf sound" or the
"Westminster sound. " Pedagogically, some of the most important concepts of the period were the straight-tone singing,
the dark choral tone, the emphasis upon blending of similar
voices, the vowel-is-the-tone concept of singing, and music
education's concern with immature voices and the resultant
soft-tone approach to choral voice training.

    Although many of the concepts of a cappella choral
training which dominated the 1930's continue to the present

time, the decades that followed became a period of diver-
sification and were not dominated by a major concept. The
most significant new element, however, was the professional
choir and its trained and mature voices, most notably the
ensembles directed by Fred Waring and Robert Shaw. This
trained-voice influence was the point of departure for criticisms of the soft-tone approach to choral voice development,
straight-tone singing, and the over-emphasis upon the blending of similar voices.

The professional choir influence also brought to choral singing an expanded repertoire which called attention to
the limitations of the A Cappella Era of the 1930's. The
expanded repertoire included more secular and dramatic
forms which, combined with the popularity of radio broad-
casting and recording, encouraged two significant developments in choral technique: 1) new procedures of diction,
and 2) a more variable tone quality which would be appropriate for the music being performed.

Combined with the vowel-is-the-tone emphasis of
the A Cappella Era, the new attention to choral diction,
which was the special emphasis of Fred Waring and his
radio-broadcasting Pennsylvanians, shaped a major peda-
gogical approach in our profession. It may appropriately
be called the diction approach to choral training.

The second development, an emphasis upon a more
variable tone quality, went hand-in-hand with the expanded
repertoire and expertise of interpretation which was most
eloquently demonstrated by Robert Shaw and his professional
Chorale. This variable tone quality was basically achieved
through an interpretative approach to choral training which
developed various tone qualities (in this context they were
frequently referred to as tone colors) by emphasizing the
imaginative and emotional response of the singers to the
expressive and dramatic qualities of the text and music.

PATTERNS OF TECHNIQUE

Perhaps the most challenging part of this study was
the search for an organizational framework which would be
appropriate for the varied concepts and complex statements
concerning the development of choral technique, especially
in the area of tone quality. Here all the semantic problems and hidden intrigues of the vocal art come to our

attention. However, a study of the authors' statements
indicates four basic ways in which their recommendations
for developing vocal technique were approached and suggests that each statement could be better understood by
analyzing it from the point of view of these four approaches:

1. through concept of tone
   (mental concepts, imagination, imitation, emotion
   and expressive intent)

2. through resonance sensations
   (placement, chest resonance, head resonance,
   height, deep-set, forward tone)

3. through concern with the physical structure of the
   resonators
   (freedom from tension, position and control of the
   physical structure of the resonators)

4. through vowel study.

Not only do these four basic groupings provide a satisfactory
organizational plan for discussing and presenting the authors'
statements, but they are also a great aid in understanding
the inherent ambiguities involved in descriptions of this aural
art. The following statements will illustrate how these four
factors may be employed:

> The vowel ee (vowel) aids in establishing a bright
> quality (concept) through a high-arched resonance (reso-
> nance sensation) and raised soft-palate (physical struc-
> ture).

> The vowel oh (vowel) opens the throat (physical
> structure) and adds depth (resonance sensation) and
> richness (concept) to the tone.

A study of these statements indicates the usefulness
of this four-point framework in comparing the methods used
by different conductors. Indeed, it can be shown how the
teacher who emphasized the vowel, its modifications and
pronunciation in his teaching was working for goals similar
to those of the teacher whose terminology stressed concepts
of tone, tone color and expressive qualities, or the one who
emphasized voice placement through the imagery of resonance
sensation. Further, this study documents the concomitance
of at least some of these factors so that a reader may see

opportunities to vary his approach to rehearsal problems by
changing the terminology with which he analyzes the problem and prescribes solutions. The following table indicates
the concomitance of the four approaches:

Concept of Tone	Resonance Sensations	Physiological Factors	Vowel
bright ringing	> forward, high-arched >	raised soft palate	> ee ay
mellow dark	> deep-set >	open throat	> oh oo

The present study shows the extent to which the art
of choral teaching may be analyzed. This inventory of the
choral training process shows that a wide range of psychological and physiological factors may be considered relevant
to some phase of singing. Through selection and emphasis
of particular factors and terminology the individual conductor
formulates his approach to the art. This study suggests
that the vocal training of the choir has been approached in
three basic ways: 1) the interpretative approach, 2) the
diction approach, and 3) the voice approach.

The interpretative approach to choral training derives its terminology from the music and the text which is
being sung. Tonal ideals are expressed in terms of tone-
color, timbre, mood descriptions, and other interpretative
qualities such as lyric, dramatic, sombre, intense, and
subjective. The expressive, imaginative, and communicative
responses of the singer are emphasized.

The diction approach to choral training derives its
terminology and procedures from a study of diction. Tonal
ideals are expressed in terms of vowel qualities, vowel
colors, or vowel placement. The desired tone quality may
be patterned after a particular vowel. Uniformity of vowels,
phonetic study, and vowel modifications are emphasized.
This approach has been widely used by choral conductors
because the terminology concerned with diction can be understood and communicated to a group more objectively than
the terminology of the other approaches.

The voice approach to choral training derives its
terminology and procedure from a study of voice production.
Tonal ideals are expressed in terms such as head tone,

chest tone, forward resonance, and depth of resonance. Freedom from tension, proper breathing, an open throat, and resonance placement are some of the points of emphasis. The voice approach is usually employed by those choral conductors who are also accomplished singers and/or voice teachers.

CHAPTER 2

TONE QUALITY

All sounds possess four psychological characteristics which are identified as pitch, loudness, time, and quality; they represent the frequency, amplitude or intensity, duration, and form of the sound wave. This fourth factor, the quality or form of the sound wave, is the topic of this chapter. According to Webster, quality is that property of a tone which may distinguish it from another tone having the same pitch, loudness and duration. It is the identifying character of the sound. From a physical point of view, tone quality is concerned with the number, distribution, and intensity of partials or overtones.

The practicing musician, however, does not limit himself to the psychologist's or acoustician's analysis of tone when he discusses his concepts of tone quality and his procedures for its development. For example, Bartholomew gives the following definition of tone quality:

> Thus we can sum up by saying that good tone quality is characterized by the vibrato, or life, or warmth; by the low formant, or 'resonance,' or roundness, or sonority; and by the high formant, or 'ring,' or shimmer; and is in addition capable of producing a powerful tone. (10, p. 83)

This definition of tone quality includes intensity and vibrato (variation of pitch, intensity, and timbre) as well as overtones or partials. It is an indication of the varying concepts of tone quality which were found in the writings analyzed. Further evidence of this variation may be found in the adjective descriptions of good choral tone quality presented in Table 2.

The terms tone quality, tone color, resonance, and timbre are sometimes used interchangeably. They refer

8

TABLE 1

Author-Coverage Table for Tone Quality Showing the
Chapter Outline Which Was Evolved from the Data,
the Number of Authors Who Discussed Each Sub-Topic
of the Outline, and the Page Number of This Study's
Presentation of the Data. 198 Authors are Represented

			No. of Authors	Page
I.	Characteristics of choral tone quality			
	A.	Adjective descriptions of tone quality	128	10
	B.	Vibrato as a characteristic of tone quality	39	14
	C.	Blend as a characteristic of tone quality	102	17
II.	Recommendations for developing choral tone quality			
	A.	Through concept of tone		
		1. Mental concept and imagination	60	19
		2. Aural training and imitation	84	22
		3. Emotion and expressive intent	49	24
		4. Quality concepts and concomitant factors	70	28
		5. Quality concepts as a factor in blend	67	28
	B.	Through resonance senation		
		1. Descriptions of resonance sensation	90	31
		2. Resonance sensation and concomitant factors	54	33
		3. Humming as a technique in vocal training	51	33
	C.	Through concern with the physical structure of the resonators		
		1. Freedom from tension	80	36
		2. Freedom from tension and concomitant factors	49	37
		3. Position and control of the physical structure of the resonators	81	39

(directly or indirectly) to the identifying character of the sound. However, as will be seen in this chapter, some authors designate a specific or limited meaning for these terms. A tabulation of the authors' use of them in reference to choral tone reveals the following results:

	Number of Authors
Tone quality	129
Tone color	81
Resonance	55
Timbre	17

CHARACTERISTICS OF GOOD CHORAL TONE QUALITY

Adjective Descriptions

Many problems are encountered in formulating verbal descriptions of an art form; indeed, the descriptions of an aural art present almost insurmountable semantic difficulties. The adjectives employed are mostly borrowed from the visual and other arts, where color, texture, dimension, shape, and volume are visible or tactile properties. These borrowed adjectives include such terms as bright, dark, round, deep, pointed, velvety, straight, broad, and full. A study of this kind can not hope to indicate or even suggest all of the meanings which these adjectives imply.

As reported in Table 1, adjective descriptions of good choral tone quality were extracted from the writings

of 128 authors. A list of these adjectives is presented in
Table 2. The various meanings which may have been attached to the adjectives make it difficult to classify them
into definite groupings; however, the following eleven groupings were considered a reasonable means of presentation:
1) color, 2) timbre, 3) resonance, 4) volume, 5) density,
6) high overtone formant, 8) low overtone formant, 8) blend,
9) vibrato, 10) physical effort, and 11) interpretative potential.

There were at least two directions in which the adjective list could have been greatly expanded, namely, the
inclusion of less desirable qualities and mood descriptions.
Normally, undesirable qualities such as breathy, hollow,
hard, hushed, muffled, shallow, hooty, dull, strident, and
white were not included, although they appeared in the
writings either as faulty qualities or qualities to be sought
for a special effect. Various mood descriptions were used
to describe tone quality: a desired tone may be mournful,
gay, sombre, sad, tranquil, pensive, bold, or bitter. This
list of adjectives could be nearly endless, but those reported
in Table 2 were the ones considered most significant because of the frequency of their appearance in the writings.

Comprehensive Descriptions. Few authors give a
description of choral tone quality which could have been re-
garded as comprehensive. The complexity of such descriptive efforts, as evidenced in Table 2, and the need for a
variable tone quality for interpretative purposes are perhaps
the reasons for the lack of comprehensive statements.

Nitsche says of good tone, "... generally defined, it
is full, free, and resonant." (278). Rowles uses the adjectives rounded, resonant" smooth, unified, light, and floating
to describe his tonal ideal (344). "Good tone must be characterized by the essential qualities of resonance, purity,
and freedom from restriction," according to Leeder and
Haynie (233, p. 72). Vennard gives two opposite essentials
of good tone: freedom and intensity or maturity (411).
Coleman's adjective usage includes flowing, smooth, easy,
natural, uniform, even, bright, ringing, and full (63 and
66).

Christy, Cleall, Evanson, Finn, Garretson, Howerton, Krone, Manson, and Wilson are among the writers
whose descriptions of choral tone quality employ such terms
as light, bright, or brilliant on the one hand, and dark,

TABLE 2

Adjective Descriptions of Good Choral Tone Quality Presented
in Possible Groupings of the Attributes of Tone Quality

Attributes of tone quality	Possible adjective descriptions
1. Color	- bright, brilliant, light, lustrous, sparkling, colored, dark, warm, rich
2. Timbre	- flute-like, organ-like, reed-like, horn-like, string-like, natural, child-like, mature
3. Resonance	- chest, head, nasal, covered, yawny, focused, projected, ringing, deep, deep-set, high, forward, full-bodied
4. Volume	- big, broad, deep, full, large, round, thick, sonorous, small, thin
5. Density	- clear, concentrated, metallic, pointed, precise, intense, mellow, velvety, silken
6. High overtone formant	- bright, sparkling, ringing, pointed, carrying quality
7. Low overtone formant	- deep, broad, round, sonorous, warm, full, mellow, dark
8. Blend	- blended, homogeneous, uniform, unified
9. Vibrato	- even, smooth, steady, straight, spinning, pulsating
10. Physical effort	- easy, effortless, free, natural, relaxed, floating, buoyant, firm, strenuous, intense
11. Interpretative potential	- appropriate, expressive, emotional, flexible, variable, controlled, consistent, objective, subjective, lyric, dramatic

mellow, warm, and full on the other. Wilson expresses this
dichotomy in this statement: "Beautiful singing tone must
have, besides fullness and roundness, 'top' or focus. This
quality ... adds brightness, sparkle and bell-like quality to
the tone" (456). Kortkamp, in discussing Bartholomew's
definition of good voice quality, refers to the high and low
formants of overtones in the definition as the "sending" and
"blending" qualities of the tone (215, p. 52). Another expression of this dichotomy is "forward resonance" in combination with qualities of depth, roundness, or full-bodied
resonance.

Borchers (21), Kettring (206) and Williamson (434)
discuss choral tone quality in terms of the structure of the
sound from the bass to soprano. Williamson's description is:

> ... the bass section is the basic element of the
> choir. The voices between the bass and first so-
> prano impart rich tone-colors to the ensemble,
> while the first soprano brings the whole structure
> to a focus through the shimmering clarity of a pure,
> crystal-clear thread of tone (434).

He also describes the choral tone quality as "sounds that are
rich and colorful" and refers to the "architectural structure"
as a "tapestry of tone" (439 and 443).

The Need for Variety of Tone Quality. In 1939, statements emphasizing the need for variety of tone quality began
appearing in the writings. These statements frequently accompanied criticisms of the monotonous, stereotyped, and inflexible tone quality produced by some choirs. Howerton, in
1939, charged that "Russian liturgical anthems, Negro spirit-
uals, sixteenth century motets, Bach chorales, twentieth century tone poems, Elizabethan madrigals are all sung with the
same tone color ..." (175). In 1944, he added, "One of the
greatest deficiencies in the singing of the average choral
group is a lack of versatility in tone production" (178, p. 28).
The same year, Waring declared:

> ... we also sing in the dramatic or emotional
> range--using choral tone that is bright or dark,
> mellow or harsh, strident or subdued, according
> to the demand of the song.... I rather doubt that
> there is any such thing as absolute or pure beauty
> in choral tone. It can have only dramatic integ-
> rity, and it is beautiful only when it actually says

what it is trying to say (418).

Borchers, also in 1944, noted that the range of choral expression was being severely limited by overzealous attention to blend and solidarity of tone (21). In 1945, Shaw warned:

> Many choirs, I find, make the mistake of trying to develop a single, fixed color of their own, as a sort of hallmark. I think it is better to avoid any fixed norm and to try for as great a variety of color as possible (353).

He further advised, "... avoid the cardinal sins of choral singing--fixed, inflexible (and therefore monotonous) tone quality; undramatic neglect of the lyrics; and flabby rhythm" (Ibid.). Klein, in 1957, asked for a "quality that is appropriate to the music sung, rather than establishing a stereotyped quality that makes every composition sound the same" (212). In 1959, Ehret acknowledged the need for variety of tone quality, criticizing "the monochromatic renderings so common to choral performances" (114, p. 18). According to Wilson, some choirs sound "like a pipe organ with only one stop or registration" (450, p. 137).

Vibrato as a Characteristic

As reported in Table 1, thirty-nine authors discuss the vibrato as a characteristic of choral tone quality. Any deviation of pitch, intensity, or quality in ensemble singing may destroy the homogeneity of the sound. The focal point of the problem is the degree of deviation allowed and the terminology used to describe or identify it. There is agreement among the authors that a voice with a "tremolo" or excessive wobble is undesirable in ensemble singing. In regard to vibrato, however, there are conflicting opinions and an apparent misunderstanding of the various viewpoints.

Discussions of vibrato and straight-tone singing have always centered around the St. Olaf Choir and its founder, F. Melius Christiansen. The writings of Christiansen, Goetz (who reported the proceedings of the summer Christiansen Choral Schools), and Bergman (Christiansen's biographer) repeatedly refer to tremolo and vibrato as negative choral attributes and the "straight" tone as the ideal. Christiansen states that "the vibrato voices are the greatest menace we

have to contend with in our choir work.... We must have
straight voices, ..." (51). Goetz quotes Christiansen at a
round table discussion during a summer school: "Only
straight-line voices should be chosen. There is a great difference between solo and ensemble.... There must be no
tremolo or vibrato in a cappella singing, not a single 'wobble'" (137). Bergman says that foremost among Christiansen's thinking was that "the voice must be straight" (15, p.
145).

Smallman and Wilcox state that the "straight-line tone"
is the ideal tone for choral singing and condemn the tremolo
but do not mention vibrato. They ask for "simple purity
without variation of any kind from the beginning to end ...
an even, unwavering, spinning tone ..." (358, p. 193). According to Krone, "The ability to sing in tune and to sing a
'straight' tone without a tremolo or distinctive vibrato is essential" (225, p. 19). He also says:

> A certain amount of vibrato is undoubtedly desira-
> ble in a solo voice to give it individual color, but
> the owner of such a voice is of little value in an
> ensemble unless he is willing to subdue himself
> (Ibid., p. 80).

The published writings show that F. Melius Christiansen's statements authenticate the "straight" tone terminology
which has been used and also show that vibrato as well as
tremolo are considered undesirable characteristics of choral
tone quality. However, his son, Olaf Christiansen, made the
following statement in 1965:

> You have all heard of the term straight tone used
> in describing certain choirs--especially here in the
> midwest. What might sound like a straight tone is
> the result of listening to each other, thus getting
> in tune--making a pure unison. All individual
> voices should have a natural vibrato, but, by limit-
> ing the extent of deviation above and below the cen-
> tral pitch, it is possible to make a whole section-
> tone sound like a single big voice (53).

He further states, "There is no such thing as a
straight tone among well-trained singers. I would not have
a STRAIGHT voice in my a cappella choir, but I demand
trained voices, super-trained singers" (Ibid.).

Other authors, while frequently acknowledging the problems of tremolo or excessive vibrato in ensemble singing, state that the vibrato is a favorable characteristic of choral tone quality. Their viewpoints are summarized in the following statements:

A normal vibrato is part and parcel of the free voice; it will blend, and it is not to be avoided anywhere (King 208).

The vibrato is essential in good tone quality; ... (Archie Jones 191, p. 33).

Great choral leaders do not want a "bleached" tone. They want the singer to have personality in his voice (Angell 3).

Do not confuse tremolo with vibrato, which is perfectly acceptable and in many cases desirable (Ehret 114, p. 35).

Beware of being known as a "straight" toner, ... (Klein 212).

A resonant, ringing quality actually depends upon a normal vibrato (Wilson 456).

... the practice of many contemporary [1945] choral conductors of inducing their choristers to use the so-called "straight tone" (a tone repressed to eliminate the natural vibrato) is causing permanent harm to the voices ...
     The true vibrato does not prevent the desired blend (Wilcox 429).

The vibrato is a fundamental characteristic of the human voice....
     Some successful choral directors have solved the problem by deliberating cultivating a so-called "straight" tone without any vibrato.... It is ... infinitely preferable to singing with excessive vibrato. Excellent as the choirs may be when they sing with this "straight" tone, however, they could sound even better if the voices possessed that full richness of tone that comes from correct, natural singing with full body coordination. In such singing there is always a vibrato that is pleasing because

it is almost unnoticeable, ... (Howes 181).

A study of the publication dates of the writings concerning the vibrato in choral singing reveal two significant
points: 1) Since 1945, no author has recommended straight-
tone choral singing, and 2) Since 1945, there have been frequent criticisms of straight-tone singing and statements favor-
ing the use of vibrato.

Blend as a Characteristic

As reported in Table 1, 102 authors discuss the blend
of choral tone quality. In any artistic group performance
there is a need for some degree of unity. In choral singing,
this unity is needed in various phases of the performance,
the basic ones being pitch, balance of dynamics, diction, and
tone quality. This unity of ensemble with regard to tone
quality results in a characteristic of the sound identified as
blend. The authors sometimes use the terms blend, uniformity, and homogeneity of tone quality as being nearly sy-
nonymous:

> Blend refers to the uniformity of the quality of tone
> within and between voice sections; ... (Wilson 450,
> p. 223).

> Homogeneity is a quality of vocal excellence which
> the choirmaster must achieve and maintain, ...
> (Finn 122, p. 70).

> ... without homogeneous tone there cannot be ef-
> fective singing (Davison 85, p. 57).

> Basic tonal blend is achieved when the individual
> tonal characteristics of each voice are fused into
> one sound (Ehret 114, p. 34).

> Good tone depends on uniformity. The singers
> must sound alike (Rodby 335).

> In order for a choir to be tonally effective, it must
> possess uniformity of good tone quality (Sunderman
> 376, p. 24).

As with the problem of vibrato, the focal point of the
problem of blend is upon the degree of uniformity which is

needed. Philips declares that "in all work in tone-production, uniformity is a vice ... the ensemble gains in vitality
by being made up of individual tone of varying quality" (299,
p. 103). Borchers asserts: "It is a fetish with some organizations to develop a certain type of uniform tone quality
throughout the chorus in order to achieve solidarity and
blend" (19). Bellows agrees that "the director should not insist on the same quality of tone from all voices" (12). "Individual voices may differ as much as they may; in the group
they will blend, if correctly produced," according to Archie
Jones (191, p. 30). Finn writes: "Differences in quality do
not usually mar the blend of any choral line. On the contrary, they tend to enhance its musical value" (122, p. 167).
Sateren agrees and warns that "a choir of homogeneous quality will sound monotonous. It is a mistake to confuse
blended voices of heterogeneous quality with homogeneity"
(347, p. 7).

Waring expresses the following viewpoint:

> It is by no means the ideal of the fine choral lead-
> er to have a chorus composed of voices as identical
> as eggs. In fact, just the opposite is the ideal.
> It is this which gives 'character' to the chorus, if
> the voices are uniformly of high quality (421).

The subsequent section, "Recommendations for Developing Choral Tone Quality," includes coverage of the three
most frequently discussed approaches to the development of
blend: 1) aural training and imitation, 2) quality concepts as
a factor in blend, and 3) uniformity of vowels for blend.

RECOMMENDATIONS FOR DEVELOPING
CHORAL TONE QUALITY

A study of the recommendations for the development
of choral tone quality indicates four basic ways in which the
problem is considered:

1. Through concept of tone.
2. Through resonance sensation.
3. Through concern with the physical structure.
4. Through vowel study.

The data are organized in these four basic sections.
It should be stressed that this is not an attempt to determine

separate "approaches" or "methods" but rather an effort to
organize and present the various recommendations and search
for relationships which exist among the factors involved.

Concept of Tone

The factors involved with concept of tone are: 1)
mental concepts and imagination, 2) aural training and imitation, 3) emotion and expressive intent, 4) quality concepts
and concomitant factors, and 5) quality concepts as factors
in blend.

For the purposes of this presentation, the mental,
aural, and/or conceptual aspects of what is sometimes referred to as "tonal imagery" are included in this section.
The physical aspects of imagery, such as tone placement,
head resonance, forward resonance, and "singing in the
mask," are considered in the section on resonance sensations.

Mental Concepts and Imagination. The role of proper
concepts of tone and imagination as factors in the development of good choral tone quality was acknowledged by sixty
of the authors analyzed. Although the authors agree that the
singers should develop proper concepts, this aspect of vocal
training yields a divergency of views. The disagreement is
concerned with the extent to which a preconceived concept of
tone quality should influence the vocal development of an individual or an ensemble. Arnold Jones warns:

> So the choral conductor can have no preconceived
> idea of what the individual or the choral tone should
> be, but merely teach correct tone production and
> allow the voice to emerge naturally, ...
> The choral director has no right to superimpose
> his idea of tone upon an individual or a chorus.
> To do so is to work from tone quality backward in-
> to tone production (193).

Ehmann agrees with Jones:

> One should never try to force a preconceived sound
> from a singer. If every pot, jar, or tumbler has
> its own unique timbre, then it is certainly true that
> every human body has its own unique timbre (112,
> p. 33).

Perhaps the issue is the competence and experience of the choral conductor and the type of ensemble he plans to develop. Garretson emphasizes that "it is essential that the director develop his concept of tone through private voice study and by listening to numerous choral recordings, and then strive toward that goal" (130, p. 76). Wilson suggests that "the safest thing to do in building tone is to use the great vocalists as models" (449).

Draper's viewpoint of the role of preconceived concepts is expressed in his contention that "before the director can audition, he must have a good mental concept as well as a tonal picture of what he expects from the group as far as basic color is concerned" (97). He adds that "through the audition the director must decide on balance and uniformity of tone color from each section." Holley says that "the choral leader adapts the shadings of color and quality of his mental tonal picture to the varying and unpredictable human-voice material he happens to work with at a given time" (168). Finn declares: "It is impossible to lead singers to the attainment of vocal distinction unless the leader himself be a master-judge of timbres" (122, p. 39). According to Veld, "A thoroughly qualified choral conductor will require: ... a mental concept of tone and its subsequent physical adjustment, ..." (408). Earlier, he had stated, "The tone of the singer depends primarily upon his mental concept, ... We sing only as we think" (407).

Perhaps the writers assume the responsibility of cor-rect tone concepts as they advise:

> Urge that a more definite mental idea of the desired tone be maintained when approaching the tones (Cain 37, p. 83).

> An ideal of tone quality must be established, ... (Hammermeyer 150).

> The singer should try constantly to remember that all singing tone is a matter first of mental concept (Jones, Rhea and Rhea 192, p. 6).

> The choral director is successful if he can establish a concept in the mind of the student that enables him to utilize the singing act at its greatest capacity (MENC 275, p. 40).

> The mental concept is the only guarantee of suc-
> cess (Sunderman 376, p. 13).

> The essential thing is to implant firmly in their
> minds the 'tone pattern'--to give them the concept,
> ... (Fuhr 128, p. 54).

> Even before he begins to read the text or sing the
> song, the student must have a proper conception of
> the tone he is going to produce (Peterson 295, p.
> 26).

> Young singers should have a mental concept of the
> vowels they are to produce and a sensation of
> where they feel the resonance of the tone (Mack
> 246).

The role of imagination in developing choral tone
quality is emphasized by Waring:

> I believe that choral tone is immensely more re-
> sponsible to imagination than most conductors have
> realized, and that choral groups in the main have
> worked almost solely in the range of dynamics and
> pitch and not nearly enough in the range of drama
> (418).

Hillis makes the following recommendation: "The previsual-
ization of the color of the required sound must be intense,
and you must somehow make yourself capable of producing
that required color anywhere in your vocal range" (162).
Pitts comments on groups which have a good quality of tone
but "color or feeling is missing. This can only be secured
through developing the imagination of the singer" (303). Kortkamp would have us

> ... simply imagine we will hear our voices the way
> we want them to sound--simply picture in our minds
> the kind of "tone" we want to produce and let the
> unconscious adjustments take care of themselves--
> which they will (221).

Fischer advises, "Imagination is essential in singing to por-
tray in tone whatever meaning is inherent in the text and
music" (126). Shields recommends, "If we will just appeal
to the imagination, we will find an abundance of tone color
coming to our aid" (354).

Coleman, Howes, Williamson, Finn, Fuhr, and Bach suggest that the beauty of the music is transferred to the tone quality. Coleman proposes that "the best way of producing beautiful tone is by singing beautiful tunes" (63, p. 30). Williamson is emphatic about his recommendations:

> If the singer or the conductor wishes to have a beautiful quality of tone in his choir no matter what the age of the group is, he can very easily achieve this desire. All that he needs to do is to make of each phrase a legato line in which every sound is present in its relative value (439).

Finn suggests, "Another useful device for the promoting of warmth and breadth of tone is the employment of favorite phrases from the repertoire which the singers have been studying" (122, p. 66). Bach (6) and Fuhr (128, p. 58) recommend Palestrina motets, and Howes (179) recommends plainsong as being "conducive to the production of beautiful vocal sounds."

Aural Training and Imitation. The role of aural training and imitation in the development of choral tone quality embraces the factors of listening for concepts of tone, imitation as a teaching technique, and listening as a factor in achieving choral blend. Eighty-four of the analyzed authors express views concerning this aspect of choral training.

The role of tonal concepts was discussed in the preceding section of this chapter; hearing good singing plays an important part in the development of these concepts. Vandre claims that "all good singing begins with the ear ... " (405, p. 1). Smallman and Wilcox state, "In all study of singing, the ear must be the constant guide and supreme judge" (358, p. 11). Steckel makes a similar statement (364) and Coleman declares, "Soft singing and listening to each other will do more than anything to induce correct tone" (66, p. 57).

In reference to listening to the singing of the teacher, other students, and recording and radio artists, Van Bodegraven and Wilson say:

> Such practice can be called teaching by imitation or it can be thought of as building correct concepts. If the students are encouraged to imitate someone's tone, certain dangers must be guarded against. The characteristics of freedom, reso-

nance, and expressiveness are to be imitated but
not the timbre or tone quality itself (404, p. 80).

Williamson also warns, "I believe that the conductor should
... never sing in such a way that his group will imitate him
and thus destroy the expression of the individual" (447). Dunham agrees: "Attempts to imitate an ideal sound are doomed
to dismal failure" (101). Peterson comments that "there is
no beauty in imitation" (295, p. 101). Of the authors who
discuss the role of imitation in the development of choral
tone quality, the majority do not share the preceding authors'
reservations:

> The conductor should have a good voice and know
> how to use it.... The conductor's tone will be
> imitated, especially by immature singers (Vennard
> 411).

> The wonderful power of imitation, characteristic of
> most children and young folk should be made use
> of ... (Wodell 464).

> ... what I do first is to mimic any less-than-de-
> sirable tone, immediately following it up, in con-
> trast, with the tone I want.... I have had very
> good results from this method of imitation, con-
> scious exaggeration of faults, corrective drills, and
> final improvement (Wilhousky 431).

> Showing them by example ... is worth more than
> any amount of discussion (Evanson 120).

> Sound pedagogy utilizes this tendency by proposing
> good examples to be copied ... (Finn 122, p. 65).

> The director should demonstrate the kind of tone
> he desires (Becker 13).

> The choirmaster should be able to illustrate, by
> singing, exactly what effect is required from the
> singers, from soprano to bass (Woodgate 466, p.
> 2).

The role which imitation plays in the development of
ensemble blend is much more subtle. The imitative process
becomes absorbed in a broader and more comprehensive
technique, that of careful listening in order that a homogene-

ous quality can be achieved. The authors who make statements concerning the need for careful listening as a requirement for blending the tone quality of the ensemble recommend a variety of techniques which encourage better listening. The recommended techniques are:

1. Unison singing and/or section rehearsals.
2. Two-part and three-part singing.
3. Unaccompanied singing.
4. Humming.
5. Sustaining chords or singing chordal music.
6. Soft singing.
7. Matching and imitating the tone quality of pairs,
   rows, sections, a model singer, or quartet.
8. Grouping the singers in quartets, circles, "scrambled," or changing the positions of sections.
9. Working with a tape recorder.

Emotion and Expressive Intent. The changes of the
quality of the speaking voice as it reflects the mood and
meaning of what we say may be observed during the course
of most normal conversations and, in a more obvious way,
by observing dramatic productions on the stage or through
the mass media. Archie Jones points out this versatility of
the voice:

> But a voice can produce many timbres. It can
> laugh and weep; it can wail and shriek; it can yell,
> or it can groan. Always it is human; always it is
> different in timbre, guided by the sentient and spir-
> itual being whose organ it is (191, p. 19).

The choral conductor who can elicit this inherent versatility of the voice will have found a key factor in the development of appropriate tone quality for the variable expressive demands of the literature. Forty-nine authors make
statements concerning the role of emotion and expressive intent in the development of choral tone quality. The following
are representative:

> It will be seen at once that the tone-colour of the
> voices will be different according to the emotion
> indicated (Coleman 63, p. 35).

> Color is improved by regarding the works to be
> performed as dramatic expressions which impart
> a story, a mood, and thoughtful significance in ad-

dition to the sensation of tone (Shaw 353).

Every feeling he has about the music colors the tone as he sings (Rieder 325).

If there is no emotional reaction, there is poor tone quality (Van Bodegraven and Wilson 404, p. 81).

Lead them to a proper interpretation and good tone will come automatically (Rowles 344).

... tone quality ... may ... be markedly improved by placing emphasis on the expressive, communicative aspect of singing (Craig 72).

Sense the emotional context of the phrase as you read the text during inhalation, and give expression to the resulting emotion through voice, eyes and face ... (Dann 76).

... the tone colors will change as the emotions vary.
   No vowel sound can be correctly produced unless it carries the color of the mood that the composer felt when he created the music (Williamson 448 and 441).

Singers must and can readily learn to put themselves literally in the control of the song-mood, thus relinquishing to the subconscious the task of selecting the appropriate vocal elements (Finn 122, p. 106).

   Table 3 shows that twenty authors use the term "tone color" when discussing the emotional qualities of the choral tone. Becker says that "by tone color is meant the voice quality appropriate to the sentiment of the words" (13). Pitts states, "Tone color comes only through the feeling and imagination ..." (313). Coleman agrees: "'Tone-colour' is the character of the voice which is automatically assumed when the singer experiences an emotion" (66, p. 49). According to Howerton, "By the use of color we mean the transference to the tone of the emotional or descriptive quality indicated by the meaning of the word" (178, p. 50). Ehret suggests a similar meaning: "Appropriate tone color exists when the quality and character of the voice emotionally reflects the sentiment of the words and the expressiveness of the music" (114, p. 47).

TABLE 3

Concepts of Choral Tone Quality and Concomitant Factors; The
Number of Authors Recorded for Each Factor in Parentheses

<u>Bright</u> or <u>brilliant</u> - (24)
    Vowel - <u>ee</u> (18), <u>ay</u> (10), <u>ah</u> (4)
    Resonance sensation - forward (7), height-head (4),
        nasal resonance (1)
    Physical factor - high palate (2), open mouth (1),
        raised upper lip (2)

<u>Clarity</u> and <u>precision</u> - (4)
    Vowel - <u>ee</u> (3)
    Resonance sensation - forward (1)

<u>Colored</u> - (30)
    Vowel - <u>oh</u> (5), through vowel modification (5), <u>oo</u> (1)
    Resonance sensation - depth-low (2), forward (1)
    Physical factor - small mouth opening (1)
    Concomitant concept - from emotions (20), from
        imagination (8), vibrato (3), covered (2), darkened
        (1), rich (1)

<u>Dark</u> - (21)
    Vowel - <u>oo</u> (13), <u>oh</u> (9), <u>aw</u> (7), <u>ah</u> (4)
    Resonance sensation - depth-low (2)
    Physical factor - lowered jaw (3), open throat (1)
    Concomitant concept - sombre (3), heavy (2), rich
        (2), mature (1), covered (1), colored (1)

<u>Floating</u>, <u>light</u>, or <u>buoyant</u> - (9)
    Vowel - <u>oo</u> (4), <u>oh</u> (1)
    Resonance sensation - use downward vocalization (5),
        forward (3), head-height (2)

<u>Full</u> - (13)
    Vowel - <u>aw</u> (6), <u>oh</u> (4), <u>ah</u> (4), <u>oo</u> (1)
    Resonance sensation - depth-low (1)
    Physical factor - open throat (3), low jaw (1)
    Concomitant concept - rounded (3), mellow (1), warm
        (1), heavy (1), subjective (1)

<u>Intense</u> - (3)
    Vowel - <u>ee</u> (1)
    Resonance sensation - forward (2)

Mature - (2)
>   Resonance sensation - depth-low (1)
>   Concomitant concept - dark (1), round (1)

Mellow - (6)
>   Vowel - oo (5), oh (2), ah (1)
>   Resonance sensation - depth-low (3)
>   Physical factor - open throat (3)
>   Concomitant concept - blended (2), rich (1), warm (1),
>   full (1)

Pointed - (2)
>   Vowel - ee (2)

Projection and carrying power - (8)
>   Vowel - ee (5)
>   Resonance sensation - forward (4)

Rich - (7)
>   Vowel - oh (2), oo (2), ah (1)
>   Resonance sensation - depth-low (2)
>   Physical factor - open throat (2)
>   Concomitant concept - dark (2), mellow (1), warm (1)

Ringing - (12)
>   Vowel - ee (7), ay (4), ah (1)
>   Resonance sensation - forward (7), nasal resonance
>   (1), height-head (1)

Round - (12)
>   Vowel - oh (6), ah (4), oo (4), aw (2)
>   Resonance sensation - depth-low (2)
>   Physical factor - open throat (1), open mouth (2)
>   Concomitant concept - full (3), mature (1), subjective
>   (1)

Subjective - (4)
>   Vowel - as in "lot" (1)
>   Physical factor - relaxed jaw (1)
>   Concomitant concept - expressive (4), full (1), round
>   (1), somewhat covered (1)

Vibrant - (3)
>   Resonance sensation - humming (1)
>   Physical factor - narrow throat (1)
>   Concomitant concept - metallic (1), dramatic (1)

TABLE 3 (continued)

Warm - (4)
Vowel - <u>oo</u> (1), <u>oh</u> (1), <u>ah</u> (1)
Resonance sensation - upward vocalization (1), low
    voice (1), humming (1)
Physical factor - open throat (1)
Concomitant concept - rich (1), mellow (1), full (1)

Quality Concepts and Concomitant Factors. The list
of adjective descriptions of good choral tone quality presented
in Table 2, is an indication of the variety of tonal concepts
held by the contributing authors. Although the improbability
of precise meanings and definitions for these adjectives is
recognized, there are instances in which authors state a
specific concomitant relationship between an adjective description of tone quality and a particular vowel, resonance
sensation, physical factor, or another adjective. For example, Evanson proposes that "for the brightest color, <u>ee</u> is
the best vowel ... The darkest vowels are <u>o</u> and <u>oo</u> ..."
(120). Christy recommends that "<u>ā</u> and <u>ĕ</u> are best for developing brilliance and pronounced head resonance" (58, p.
50). According to Grace, <u>aw</u> develops fullness (140, p. 12).

By tabulating those statements where concomitant relationships are established, the meaning and use of the terms
are at least somewhat clarified and the relationships between
concepts of tone, resonance sensations, physical factors, and
vowels are made more precise. Such a tabulation is reported in Table 3, in which seventy authors are represented.

Quality Concepts as a Factor in Blend. The role of
quality concepts in developing choral blend received the attention of sixty-seven authors.

Finn, J. W. Jones, Wilson, Cleall, and Peterson emphasize that a major factor in developing the blend of the
choral ensemble is the use of lyric voices or a lyric style
of singing. Peterson calls it "Bel Canto style" (295, p. 102).
Wilson says that after this lyric quality has been attained,
the quality should be enriched with a rounder, fuller resonance. He criticizes those who continuously use the light,
lyric quality for its ease of blending and do not develop a
full, vigorous tone (450, p. 229; also 460). Finn supports

the basically lyric approach to ensemble tone, adding:

> Voices of the lighter colors cannot be safely
> broadened to include all the dramatic elements, on
> the one hand, but, on the other, the dramatic
> voices can be so exercised as to function as lyrics
> when necessary. The lyricizing of the broader
> voices does not involve the destruction of the dra-
> matic elements (122, p. 117).

J. W. Jones asserts that his recommendation of a
basically lyric "choral voice" is fundamentally different from
the generally accepted practice of a "blend resulting from the
so-called dark, rich tone, acquired often times from concentration on lowering the jaw and adjusting the necessary muscles" (202). Wilson agrees that some conductors attempt to
achieve blend quickly by "closing or darkening all the voices
to a neutral ooh or oh quality ..." (450, p. 223). He criticizes this technique for its effect on the individual voices and
its lack of variety, which makes all compositions sound the
same.

Davison, F. M. Christiansen, Epstein, Dyer, and
Page express viewpoints which are more favorable to this
darker tone quality. Davison characterizes "subjective tone"
as having a full and pervading roundness, a relaxed jaw and
resulting long face; it is a somewhat covered tone which
"guarantees the destruction of individual idiosyncrasies of
tone production and yields one magnified choral voice as no
other tone can" (85, pp. 57-59). F. M. Christiansen notes
that "the dark-toned voices may sing somewhat louder than
the light-toned ones because they blend more easily" (51).
Hjortsvang suggests exercises based upon the vowel oo for
"tone deepening, " which gives a more mellow sound and better blending (165, p. 79). Dyer and Epstein recommend a
"covered" quality of tone; Epstein explains that "it is a
pleasing sound and allows for blending of different voice
qualities" (Dyer 103; Epstein 119, p. 36). Page describes
two systems of vocalization which he calls the Italian and
French systems:

> The Italian method is based upon great freedom,
> and a natural, balanced resounding of the sound
> waves. The tone quality is bright and the vowel
> is articulated naturally.
>   The French system relaxes the soft palate and
> permits much direct resounding in the nasal phar-

ynx. The resounding is covered or muffled. This
is supposed to add color or richness to the tone.
... In group singing it is argued that it is possible to get a "oneness" of quality from the covered method that is not possible in the brighter or
more natural use of the voice. I hardly believe
this to be true. Good quality may be obtained by
either method (291).

Molnar, Hintz, Goetz, Fuhr, Liehmohn, and Rodby
recommend the grouping of similar voice qualities within the
various sections as an aid to better blend. Rodby advises,
"By putting the same types of vocal texture together you have
automatically taken care of a big part of the blending problem" (333). Hintz explains this technique further:

Very often, the reason why a voice continues to
'stick out' is that the individual is seated in a
section of the choir where no possibilities are of-
fered to blend his or her voice to the ensemble as
a whole.... A voice is most valuable to a good
group tone if placed in a section of the choir where
individual difficulties are most easily overcome because of a similarity of tone quality (164).

Molnar recommends grouping the singers according to
the "basic sound of the voice," classifying them as flute-
type, string-type, and reed-type. He advises placing the
"flutes" in the front row, the "strings" in the second row,
and the "reeds" in the back row, believing that the "voice
blends with those on either side of it, rather than those in
front or back of it" (264; also 265, 266).

Krone, Ehret, Finn, and the Music Educators National Conference state their opposition to the grouping of
similar voice qualities. Krone and Ehret recommend classifying the singers according to flute-type and reed-type
(Ehret adds string-type) and then alternating the types within
the section (Krone 225, p. 32; Ehret 114, p. 35). According to the Music Education Source Book, "It is felt that a
better blend of voices is secured if singers of unlike ability
and dissimilar voice quality are placed together" (273, p.
103). Finn proposes a "principle of apposition" in which op-
posites are exercised together so that one borrows quality
from the other. He applies this to lyric-dramatic voices,
thin-full qualities, light-dark qualities, softer-louder voices,
upward-downward progressions, legato-staccato singing, and

reed-flute-string qualities (122, pp. 61, 63, 165, 171, 172, 180).

Resonance Sensations

Whether approached through the science of acoustics or through the empirical methods of the vocal studio or choral rehearsal, it may be observed that the initial vibration from the larynx is reinforced in the resonating cavities of the singer. Ninety authors describe the physical sensations of resonance in the development of choral tone quality. The terminology and the type of description vary. Some authors ask for a "placement" or "focus" of the tone in a direction (usually forward or high) or to a particular point of the anatomy (teeth, lips, mask). Other authors refer to "head resonance," "nasal resonance," or "chest resonance." Others ask for a certain dimension of resonance such as "height," "depth," or "forwardness." These descriptions, combined with the more subjective adjectives such as "full," "round," "ringing," and "concentrated," are the basic terminology employed in dealing with resonance sensations.

The authors' descriptions of resonance sensations are summarized in Table 4. The table shows that the dominant concern is to elicit "forward" or "head" resonance sensations. For a majority of the writers, terms such as "forward tone," "forward resonance," "forward placement," "focused in the mask," or statements which emphasize the importance of forward, nasal, or head resonance are the key factors in their concern with the physical imagery of vocal resonance.

Of the authors who recommend a quality of "depth" to the tone, Tkach, Wilson, Jones-Rhea-Rhea, Cleall, Kortkamp, Garretson, and Peterson also ask for a combined quality of "height," "forwardness," or "head resonance." Wilson explains: "... along with this open-throated, deepset vowel feeling, there must be a high, forward sensation of the resonance of the tone" (445). According to Peterson, "The vocal tone must always have a feeling of height, depth, and forwardness" (295, p. 43). Krone, Wilson, and Peterson also refer to this composite sensation as a "circle of resonance." Krone describes it: "... the feeling that it is produced from the throat up into the resonance cavities of the face and down in an arched formation to vibrate at the upper teeth and nose" (225, p. 72). Howerton also describes

TABLE 4

Descriptions of Resonance Sensation

Number of
Authors

1. Physical location of resonance sensations. . .
   a. "Head" resonance, quality, or tone   31
   b. "Nasal" resonance   17
   c. "Throat" resonance or quality.   2
   d. "Chest" resonance, quality, color, or tone   15

2. Dimensions or directions of resonance sensations
   a. "Forward" resonance sensations.   49
   b. "High" (height) resonance sensations. . . .   11
   c. "Low" (depth) resonance sensations   16

3. Author use of terms
   a. The term "placement" was used.   38
   b. The term "focus" was used.   32

this "arching" of the tone into the upper resonators (177, p. 15). Coleman makes the point that "the end in view is ... the development of the full use of all the resonating cavities" (63, p. 6). Sunderman agrees: "... the singer should have the feeling of tone resonating in as many areas as he is consciously able to use" (376, p. 37).

Of the authors who use the term chest resonance (or quality, color, or tone), Tkach (398, chest quality), Epstein (119, chest tones), Holcomb (166, chest voice), and Phillips (299, chest resonance) all warn of the problems which arise from the improper use of this quality. Tkach explains, "This quality should never be used alone for it limits the range and eventually ruins the voice. It should always have the mixture of the nasal and head resonance" (398, p. 62). In analyzing the vocal problems of the North Central High School Chorus, as reported in the 1931 Music Supervisors National Conference Yearbook, Williamson declares:

> In developing these vowels and colors, the conductor himself knows that certain resonances are essential. I find in the soprano section a flat resonance in the voice box. The nose is entirely

ignored. The chest is entirely ignored. In the
bass section I find the entire ignoring of chest
color. The bass section more than any other section defines the intonation, and the virility and
masculinity of the group. To take care of the
bass section we must understand that there must
be almost a superabundance of chest color with
these voices, never to the point where the tone becomes pharyngeal, but just a normal amount for a
chest voice (447).

Resonance Sensations and Concomitant Factors. Specific factors concomitant with various resonance sensations
were extracted from the writings of fifty-four authors. For
example, Krone advises that "both m and n are extremely
useful in inducing forward placing of the vowel ..." (225, p.
59). Wilson recommends the vowel ooh (as in who) as a
means for achieving a "deep-set vowel" (450, p. 175). Peterson says, "The 'oo' vowel sound has warmth of tone and
qualities of head resonance" (295, p. 29).

Table 5 is a tabulation of factors which were stated
as being concomitant with various resonance sensations. For
purposes of clarity in tabulating these factors, four basic
categories of resonance sensations were established:

1. Forward resonance sensations (e. g. the mask,
   teeth, lips, forward placement)
2. Height-head resonance sensations (e. g. head tone,
   head resonance, deep resonance)
3. Depth-low resonance sensations (e. g. deep-set,
   depth of resonance, deep resonance)
4. Nasal resonance sensations

The concomitant factors are grouped to show their
relationship to the other approaches to tone quality development discussed in this chapter.

Humming as a Technique in Vocal Training. Fifty-one
authors discuss the use of the voiced consonants m, n, and
ng in the vocal training of the choir. This device, commonly
referred to as humming, is employed by sustaining the consonant or by using the m and n as prefixes to a vowel. The
recommended values of humming in the vocal training of a
choir are presented in Table 6, which shows that humming
was most frequently recommended as a technique for establishing or developing resonance sensations. The following

TABLE 5

Resonance Sensations and Concomitant Factors, The Number
of Authors Recorded for Each Factor in Parentheses

Forward resonance sensations - (34)
    Vowel - ee (18), oo (5), ay (5), ah (1), oh (1)
    Quality concept - bright (7), ringing (7), intense (2),
        projection and carrying power (4), concentrated
        (1), clear (1), precise (1), colored (1), covered
        (1), light (1), buoyant (1)
    Physical factor - open mouth (1), raised upper lips (2)
    Concomitant resonance sensation - humming (21),
        frontal consonants (6), downward vocalization (4)

Height-Head resonance sensations - (32)
    Vowel - oo (7), ah (7), ee (4), ay (2), oh (1)
    Quality concept - bright (4), ringing (1), floating-light
        (2)
    Physical factor - high soft palate (4), open mouth (3)
    Concomitant resonance sensation - humming (14),
        downward vocalization (5), arched sensation (4),
        yawn sensation (3), snoring sensation (1), surprise
        sensation (1)

Depth-Low resonance sensations - (13)
    Vowel - oo (9), oh (7), ah (4), aw (2)
    Quality concept - mellow (3), dark (2), rich (2),
        round (2), mature (1), full (1)
    Physical factor - open throat (6), open mouth (4)
    Concomitant resonance sensation - yawn sensation (3),
        deep-set vowel sensation (3), humming (1)

Nasal resonance sensations - (13)
    Vowel - ay (1)
    Quality concept - bright (1), ringing (1), thin (1)
    Concomitant resonance sensation - humming (13)

TABLE 6

The Values of Humming in Choral Training

	Number of Authors
1. Humming established or develops resonance sensations	39
a. Forward resonance sensations 22	
b. Nasal resonance sensations 13	
c. Head resonance sensations 13	
d. "Placement" of the tone 12	
2. Humming relaxes the physical structure of the resonators	13
3. Humming aids the development of choral blend .	11

are representative statements:

> After the hum is established, it should be turned into the vowel with the vowel keeping the forward placement of the hum (Jeffers 188).

> To develop <u>resonance</u> and to help form the tone, humming ... is good (Dykema and Ghrkens 104, p. 92).

> This soft 'm-hum' gives a complete sensation of resonation from the abdominal lift directly to the sensation of the vibrations of the hum somewhere back of the nose and above the roof of the mouth (Arnold Jones 193).

> M's and N's are good consonantal prefixes for bringing forward resonance into the tone (Ehret 114, p. 44).

> ... it will be found also that humming adds the required amount of nasal resonance (Staples 361, p. 44).

> The use of 'n' intensifies vibration of tone in the

nasal cavities, bringing out head resonance and
giving a distinct impression of the tone's being
forward (Blauvelt 19).

Cain and Wilson state that humming should not be
used in the development of tone quality (Cain 37, p. 88;
Wilson 450, p. 185). Wilson articulates his dislike of the
technique, saying that the singing "resonance sensation is
frontal but seems higher than the humming sensation. In
fact, continuous use of humming has a tendency to deaden
the voice, but not build it" (454).

The hum is also valued for the relaxation it can bring
to tone production. Thirteen authors state this viewpoint
which is discussed in the section below, "Freedom from
Tension and Concomitant Factors."

Eleven authors state that humming aids the development of choral blend. Although it is not always made explicit why blend is improved, Arnold Jones says, "It is this
hum sensation that produces the blend in the choral tone ..."
(193). Kortkamp suggests that the choristers "mix some
'hum' into your quality" as an aid to blending the voices
(215, p. 101). Hosmer says:

> Bearing in mind the ideal of the forward tone--or
> tone 'in the masque,' quickest results for unified
> choral tone come through a hum, alternating on
> signal with 'ah' with a very loose jaw (172).

Other authors suggest that humming enables the singers to
hear the other voice-parts better and thus improves the
homogeneity of tone quality.

Physical Structure of the Resonators

Recommendations for the development of choral tone
quality which are concerned with the physical structure of
the resonators are organized and tabulated in four groupings:
1) freedom from tension, 2) freedom from tension and concomitant factors, 3) position and control of the physical
structure of the resonators, and 4) position of the physical
structure of the resonators and concomitant factors.

Freedom from Tension. Concern with freedom from
tension in tone production is expressed by eighty authors.

Phrases such as "free tone," "freedom of production," "free, relaxed jaw" and "relaxed throat" are frequently found in the writings. Some authors emphasize that freedom of production is the initial objective of vocal training and the basis of all good singing. Finn declares, "The first purpose of vocalization has been seen to be the removal of impediments to the free muscular activity of the vocal mechanism" (122, p. 242). Dann agrees: "The most dangerous foe to tone production, the severest handicap to singing, the cause of the most mistakes in voice classification, is tension--stiffness, muscular interference" (80).

Freedom from Tension and Concomitant Factors.
Table 7 is a compilation of the authors' recommendations for developing or maintaining a free vocal production. As reported in Table 1, forty-nine authors are represented in this tabulation.

The use of various vowels for inducing freedom from tension is recommended by twenty authors: oo is recommended for freedom of production by eleven authors; ah, seven authors claim, relaxes the jaw; and oh is claimed to relax the jaw by six authors.

The role of proper resonance sensations in developing freedom of tone production is indicated in the recommendations of twenty-one authors: thirteen recommend humming, six designate forward resonance, five advocate downward vocalization, and four recommend the use of frontal consonants such as f, p, and y. These techniques are also recommended for developing forward or high resonance sensations. Although it is seldom stated explicitly, some authors speak of a relationship between forward resonance sensations and a relaxed jaw and throat:

> The usefulness of correct humming for inducing relaxed production and nasal resonance has long been understood by specialists (Finn 122, p. 32).

> A close relationship between the vowel and the release of the "hum" offered by the m at the beginning of each vowel must be maintained. It proves helpful in the development of "height," or "vault," in singing, and consequently in eliminating tension in the regions of the throat (Veld 408).

> Good humming is beneficial in several ways: it in-

TABLE 7

Freedom from Tension and Concomitant Factors

	Number of Authors
1. Particular vowels are concomitant with freedom from tension	20
a. Vowel oo for freedom of production 11	
b. Vowel ah for relaxing the jaw 7	
c. Vowel oh for relaxing the jaw 6	
2. Correct resonance sensations are concomitant with freedom from tension.	21
a. Humming 13	
b. Forward resonance sensations 6	
c. Downward vocalization 5	
d. Frontal consonants. 4	
3. Correct mental concepts are concomitant with freedom from tension	10
4. Soft singing is concomitant with freedom from tension	14
5. Proper breathing is concomitant with freedom from tension	13
6. Bodily movement exercises develop freedom from tension	13

duces freedom ... it prevents throatiness ... forcing being impossible, it forms and develops tone that is both soft and vital (Grace 140, p. 9).

M, n, and ng, ... facilitate the beginning of phonation without excessive muscular tension. Because of this "relaxing effect," choir members should endeavor to retain the humming sensation while singing (Garretson 130, p. 85).

Adjective descriptions of good choral tone quality such as easy, buoyant, effortless, free, floating, natural and

relaxed suggest that the proper mental concept is also a
factor in developing or maintaining freedom from tension.
Fuhr discusses his concepts of tone, emphasizing the "fundamentals of ease and quality" and the "concept, first of a
sensation of absolute freedom in tone emission, and second,
of a quality that seems to float on the breath" (128, pp. 54
and 59). Coleman advises, "A happy, smiling expression,
with a loose open throat, and free movement of the lower
jaw.... There must be none of that 'do or die' expression,
no straining, no tension" (64, p. 13). Short's warning is to
"keep the students alert and in a happy mood, or the tone
quality will suffer" (355). Finn also advises keeping "the
choristers relaxed and in good humor" (122, p. 36). Hjortsvang recommends that the rehearsal begin with a well-known
number which "will open up the voices and give a feeling of
freedom and joy in singing" (165, p. 82).

The role of the "soft tone" in choral training is discussed in the chapter on dynamics. Table 7 shows that
fourteen authors recommend soft singing as a key factor in
the avoidance of tension in singing; among the spokesmen for
this technique are Beach, Finn, Fuhr, Grace, Coleman, and
Dykema and Gehrkens. The focal point of their recommendations is expressed in Finn's statement that "the corrective
pianissimo must always be at hand to neutralize the tendency
to force which is usually a concomitant of early efforts at
mezzo-forte and forte" (122, p. 52).

Sunderman's contention that "it is impossible to sing a
free tone without the proper breath support" is representative
of the viewpoint expressed by thirteen authors (376, p. 24).
This factor is discussed further in Chapter 3.

Thirteen authors recommend techniques which deal directly with the problem of tension. They suggest body-movement exercises such as massaging the neck, yawning, rolling
the tongue around, "yah-yah-yah" exercises, shaking the
body, and bending forward from the waist with the head hanging limply down.

Position and Control of the Physical Structure of the
Resonators. Table 1 shows that eighty-one authors make
recommendations for the development of choral tone quality
which are concerned with the position and control of the
physical structure of the resonators. Singing is, among
other things, a beautifully coordinated physical act. However, the writings reflect a wide variation of opinion con-

cerning the amount of attention which should be given to the
physical aspects of choral training. The following statements are indicative of this variation:

> ... the singer must think of the tongue as an
> active muscular apparatus, moving quickly and
> precisely, lying low in the mouth, depressed in
> the center, with the tip moving freely and lightly
> against the lower teeth (Howerton 177, p. 14).

> Specific instructions may be given to members con-
> cerning the vocal act of which he has conscious
> control, such as the jaw, the lips, the tip of the
> tongue, and the head. Beyond this it is better to
> develop physical imagery through tonal techniques
> (Wilson 450, p. 162).

> References to mouth positions and other physical
> factors must be considered as hints to help the
> vocal organ in its search for a way to satisfy the
> requirements of the ear (Smallman and Wilcox 358,
> p. 11).

> If we were more concerned about the development
> of the correct concept in the mind of the singer
> and very much less about the physiological process
> or processes through which his tone goes, we
> should soon discover that our bodies--which, after
> all, only reflect our thinking--would react and
> respond much more readily to the demands that
> good singing makes (Veld 407).

The results of an analysis and tabulation of the authors' statements concerning the position and control of the
physical structure of the resonators are reported in Table 8.
The only explicit point of disagreement concerns the "open
mouth." According to Sunderman, "B l a t a n t, white and
colorless tones ... are the result of open mouth singing"
(376, p. 34). Williamson expresses the following viewpoint:

> It is the general belief that a wide-open mouth
> makes good singing. Lamperti, who was one of
> the world's greatest teachers, made this statement
> several hundred years ago: 'The greatest fault we
> have in singing today is the too wide open mouth.'
> I believe that is still true ... I find the American
> boys and girls ... overwork the jaw instead of

TABLE 8

Position and Control of the Physical
Structure of the Resonators

		Number of Authors
1. Recommendations concerning the throat . . .		50
a. Relaxed throat	33	
b. Open throat	31	
2. Recommendations concerning the mouth or jaw		50
a. Relaxed jaw	33	
b. Open mouth or jaw	36	
c. Criticisms of wide mouth opening	2	
3. Recommendations concerning the tongue . .		20
a. Relaxed tongue	14	
b. Tongue forward	6	
c. Tongue low	4	
4. Recommendations concerning the soft-palate .		11
a. Soft-palate should be high or raised . . .	11	
5. Recommendations concerning the lips		13
a. Relaxed lips	5	
b. Lips away from teeth	9	
c. Upper lip raised	4	

working the tongue (447).

Thirty-six authors express a conflicting viewpoint,
recommending a mouth and jaw that are basically open; in
fact, twelve authors suggest a measurement of two finger's
width.

Positions of the Physical Structure of the Resonators
and Concomitant Factors. Table 8 shows that three basic
positions of the physical structure of the resonators are considered desirable: open throat, open mouth, and a high or
raised soft-palate. Forty-seven authors state factors which
are concomitant with these positions. For example, Evanson
says, "o and ah induce free jaw and open throat" (120).

TABLE 9

Positions of the Physical Structure of the Resonators
and Concomitant Factors: The Number of Authors
Recorded for Each Factor in Parentheses

Open throat - (28)
    Vowel - ah (9), oo (7), oh (4), aw (1)
    Resonance sensation - yawn sensation (12), depth (6),
        deep-set vowel (3), humming (1), sigh sensation (1)
    Quality concept - full (3), mellow (3), rich (2), dark
        (1), round (1), warm (1)

Open mouth - jaw - (31)
    Vowel - ah (21), oh (2), aw (1)
    Resonance sensation - yawn sensation (7), depth (4),
        sneeze sensation (1)
    Quality concept - dark (3), round (2), full (1), bright
        (1)
    Concomitant physical factor - insert two fingers (10),
        insert thumb (2)

High or raised soft-palate - (7)
    Vowel - ah (5)
    Resonance sensation - downward vocalization (4), yawn
        sensation (4), consonant r following the vowel (3),
        high-arching sensation (4), breathe in and up sensa-
        tion (2), snore sensation (1), smile behind the teeth
        sensation (1)
    Quality concept - bright (2)
    Concomitant physical factor - open mouth (3)

Jeffries discusses the need for an open throat, recommending, "Induce the sensation of yawning" (189).   Dykema and
Gehrkens write: "It is often good to use a descending exercise at first because it seems easier to keep the throat open
on the descending scale" (104, p. 91).   Tkach is among the
authors who recommend, "The jaw should be open the width
of two fingers.... Test with fingers between the teeth, index
finger down" (397, p. 9).

    Table 9 is a compilation of the factors which are said
to be concomitant with an open throat, open mouth, and a
raised or high soft-palate.

Vowel Study

In this section, the development of choral tone quality
is approached through vowel study. There are three groupings and tabulations of the data: 1) tone quality through vowel
study, 2) vowels and concomitant factors, and 3) uniformity
of vowels for blend of tone quality.

Tone Quality Through Vowel Study. One hundred and
eight authors approach the development of choral tone quality
through the vowel. The importance of the vowel is expressed
in the following representative statements:

> The vowel is responsible for the quality of the tone
> ... (Strickling 372).

> Beautiful singing is a result of perfect diction
> (Kettering 205).

> The vowel, being the chief sustaining factor, thus
> becomes the most important consideration in tone
> production (Peterson 295, p. 99).

> An essential factor in good singing is that the tone
> be sustained on the vowel, and that the vowel
> should be pure and its form not changed until it
> is time for the next vowel or consonant (Mowe
> 269).

> The quality of the tone and the singing lyric pos-
> sibilities of the voice are determined largely by
> the way the vowels are handled (Smallman and
> Wilcox 358, p. 8).

> Quality of tone is dependent upon the correct forma-
> tion of the vowels ... (Howerton 178, p. 7).

> The vowel is the key to beautiful tone production
> (Van Bodegraven and Wilson 404, p. 77).

> Good tone depends upon a pure, vital, and resonant
> vowel (Christy 58, p. 46).

> If the word is pronounced correctly and enunciated
> properly, focus, projection, and position will all
> be proper (Lawson 232, p. 245).

The development of tone quality through vowel study
involves two interrelated methods: pronunciation or phonetic
study, and vowel modification.

In 1931, Williamson wrote, "I believe all tone purity
has to do entirely with breathing and pronunciation, and
nothing else" (447). He recommends that vowel colors be
developed by using the words soon, so, saw, psalm, say,
and see for the long vowels and soot, sod, sung, sat, set,
and sit for the subordinate vowels. "Work, first, for certain vowel colors. I will say, 'No, you are singing the a
sound as in sat; I want the sound as in sung'" (Ibid.). By
using such an approach, he avoids references to resonance
sensations or physical postures and uses "a language which
the whole group can understand" (Ibid.).

Describing the work of Waring, J. W. Jones emphasizes two fundamentals of his approach: "First, basic,
pleasant, natural utterance... Second, the ultimate in the
use of ... vowel phonetics; and the reduction of every sound
to its absolute, purest basic" (203). He describes the procedure as being natural, pure, and simple, and declares
that the result is one of startling beauty. Other statements
of the approach to tone quality through pronunciation and
phonetic study include:

> To clean up pronunciation and enunciation is to im-
> prove tone quality (King 209).

> It will be noted that I have tackled the whole ques-
> tion of voice production, or vocal tone, through
> the discussion and analysis of pronunciation: for
> the reason that, in a general way, there is no tone
> that does not come through words--word is tone
> (Cleall 62, preface).

> Through applying phonetic understanding, bad vocal
> habits may be overcome and correct vocal habits
> may be established (Whittlesey 427, p. 88).

> ... faultless diction in singing reduces the possi-
> bility of bad tone production to an almost minus
> quantity (Grant 141).

The procedures employed in vocal training frequently
encompass a type of "modification" or "transfer" in which
certain favorable characteristics of one sound are carried

over to adjacent sounds. Although this pervades many of the
recommendations for the development of tone quality, especially those concerned with "placement" of resonance sensations, it is perhaps most clearly stated when dealing with
the characteristics of the various vowels:

> I have my students think ee when they are singing
> a and that immediately places the tone forward and
> into the focus it should have (Jeffers 188).

> ... if the vowel 'ee' sounds shrill, it needs the
> blending of 'oo' to give it the proper color....
> Vowels which are too bright or shrill lack the 'o'
> or 'oo' coloring, and vowels which are too dark
> and sombre lack the 'ee' or 'ay' coloring (Tkach
> 398, p. 8).

A simple means of improving an unsatisfactory
vowel sound is to suggest some other vowel color
to be blended with it, or to suggest that it be sung
more in the mold of some other vowel form (Fuhr
128, p. 76).

Each vowel has its own position or spot and so the
position and strength of one vowel can be utilized
to equalize or overcome the disadvantage of another
vowel. For example, the high focus of the ee vowel can help to bring forward the ah vowel which
tends to stay back in the throat (Ehmann 112, p.
34).

To procure subjective tone the chorus must approach each a, e, i, and u as though it were the
letter o as in 'lot'; but the o will be abandoned
just at the second the second vowel is attacked
(Davison 85, p. 58).

The whole art of tone-color in choral terms is
concerned with the choice of one vowel or another
as the type of sound to which the remaining vowels
are keyed (Cleall 62, p. 32).

Vowels and Concomitant Factors. Fifty-nine authors
attribute specific quality concepts, resonance sensations, or
physical factors to individual vowels, thus indicating how
they can be employed in the development of tone quality.
Table 10 is a compilation of six vowel sounds and concomi-

tant factors. The following quotations are representative of
the data from which this table was compiled:

> Beginners find oo the easiest vowel on which to
> get good tone, perhaps because this vowel tends
> to head resonance and to an 'open' throat (Phillips
> 299, p. 112).

> The most effective vowel for bringing the tone for-
> ward, that is, focused upon the front of the mouth,
> is undoubtedly 'oo' (Staples 361, p. 39).

> Correct placement of tone, resonance, and control
> of the breath, lead to the essential element of pure
> vowel sounds. Start with 'oo' with lips pursed and
> the tone focused; the change to 'oh' and then to 'ah'
> requires dropping the jaw (Dunham 102).

> For projection of tone outward and hence, clearness
> and precision, 'ee' is the best (Cain 37, p. 86).

> E: as in need. This is the most brilliant vowel
> and is useful for brightening dark, hooty, throaty
> voices (Krone 225, p. 63).

> If a choral group sings with a nasal, white, or
> colorless tone, then vowels with extreme forward
> placement such as ee and i should be utilized spar-
> ingly in vocalization, and the vowels formed lower
> in the throat, such as aw, oh, and oo should be
> utilized (Garretson 130, p. 94).

> The use of FAW as a vocalization word will help
> the singers to open their throats, to keep their
> jaws down, and to achieve full tones (Swarm 380,
> p. D2).

Twenty-seven authors recommend a specific vowel as
"the first vowel to develop for tone quality," or "the basic
vowel for tone quality development." The recommendations
are: 1) AH vowel--eleven authors; 2) OO vowel--seven authors; 3) OH vowel--six authors; 4) EE vowel--two authors;
and 5) AY vowel--one author. The compilation of the vowels
and their concomitant factors in Table 10 indicates at least
some of the reasons for these recommendations.

Uniformity of Vowels for Blend of Tone Quality. Fifty-

TABLE 10

Vowels and Concomitant Factors: The Number of Authors
Recorded for Each Factor in Parentheses

<u>EE</u> (as in me) - (31)
  Quality concept - bright (18), ringing (7), projection
    and carrying power (5), point (2), clarity and pre-
    cision (3), hard (1), concentrated (1), intense (1),
    virile (1), vital (1), ping (1), string quality (1)
  Resonance sensation - forward (18), height-head (4)

<u>AY</u> (as in day) - (17)
  Quality concept - bright (10), ringing (4)
  Resonance sensation - forward (5), head (3), nasal (1)

<u>AH</u> (as in father) - (36)
  Quality concept - round (4), dark (4), bright (4), full
    (4), rich (1), mellow (1), ringing (1), solid (1),
    reed quality (1), warm (1)
  Resonance sensation - head-height (7), depth-low (4),
    forward (1)
  Physical factors - open mouth-jaw (21), open throat
    (9), relaxes jaw (7), high soft-palate (5)

<u>AW</u> (as in saw) - (12)
  Quality concept - dark (7), full (6), round (2), virile
    (1), horn quality (1)
  Resonance sensation - depth-low (2)
  Physical factor - open throat (1), open mouth (1)

<u>OH</u> (as in so) - (28)
  Quality concept - dark (9), round (6), adds color (5),
    full (4), develops blend (3), mellow (2), rich (2),
    floating (1), warm (1), virile (1), solid (1)
  Resonance sensation - depth-low (7), forward (1),
    head (1)
  Physical factor - relaxes jaw (6), open throat (4),
    low jaw (2)

<u>OO</u> (as in soon) - (40)
  Quality concept - dark (13), mellow (5), round (4),
    floating or buoyant (4), develops blend (3), rich
    (2), sombre (1), flute quality (1), warm (1), adds
    color (1), full (1)
  Resonance sensation - depth-low (9), height-head (7),
    forward (5), easily placed (2)
  Physical factor - freedom of production (11), open
    throat (7)

one authors state that blend of tone quality can be achieved
through uniformity of vowels. The following are representative statements:

> To achieve a well-blended tone, singers must first
> be made aware of the correct sound or sounds in
> each vowel (Waring 420, p. 6).

> When the director secures uniformity of good dic-
> tion among the untrained singers, a choral blend
> is well on its way (Peterson 295, p. 100).

> All choral organizations should learn to sing vowels
> with a homogeneous quality (Christy 55).

> Singing a choral selection on the vowels only is a
> useful device for achieving uniformity of vowel pro-
> duction and improving tonal blend (Garretson 130,
> p. 91).

> Explain that blend of tone is largely dependent upon
> the exact uniformity in the shape of the vowels
> (Coleman 63, p. 58).

> Good choral tone depends upon the vocal talent and
> training of each member of the group, plus the
> ability of the conductor to inspire uniformity of
> vowel quality ... (Vennard 411).

> Choral blend is ... the result of uniform phonetics,
> each produced naturally and resonated naturally by
> each voice. By this means, the individual quality
> of voices disappears in a general tonal line (J. W.
> Jones 203).

> To achieve vowel unity, we vocalize every day on
> all vowels.... When we come to a vowel sound in
> a song that gives us trouble, we stop to correct
> the enunciation until we get the unified sound that
> gives us a clear and understandable word (O. C.
> Christiansen 52).

CHAPTER 3

BREATHING

Breathing is the repetitious act of taking air into the lungs, or inhaling and letting it out, or exhaling. Although breathing is normally an involuntary process, certain aspects of it may be consciously controlled: the amount of air inhaled or exhaled, the speed of inhalation or exhalation, and certain concomitant physical movements. Singing is dependent upon this act since it is the exhalation of the breath from the lungs which generates the vibrations in the larynx; therefore recommendations for the development of proper breathing are frequently an integral part of discussions of vocal training.

CHARACTERISTICS OF GOOD CHORAL BREATHING

General Descriptions of Breathing

The seventy-eight authors who give general descriptions of good choral breathing are concerned with the amount of breath inhaled, deep breathing, breath control and breath support.

Concerning the amount of breath which is needed for singing, the following statements indicate the varying viewpoints:

The normal breath must be taken and control established (Cain 37, p. 101).

It might be sufficient to say that each singer should maintain a sufficient supply of breath for any given phrase to be sung (Klein 212).

The amount of breath taken is of little consequence, but the manner in which the breath is allowed to escape is important ... (Coleman 66, p. 55).

49

TABLE 11

Author-Coverage Table for Breathing Showing the Chapter
Outline which was Evolved from the Data, the Number of
Authors who Discussed Each Sub-Topic of the Outline, and
the Page Number of this Study's Presentation of the Data.
117 Authors are Represented

	Number of Authors	Page
I. Characteristics of choral breathing		49
A. General descriptions of breathing	78	49
B. Positions and movements of the body structure	73	54
II. Recommendations for developing choral breathing		55
A. Developing breathing through singing	20	57
B. Establishing correct breathing action	45	58
C. Breathing exercises	55	60
D. Staggered breathing	37	64

Take only enough breath to sing the phrase easily;
too much is a detriment (Christy 58, p. 41).

Do not pack the lungs with breath (Earhart 105,
p. 2).

Usually when a singer thinks he has a big breath
he merely has tight muscles (Williamson 448).

The ability to sustain a long phrase is not a matter
of lung capacity. It is a matter of controlling the
breath. Singers should not cram the lungs full of
air (Peterson 295, p. 17).

Deep breaths should be taken before each phrase

... always take more breath than is needed. In this way, the breathing organs will be developed and eventually it will be found that a sufficient breath capacity will be present (Archie Jones 191, p. 24).

For singing they should be completely filled, 'from the bottom upwards, ' as it were (Phillips 299, p. 108).

A tabulation revealed that thirty-eight authors recommend deep breathing. Although this recommendation frequently may be interpreted as a directive for inhaling a larger amount of air, it is also an indirect approach to maintaining a stationary chest and shoulders with the desired expansion of inhalation below the sternum or breastbone. The following quotations illustrate the use of the term:

Even at the risk of being tiresome the conductor should din into the ears of his chorus the maxim, 'Breathe naturally, deeply, and often' (Davidson 85, p. 60).

All breathing should be as deep as possible (Woodgate 466, p. 8; also Jones, Rhea and Rhea 192, p. 24).

Keep the shoulders down and take a deep breath. It will be noticed that the ribs are well expanded, the chest high, and the waistline enlarged (Pitts 308).

Breathe deeply, or in other words, around the waistline (Wilson 456).

Deep breathing involves outward expansion of the ribs combined with downward pressure on the diaphragm (Rowles 344).

Deep breathing ... is largely a matter of poise of the body, which, if correct, allows the diaphragm, ribs, and back to coordinate in providing room for a developing, easy lung expansion ... (Fuhr 128, p. 51).

The terms breath control and breath support are used in various ways. The following statements show the conflicting viewpoints concerning these terms:

> This method of breath control is commonly re-
> ferred to as the diaphragmatic-intercostal method,
> which indicates that the breath is controlled by the
> interaction of the diaphragmatic and the inter-
> costal, or rib muscles (Howerton 178, p. 3).

> The central focus is the diaphragm (or solar plexis)
> and control of breath begins here (Woodgate 466,
> p. 8).

> The best breath control is achieved by a smooth
> coordination of chest and abdominal breathing and
> by a vocal production that uses a minimum of air
> ... the 'follow-through' of the breath must be pro-
> perly sustained by deep controlled breathing. The
> diaphragm is chiefly an inhaling muscle and the
> muscles of the abdominal wall expelling muscles.
> Since the front abdominal wall is the main expelling
> force, following through must be done with the front
> abdominal wall (Peterson 295, p. 17).

> Breath control during correct singing means that the
> rate of expenditure is controlled by the larynx while
> the diaphragm maintains the compression as the
> oxygen is exhausted. The whole activity around the
> waist then increases because of creating this air
> compression. The singer feels that his stomach
> and upper abdomen are being pulled in toward the
> spine (Williamson 437).

> Almost from the beginning the conductor should in-
> sist on breath-control; not in the scientific sense
> in which singing teachers use those words, but as
> meaning that the singer must at all times have
> plenty of breath on hand (Davison 85, p. 60).

> There can be no breath support unless these (ab-
> dominal) muscles are kept firm but flexible. These
> muscles should start the exhalation for the produc-
> tion of tone (Barkley 7).

> ... breath support ... a feeling of lifting; this
> lifting sensation will cause the tone to be supported
> by the breath (Morgan 268).

The authors' statements concerning breath control indicate other points of disagreement. Krone, Lewis, Sunderman, Smallman and Wilcox, and Christy state that the breath
should be held momentarily following inhalation and before
the vocal attack. Krone says to "hold the breath (not with
the throat but from the diaphragm and its adjacent muscles)
for just a moment before you attack the tone" (225, p. 53;
also Lewis 236, p. 45). Sunderman advises, "... it must
be understood that before the sound of tone is audible (before he sings) the singer holds his breath--the release of
breath and tone are simultaneous" (376, p. 38). Christy
calls this aspect of breathing "suspension" and explains:

> This occurs the moment after the inhalation
> ceases, and before exhalation begins. It induces
> proper laryngeal position and makes possible an
> easy and correct attack with the breath impulse.
> This moment of suspension is a vital factor in
> breath support and therefore in artistic singing.
> It may well be taught to groups (58, p. 42).

Archie Jones clearly states his opposition to this
technique: "It is important that the singer refrain from
holding the breath between breathing and singing, as this invariably closes the throat" (192, p. 26).

Another aspect of control in breathing is expressed in
Tkach's statement: "Expand to breathe, do not breathe to
expand" (398, p. 3; also Nitsche 278; Jacobs 184, p. 37;
Rowles 344; Krone 225, p. 53; King 209; and Steckel 364).
This concept implies a conscious control of the physical ex-
pansion. Tkach endorses conscious control:

> When exhaling, the ribs should remain expanded
> as long as possible, and when they begin to con-
> tract, they should do so very gradually. The
> thought of keeping the ribs expanded retains the
> even breath pressure (Ibid., p. 6).

However, the degree of conscious control which the writers
recommend is difficult to ascertain. Jacobs writes, "Expand and let the breath come it; do not try to take it in"
(Ibid.). Rowles adds that "we expand to breathe, a very
different thing from sucking in the air as if we were drinking through a straw" (Ibid.). Howerton recommends placing
the hands around the waist and noting the expansion as the
breath is inhaled. He states that "the fingers should move

apart because the quantity of breath taken pushes them apart, not because of mere expansion of the muscular structure" (178, p. 3).

According to Woodgate, Young, Howerton, Van Bodegraven and Wilson, Sunderman, and Smallman and Wilcox, we should "sing on the breath." Woodgate claims that the "lungs are full of air and the diaphragm sends the air from the lungs into the head" (466, p. 8). Sunderman compares the tone and breath relationship to a chip floating down stream (376, p. 26). Young refers to a violin bow in depicting the smooth and easy flow of the breath (473, p. 24). Van Bodegraven and Wilson suggest, "Breathe into the tone" and "Sing with the breath" (404, p. 79). Howerton writes that there should be a "continuous flow of breath from the diaphragm to the resonating cavities" (177, p. 66). Williamson disagrees with these concepts of the relationship between the tone and the breath:

> If we sing on our breath, as we so many times are told, our breath must travel at a speed of over 700 miles an hour, or at the speed of sound ... the truth is that sound waves move not on the air, but move through the air, in the same fashion that water waves move (436).

Perhaps King's suggestion represents a compromise as he advises "singing into the breath instead of on top of it" (208).

Positions and Movements of the Body Structure in Breathing

The specific positions and movements of the body which are concomitant with good choral breathing are stated by seventy-three authors (see Table 11). The following statements are representative:

> ... 'diaphragmatic-intercostal' method of breathing. ... The shoulders should be erect and quiet and should not rise and fall with the intake and the outgo of the breath. The diaphragm should be brought into play to avoid the tendency to 'collapse' as the breath is exhaled (MENC 273, p. 105).

> ... the entire rib area expand for the intake of the

breath. (Note that in breathing the shoulders
should never rise and fall.) ... breathe in and
out--through the mouth ... (Hume 182, p. 248).

But we find that breathing all the way around the
waist, below the arm pits and above the hips (intercostal and diaphragmatic breathing) not only
gives the greatest amount of air, but insures the
most perfect control (Evanson 120).

Correct breathing, that is to say natural breathing,
should result if the shoulders are not allowed to
rise, ... in singing the breath is taken in through
the mouth ... (Coleman 63, p. 9).

With the chest high and quiet, the students must
learn the expansion around the waistline for air in-
take, and the use of the stomach wall in tucking in
for air expulsion (Arnold Jones 193).

During inspiration, the diaphragm contracts and
pushes downward, while the contraction of the intercostal muscles lifts or raises the ribs.... During normal expiration there is supposedly no muscle
contraction necessary; the chest is decreased in
size by the elastic recoil of the thoracic wall. In
prolonged expiration, such as in singing a sustained note, the abdominal muscles gradually con-
tract while the diaphragm slowly relaxes ... (Garretson 130, p. 69).

The student should also get away from the old idea
that the diaphragm does all the work, for he now
can see that the abdominal muscles control expiration, and all vocal sound is a result of expiration
(Henson 160).

A tabulation of the specific author recommendations
for body positions and movements in choral breathing is
given in Table 12.

RECOMMENDATIONS FOR DEVELOPING
GOOD CHORAL BREATHING

The recommendations for developing good choral
breathing are organized in four sections: 1) developing

TABLE 12

Positions and Movements of the Body in Choral Breathing; The
Number of Authors Recorded for Each Factor in Parentheses

Orificial control - (14)
   Inhale through the mouth - (5)
   Inhale through the nose if time permits - (3)
   Inhale through both the mouth and nose - (3)
   Inhale through either the mouth or nose - (3)

Shoulders - (23)
   Should not move - (23)

Chest - (31)
   Should not move - (28)
   Expands during inhalation - (5)

Lower ribs - (25)
   Expand during inhalation - (24)
   Remain expanded as long as possible during exhala-
    tion - (6)

Diaphragm - (42)
   Controls the breath - (14)
   Contracts (lowers) during inhalation - (11)
   Diaphragmatic breathing - (13)
   Diaphragmatic-intercostal breathing - (9)

Back - (7)
   Expands during inhalation - (7)

Abdomen - (39)
   Upper abdomen or waist expands during inhalation -
    (27)
   Abdomen expands during inhalation and contracts dur-
    ing exhalation - (18)
   Abdomen remains firm - (6)

---

breathing through singing; 2) establishing correct breathing
action; 3) breathing exercises; and 4) staggered breathing.

Through Singing

Twenty authors state that singing is itself the best
way to develop proper breathing and warn of the dangers of
breathing exercises. The following are representative statements:

> Let us state emphatically that the procedures of
> breathing in singing should not precede or be
> separated from the act of phonation and diction.
> Singers who become overly breath conscious to the
> detriment of establishing resonance and habits of
> diction, seldom sing artistically and expressively
> (Wilson 450, p. 175).

> Formal abstract breathing exercises however, are
> not particularly helpful in developing the voice
> (Archie Jones 191, p. 35).

> In any act of exercises ... the usual result of
> such activity is several cases of paralyzed dia-
> phragms with assorted heaving chests (Treggor
> 399).

> The more one calls attention to the breathing when
> teaching the high school voice, the more artificial
> the breathing may become....
>   If any 'breath control' is necessary with school
> choral group, it can be accomplished by watching
> carefully that all students phrase properly (Loney
> 241).

> ... special breathing exercises ... are not in-
> dispensable.... The habit of good breathing, i.e.,
> the taking-in of an adequate supply of air and the
> controlled use of it--is a natural result of good
> phrasing. The long phrase leads to the long
> breath (Grace 140, p. 43).

> ... if the composition is properly phrased, the
> breathing or breath control will be cared for auto-
> matically (Boettle 20).

> The study of breath control should be approached
> through a consideration of the phrase structure of
> the particular song chosen for use (Howerton 178,
> p. 2).

Coleman and Williamson emphasize the role of emotion in the development of proper choral breathing:

> The right emotion must therefore prompt the intake
> of breath, since it is impossible to inhale joy and
> exhale sorrow with the same breath, and vice ver-
> sa (Coleman 63, p. 45).

> ... when he is annoyed he breathes one way; when
> he is in pain he breathes another way; when he is
> pleased he breathes another way; when he is bois-
> terously happy he breathes another way. Each
> time the breathing is controlled and guided by the
> emotion.
> ... all the talking we do about breathing simply
> makes the individual more self-conscious and more
> tense....
> suggest the mood and then with the group in-
> stinctively and emotionally breathe to create the
> mood suggested ... thought has been directed away
> from the body and self-consciousness, to mood and
> naturalness (Williamson 448).

Establishing Correct Breathing Action

Table 13 gives the recommendations of forty-five
authors for establishing correct breathing action. The
recommendations have a common objective: to establish or
maintain the body expansion during inhalation below the
sternum or breastbone while maintaining an inactive chest
and shoulders.

Imagery is recommended to establish correct breathing action and the proper relationship between the breath and
tone during singing. The following quotations illustrate these
techniques and their conflicting viewpoints:

> A simile which may prove useful is that of a
> spout of water with a ball bouncing on top of it.
> The water is the support (the column of air coming
> from the diaphragm) and the ball, the voice (Wood-
> gate 466, p. 8).

> Use the 'pulling the string' idea you have utilized
> in obtaining good posture also: (a) on the attack
> of each new phrase: pull the string from the toes;

TABLE 13

Recommendations for Establishing
Correct Breathing Action

Objective: To establish or maintain the body expansion
during inhalation below the sternum while
maintaining an inactive chest and shoulders.

Number of
Authors

1. Place hands around the waist above the belt . 12

2. Observe how you breathe when you lie down . 7

3. Observe breathing action during a cough, sigh,
sob, or sniff 6

4. Sing a staccato passage and observe the breathing action 6

5. Observe a baby's breathing 5

6. Observe the breathing of a sleeping person or
a pet 5

7. Pant like a dog 5

8. Place elbows on knees while sitting and observe
where you expand 5

9. Place one hand on the stationary chest and one
hand on the expanding waist 3

10. Stand and bend forward from the hips to a horizontal position; observe breathing action . . . 3

11. Observe breathing action during a vigorous
"Hey!" 2

12. Inhale quickly 2

13. Fill your belt 2

14. Clasp your hands behind head (keep shoulders
stationary) 1

15. Place hands on the back of a chair (keep
shoulders stationary) 1

16. Extend arms horizontally or over head (keep
shoulders stationary) 1

(b) on sustained notes: pull the string steadily;
(c) for accents: on sforzando accents pull the
string suddenly and powerfully; (d) on sustained
fortissimi: pull the string steadily and powerfully;
(e) on sustained pianissimi: pull the string steadily
and gently (Christy 58, p. 42).

Sing as if in the act of inhaling, that is having a
sense of drawing the tone in and over. The feel
of singing is 'in' not 'out.' ... 'Sing to yourself,
no one else wants to hear you' (Wilson 450, p.
177).

Drink in the tone; do not blow it out (McCall 254).

As you sustain (the vowel oo), imagine you are sip-
ping through a straw. Hold back with the breathing
muscles by keeping the rib cage well expanded and
shoulders down (Pitts 311).

To test your ability to think this steady movement
(of the diaphragm), try this: Sing, 'That boat sank
last night,' on some pitch, meanwhile raising an
extended arm very slowly ... transfer this same
steadiness ... into the muscular action of the diaphragm! (Kortkamp 219, p. 13).

... the old Italians were right when they placed a
mirror or lighted candle in front of the mouth, and
refused to accept the singing if the mirror clouded
or the candle flame flickered (Williamson 436).

Breathing Exercises

Exercises for the development of breathing in choral
singing may be classified according to three types: 1) sustained breath or tone exercises, 2) staccato breath or tone
exercises, and 3) exercises to develop the physical structure
of the breathing mechanism. Fifty-five authors recommend
breathing exercises of these types.

Exercises which involve sustaining and controlling the
breath are constructed around the following factors: 1) sustain various vowels or a hiss sound, or sing long phrases,
repeated phrases, numbers, or the alphabet; and 2) vary and
control the timing of inhalation, exhalation, or the time be-

tween these processes. Examples of the authors' recommendations for sustained tone or breath exercises are given
below:

> Control the emission of breath with abdominal sup-
> port. Take a full breath, begin singing with a
> soft ah, and hold the tone as long as possible
> (Ward 414, p. 96).

> A familiar hymn-tune or chant, or a phrase of
> it--even a single chord--can be used as a medium
> for practicing ... (sustaining evenly for a given
> number of beats after a quiet deep intake of
> breath) ... (Davies and Grace 83, p. 74).

> Long holding notes each preceded by the aforesaid
> deep breath ... Later on they can be sustained for
> ten seconds or more (Conway 69, p. 75).

> Take a slow deep breath, feeling the expansion all
> around the waistline, especially in the back. Ex-
> hale slowly with a steady hissing sound for 8 slow
> counts. Repeat this exercise four times (Tkach
> 398, p. 2).

> ... drills of basic vowels on long tones and scales.
> A sixteen-second time limit was set as a good
> starting point for practicing long tones (Marier
> 249).

> Practice singing from 1 to 25 on a single tone with
> a single breath. Gradually work up to singing 1
> to 50 on one breath. Try singing through the al-
> phabet also (Krone 225, p. 53).

> The tendency to allow too speedy exhalation of
> breath can be checked and presently eliminated if
> the choirmaster insist that the lungs be emptied
> slowly while he counts a given number (Finn 122,
> p. 25).

Staccato exercises are employed to establish the sensation of deep breathing and the expansions and contractions
around the waistline. Staccato exercises are also recommended to strengthen the breathing muscles. Panting and
staccato singing on syllables such as "Ha, " "Ho, " and "Dee"
are among the recommendations made. The following state-

ments are representative:

> Do some staccato vocalization each day. This
> valuable technique is usually neglected as a phase
> of vocal development. Staccato singing activates
> the muscles of the diaphragm and is invaluable in
> relieving the voice of heaviness, languor, and in-
> ertia, at the same time adding a degree of buoy-
> ancy (Ehret 114, p. 16).

> To try to arouse diaphragmatic attack the con-
> sonant 'h' may be prefixed ... (Kolb 213).

> The work of the diaphragm can be realized more
> fully if the singers are asked to ejaculate Ah rapid-
> ly, as though they were panting (Woodgate 466, p.
> 8).

> Panting and staccato 'hah' syllables help to estab-
> lish correct breathing (Vennard 411).

> Detail about the mechanics of breathing is not gone
> into. I do very little talking about it. We rather
> drill on some of the fundamentals that create a
> sense of diaphragmatic activity. By using sounds
> like Ho! Ha! Hee! slowly with good activity of the
> diaphragm and with a forceful column of air be-
> hind each syllable, the students develop the feeling
> of breath support (Erdman 118).

> ... learn to use the diaphragm. Probably one of
> the simplest ways is to pant like a dog; next pant
> and say ha-ha-ha-, etc.; then take a pitch on ha
> ... (Dykema and Gehrkens 104, p. 92).

The breathing exercises which involve techniques other
than sustaining and staccato drills frequently incorporate
these two basic techniques into a more comprehensive procedure. Olaf Christiansen recommends a "Before Singing:
Physical Conditioner" which includes reaching, stretching,
and inhaling for four counts; holding the breath and rocking
on the heels and toes for eight counts; slumping and exhaling
for four counts; and an abdominal squeeze, staying empty
for four, six, or eight counts (54, p. 4). McCall explains
that exercises designed to develop breathing should aim at
two goals: "The first is to increase the supply of air, by
deep breathing. The second is to control or master the sup-

ply by exercising the muscles and the diaphragmatic wall itself" (254). He presents breathing and singing exercises
which emphasize the expansion and contraction of the abdominal wall. Bingham proposes exercises which include
touching the toes, stretching the arms above the head, and
bending the torso to the left and right with the arms extended
horizontally from the shoulders (17). Best would have the
choir do a "rowing exercise" while seated, touching their
toes with the fingers (16). Shields agrees that the diaphragmatic and intercostal muscles must be strengthened, saying
that "work on the muscles which aid breathing must be an
unceasing task in order to secure a firm, full-bodied tone"
(354). Kindig includes sit-ups, raising the legs while lying
flat on the floor, and touching the toes from a standing position in an article entitled "Choral Rehearsal Techniques"
(207).

Smallman and Wilcox suggest that "breathing exercises
can well occupy ten minutes at the beginning of a sixty-minute
rehearsal. The exercises ... utilize singing from the very
start" (376, p. 5). "Practice concerted breathing exercises
before starting to sing and at least once during rehearsal as
an aid to relaxation, " is the recommendation of Deardorff
(87, p. 9). Guadnola expresses the opinion that warm-up
exercises which employ panting, staccato "hah" patterns, and
an indefinite pitched hum should not be confused with vocalizing. He recommends that vocalizing be left for individual
or class voice instructors, but emphasizes the importance of
non-vocal warm-ups (145). Howerton recognizes that only a
limited amount of time can be spent on posture and breathing
exercises. He recommends from ten to twelve minutes out
of each hour's rehearsal, stating that "the exercise should
always be introduced through actual music" (178, p. 4).
Finn declares:

> Each rehearsal should begin with breathing exer-
> cises, chiefly as a limbering-up measure, and in
> order to remind singers to avoid the faulty af-
> fectation of raising the shoulders.... The writer
> never fails to devote a few minutes to this bene-
> ficial practice at rehearsals, in tuning-up periods
> before services, and backstage before concerts
> (122, p. 25).

Staggered Breathing

The choral technique of staggering the group inhalations of the breath in order that longer phrases may be sung without a noticeable break is discussed by thirty-seven authors. Davison describes the technique:

> ... no attempt should be made to perform a long phrase under one breath as a soloist must do; instead catch-breaths must be taken whenever there is danger of the supply running short ... the singers may be instructed to breathe at will, each time letting themselves in fairly softly on the vowel with a rapid crescendo to the required dynamic (85, p. 60).

Davison, Young, Veld, Eisenkramer, Krone, Lewis, Garretson, Ehret, and Jones, Rhea and Rhea suggest that the timing of the breaths not always be left to chance. They advise designating when the various sections or individuals should breathe. Each section of the choir may be divided into three or four groups and a specific place in the phrase or beat of the measure may be assigned as the breathing place for each group. The group designations may be made by assigning numbers to the singers or by dividing them according to the first letter of their last name.

Although the use of staggered breathing is generally endorsed, warnings of its abuse are given by Archie Jones, Vandre, Christy, and Edeson. Jones contends that "a common fault with many choral conductors is that of allowing too many breaths. The full phrase should be sung with one breath where at all possible" (191, p. 54). Christy agrees: "All good choirs have the ability to sing long phrases on one breath" (58, p. 41). "If you want to sing badly, take a breath whenever you feel like it, " warns Vandre (405, p. 12). Edeson recommends, "Work in general to the rule 'one phrase, one breath' and make as few exceptions as possible" (109, p. 27).

CHAPTER 4

POSTURE

Posture, as a factor in choral training, is concerned
with the relative position and control of the structural parts
of the body. The parts of the body structure which commonly receive attention are the head, shoulders, chest, abdomen, feet, and back.

TABLE 14

Author-Coverage Table for Posture Showing the Chapter Outline
which has Evolved from the Data, the Number of Authors who
Discussed Each Sub-Topic of the Outline, and the Page
Number of this Study's Presentation of the Data.
77 Authors are Represented

	Number of Authors	Page
I. Characteristics of choral posture		66
A. General descriptions of posture	49	66
B. Positions of body structure	57	67
II. Recommendations for developing choral posture		68
A. Psychological approaches	30	68
B. Body-movement techniques	16	70

CHARACTERISTICS OF GOOD CHORAL POSTURE

General Descriptions

      Forty-nine authors published statements which were
tabulated as general descriptions of good choral posture.
The nature of these descriptions is illustrated in the following quotation from the MENC publication, Music in American
Education:

> Since vital, well-balanced body position is the
> fundamental basis of all singing, it must be main-
> tained in all choral rehearsing. For those who
> rehearse their groups while seated, careful atten-
> tion should be given to singing with relaxation pos-
> ture (274, p. 208).

      Dann wrote in an open letter to the 1932 Music Super-
visors' Chorus, "An active, alert, 'firmly flexible' body is
a necessity. Successful singing posture cannot be passive;
it is decidedly active, alert, very much alive" (76). Craig
refers to the physical tonus as "controlled aliveness" (72).
Fischer advises, "... insist on a vital posture ... which reflects vitality and awareness" (127). Wodell says that the
singer should keep a position which is favorable to the free
use of all his muscles, and "keep his body in the state of
freedom from rigidity, and in tonicity, or readiness to act,
which I have called (for short) responsive freedom" (464).
According to Smallman and Wilcox, good choral posture may
be described as "poise of body" or "the posture of assurance" (358, p. 3). Wilson asks for "aliveness of body and
resultant vitality in singing" (460). Morgan recommends a
position which gives "flexibility and poise for the entire
body" (268). Fuhr recommends techniques which give "poise
and erectness to the chest" and the maintenance of "muscular
tone in the abdominal wall" (128, p. 51). Perhaps Ehmann's
statement summarizes this point:

> The singer should cultivate a consciousness of his
> body, letting it become alive to music and under
> all circumstances, allowing it to be flexible, buoy-
> ant, and responsive to resonance.... A sense of
> physical alertness is a prerequisite for every sing-
> er (112, p. 1).

      The authors refer to various degrees of relaxation
and tension in their descriptions of good posture. For exam-

ple, Jones, Rhea and Rhea state, "Relaxation is the keynote
in correct posture" (192, p. 4). Woodgate advises that the
body should be relaxed (466, p. 3), and Coleman suggests
standing in "an easy attitude" (63, p. 8). Howerton does not
discuss relaxation, but emphasizes "a proper state of tension ... resilient, firm but not rigid...." He also asks for
"the maintenance of constant vitality in the physical attitude"
(177, pp. 7-8). Krone recommends that the back be kept
straight and away from the back of the chair. He states that
this "tires the back at first, but it is better to have a sore
back than a sore throat" (225, p. 53). Cleall declares that
the position of the shoulders should be back and down: "This
is a strenuous act, for the shoulders will ache and fight for
relaxation ..." (61, p. 34).

Tkach notes that relaxation is a misleading term in
singing: "One cannot be completely relaxed when singing,
because a relaxed muscle is inactive. A firmness is necessary for the action demanded of the muscle" (398, p. 7).
"A good posture is a comfortable posture," according to
Eisenkramer (116). Loney adds that "the director must keep
in mind that what may be a comfortable upright position for
one student may not necessarily be comfortable for another"
(241).

Positions of the Body Structure

The following statement by Christy is illustrative of
the recommendations which describe choral posture in terms
of positions of the body structure:

> 'The singer should stand comfortably erect, with
> the chest medium high, and with a feeling of flexi-
> bility and well being.' The shoulders should be
> back and down and the head neither thrust forward
> nor thrown back unnaturally, but balanced evenly
> on the spinal axis. In order to provide a firm and
> easy posture when standing, one foot may well be
> slightly in front and to the side of the other. The
> weight should always be forward for either the
> standing or sitting position. The body should not
> be allowed to slump down, and the legs should
> never be crossed when seated.... The singer
> should always give the impression of being per-
> fectly at ease (58, p. 43).

A tabulation of the recommended body positions is given in Table 15. It is important that the recommendations not be considered as extreme positions and their descriptive intent thus distorted. As may be noted in the above statement by Christy, the recommendations are frequently accompanied by a qualifying term such as "comfortable," "medium," "naturally," and "slightly."

RECOMMENDATIONS FOR DEVELOPING
GOOD CHORAL POSTURE

These recommendations are considered in two groupings: 1) psychological approaches, and 2) body-movement techniques.

Psychological Approaches

All techniques for the development of good posture which avoid direct attention to or positioning of a part of the body structure are considered in this section. The following statements are representative of the recommendations extracted from the writings of thirty authors:

Sit or stand 'tall and light above the hips' (Earhart 105, p. 2).

Imagine you are suspended in air by a string attached to the back of your head (Krone 225, p. 52).

A good posture 'exercise' is always (when singing) to look self-confident (Jones, Rhea and Rhea 192, p. 4).

Dr. Hollis Dann, tells his singers to 'imagine lifting the back part of the top of the head an inch, keeping the body alert and flexible, ready to spring in any direction' (Steckel 364).

... sit erectly on the chair with a feeling of almost lifting their bodies off the chair (Williamson 437).

Proper sitting or standing position should be maintained with a general psychological feeling of lightness and lifting (Klein 212).

TABLE 15

Recommended Positions of the Body Structure: The Number of
Authors Recorded for Each Factor in Parentheses

---

1. Standing or sitting

    Head - (20)
      Erect - (9)
      High - (8)
      Chin slightly drawn in - (10)

    Shoulders - (16)
      Down - (7)
      Back - (8)
      Square - (3)
      High - (2)
      Forward - (1)

    Chest - (35)
      High - (34)
      Expanded - (4)

    Back or overall Body - (39)
      Erect or straight - (35)
      Weight shifted forward - (18)

    Abdomen - (13)
      Pulled in or flattened - (12)
      Lifted - (2)

2. Standing

    Feet - (20)
      One foot forward - (16)
      Feet apart - (12)

3. Sitting
    Sit well back in the chair - (7)
    Sit forward in the chair - (6)
    Shift body weight forward - (17)
    Place feet flat on the floor - (17)
    Place feet apart - (7)
    Place one foot forward - (5)
    Place one foot beside the chair - (2)

Let the singer imagine a book balanced upon the
head, then that he is standing or sitting with the
book as high as possible (Whittlesey 427, p. 87).

The idea of 'hanging the weight from the shoulders,'
... 'Stand to the greatest possible height' (Howerton 177, pp. 8-9).

Stand so you could rise on the toes without first
swaying forward (Kortkamp 215, p. 16).

... stand so that the tension on the lowest vest
button is transferred to a corresponding tension on
the top one ... assume the position you naturally
take when you squeeze through an opening too small
for you ... (Jacobs 184, p. 14).

Body-Movement Techniques

As reported in Table 14, sixteen authors recommend
body-movement techniques for establishing the desired singing posture.

O. Christiansen, Archie Jones, Bingham, and Kortkamp recommend raising the outstretched arms above the
head, and maintaining the high chest position as the arms
are lowered (O. Christiansen 54, p. 4; Jones 191, p. 24;
Bingham 17; Kortkamp 215, p. 16). Kolb and Jones, Rhea
and Rhea achieve the proper chest position in a similar way
by clasping the hands behind the head (Kolb 213; Jones,
Rhea and Rhea 192, p. 4). Tkach suggests that a full circu-
lar swing of the arms will result in the proper position of
the chest and shoulders (398, p. 7). Hosmer, Krone, and
Wilson recommend the following techniques for achieving the
correct singing posture:

Place the hands on the hips, give a slight downward pressure, remove hands and retain resultant
posture.
Analytically, this shows shoulders comfortably
back, chest naturally raised, chin relaxed, and abdomen pulled in (Hosmer 172).

... assume a good standing posture, then move
your arms forward and up to a horizontal position.
Now swing your arms back slowly, pressing down

at the palms until your chest is up in a comfortable
position. Let your arms drop without letting your
chest fall or your shoulders sink. Keep this position, standing or sitting (Krone 225, p. 53).

Place the ends of the middle fingers together with
the elbows pointing out. Place the hands against
the stomach with the palms up, elbows still pointing out. Pull the elbows forward a couple of
inches without permitting the chest to lower or
cave it. Retain the feeling of this position when
the hands drop to the side or when sitting down
(Wilson 450, p. 169).

Howerton recommends swaying the body, with all
movement coming from the ankles, as an exercise for developing the proper tension (177, p. 9). Peterson recommends a "rag doll" technique with the head and arms dangling
loosely forward as a preliminary to assuming the singing
posture with the proper amount of looseness and muscular
suppleness (295, p. 12). To elicit the feeling of flexibility,
Maybee would begin the rehearsal with "a good stretching of
the body, with the arms aloft, rising on tiptoe" (251, p. 6).
O. C. Christiansen and Ehmann also recommend stretching-
swaying-bending exercises as physical conditioners.

CHAPTER 5

INTONATION

Intonation denotes the degree of adherence to an established pitch. It may be established by an instrument with fixed pitch, such as a pitch pipe or a keyboard instrument, or it may be conceived in the mind of the singer and listener, in which case, due to the temperament of the scale, it may deviate from the fixed pitch of an instrument. In choral singing, the problems of intonation are of two basic types: 1) the ensemble gradually lowers or raises the established pitch while singing; and 2) while maintaining an overall adherence to the established pitch, select intervals, melodic passages, chords or voice sections of the choir are not in satisfactory relationship to the composite ensemble pitch. It will be seen that a wide variety of factors may be related to problems of choral intonation.

TONE PRODUCTION AS A DEPENDENT FACTOR IN CHORAL INTONATION

Table 16 lists the phases of tone production which are stated to be dependent factors in choral intonation. Tone quality, breathing, posture, range, dynamics, and diction are all discussed with reference to intonation. Each of these phases of tone production is a basic chapter of this study and it would be redundant to elaborate upon them in this chapter; however, representative quotations are given to illustrate their relationship to intonation.

A. Tone Quality as a dependent factor

1. Approached through concept of tone.

The habitual singing of vowels with a breathy, dark, or sombre quality is a frequent cause of flatting (Christy 58, p. 58).

72

TABLE 16

Author-Coverage Table for Intonation Showing the Chapter
Outline Which Was Evolved from the Data, the Number of
Authors Who Discussed Each Sub-Topic of the Outline, and
the Page Number of This Study's Presentation of the Data.
145 Authors Are Represented

<table>
<tr><td></td><td>Number of
Authors</td><td>Page</td></tr>
<tr><td>I. Tone production as a dependent factor in
choral intonation</td><td></td><td>72</td></tr>
<tr><td>   A. Tone quality . . . . 63</td><td></td><td>72</td></tr>
<tr><td>   1. Concept of tone . . . . 23</td><td></td><td>72</td></tr>
<tr><td>   2. Resonance sensation . . . . 18</td><td></td><td>74</td></tr>
<tr><td>   3. Concern with the physical structure . 28</td><td></td><td>74</td></tr>
<tr><td>   4. Vowel study . . . . 21</td><td></td><td>75</td></tr>
<tr><td>   5. Vibrato . . . . 21</td><td></td><td>75</td></tr>
<tr><td>   B. Breathing . . . . 44</td><td></td><td>76</td></tr>
<tr><td>   C. Posture . . . . 24</td><td></td><td>76</td></tr>
<tr><td>   D. Range . . . . 25</td><td></td><td>76</td></tr>
<tr><td>   E. Dynamics . . . . 14</td><td></td><td>77</td></tr>
<tr><td>   F. Diction . . . . 28</td><td></td><td>77</td></tr>
<tr><td>II. Musicianship and the music as dependent factors in
choral intonation</td><td></td><td>78</td></tr>
<tr><td>   A. Selection of singers . . . . 29</td><td></td><td>78</td></tr>
<tr><td>   B. Development of listening skills . . . . . 90</td><td></td><td>79</td></tr>
<tr><td>   C. Unaccompanied singing . . . . 24</td><td></td><td>80</td></tr>
<tr><td>   D. Untempered tuning . . . . 19</td><td></td><td>81</td></tr>
<tr><td>   E. Key of the music . . . . 28</td><td></td><td>83</td></tr>
<tr><td>   F. Tempo and rhythm . . . . 17</td><td></td><td>84</td></tr>
<tr><td>   G. Difficulty of the music . . . . 17</td><td></td><td>85</td></tr>
<tr><td>III. Mental and physical attitudes as dependent factors
in choral intonation</td><td></td><td>85</td></tr>
<tr><td>   A. Poor mental attitude or mood . . . . . 36</td><td></td><td>85</td></tr>
<tr><td>   B. Lack of concentration . . . . 23</td><td></td><td>85</td></tr>
<tr><td>   C. Nervousness or excitement . . . . 23</td><td></td><td>85</td></tr>
<tr><td>   D. Fatigue . . . . 27</td><td></td><td>85</td></tr>
<tr><td>   E. Physical inertia or lack of energy . . . 21</td><td></td><td>85</td></tr>
</table>

TABLE 16 (continued)

Correct intonation can be secured at the expense of tone quality, but it is infinitely easier of attainment when the tone is light, floating and well-produced. When using this kind of tone, the singer can hear himself and others more accurately, a necessary condition if true intonation is to be maintained (Rowles 344).

'Flutey' voices need the brilliance of 'reedy' voices to keep them on pitch in their lower ranges....
... you will usually find the sharping tendency among 'reedy' sopranos and tenors--hence the need for a balance of 'reeds' and 'flutes' in these sections (Krone 225, pp. 79-80).

2. Approached through resonance sensation.

Focusing or forward placement of tone (also described as brightness, sparkle and bell-like quality) will eliminate continuous flatting (Wilson 456).

Use the consonant F as an aid to good intonation, i.e. 'fluent, facile, favors forward focus' (Finn 125, p. 7).

Singing in tune is not possible when the tone is coming from the back of the throat (Murray 272, p. 3).

3. Approached through concern with the physical structure.

Most flatting is caused by singing that isn't free,

relaxed, and unconstricted (Rodby 329).

Good intonation is basically dependent upon freedom
of production as well as many other factors (Winslow 463).

Variation in pitch also is likely to result from the
constantly changing shape of the singing mechanism
(Howerton 177, p. 14).

4. Approached through vowel study.

Words with the oo vowel sound, as in soon, are
the easiest to tune well. This vowel has the few-
est overtones of all vowels and consequently does
not present the type of difficulty encountered in
most vowels (Liemohn 237).

Special care must be taken that the final vowels,
e as in 'heaven,' ay as in 'name,' ee as in 'we,'
i as in 'sins,' are not allowed to drop in pitch
(Coleman 63, p. 81).

Many well known choral selections are persistent
trouble makers for all choral groups. Upon
analysis you may find the following factors present
which may contribute to the lowering of the pitch:
    a) the vowels found in the text are predominant-
ly IH (pit), EH (pet), and EE (me), sounds which
most choir members control poorly (Ehret 114,
p. 21).

5. Vibrato

To have, for example, fourteen voices singing a
tone, all with vibrato, will produce a 'wide' tone
resulting in a detriment to intonation ... the director who strives for good intonation but still
wants a tone with life and spirit will find the answer somewhere between the extremes of the bleak,
lifeless, colorless tone and the more vibrant,
warm, rich and colorful tone produced with some
vibrato (Liemohn 237).

Most desirable is a small vibrato, sufficient to
give the tone a rich quality, but not enough to dis-
rupt unification of pitch in a section (Hansen 154).

Good unisons are impossible if any of the singers
employ tremolo. All excessive vibrato is the
enemy of unison (Sateren 347, p. 4).

The proponents of the 'straight-line tone' contended
that this type of tone produced finer pitch-fidelity
and clarity ... pretty much in the limbo of the
past (Lukken 244).

B. Breathing as a dependent factor

Directly the support is decreased the voice flattens
(Woodgate 466, p. 8).

To maintain pitch and true intonation, a steady
pressure of breath against the vocal chords at all
times is absolutely necessary (Tkach 398, p. 16).

This usually cures flatting ... as it gets them in
a good humor, and causes some very deep breathing.... Have them stand, hands on hips, and
vocalize with explosive ha's, ho's, and he's (Rossel
341).

C. Posture as a dependent factor

In addition to not 'thinking' pitch, other reasons
for losing pitch are poor posture, poor breath support, and not starting on pitch (Eisenkramer 116).

Singing requires energy; ... an abundant supply of
oxygen....
The second requirement for singing in tune is
correct posture (Williamson 442).

Correct posture and breathing are also to be
stressed.... It is not possible to have good, free
motion of the diaphragm when one is sitting with
feet crossed, or in a slouching position (James
186).

D. Range as a dependent factor

Most sopranos sharp on the higher notes, especially

in loud singing. The faster the vibrations, the
harder it is for the singer to control the pitch
(F. M. Christiansen 51).

... flatting happens mostly between middle C and
the C an octave higher, and is caused, I believe,
by the influence of the untrained lower register.
When the singer exerts too much pressure on a
tone the unbalanced heaviness or weight of the lower register pulls the tone flat (Pierce 302).

There are notes in every voice which unless carefully managed are inclined to be out of tune.
(soprano: d", e" and f"; contralto: a', b', and c";
tenor: e', f♯', and g'; bass: b, c', and d') (Woodgate 466, p. 16).

E. Dynamics as a dependent factor

In loud passages they tend to sharp; in soft ones,
to flat (Wilhousky 432).

(Flatting) In the case of adults the best remedy
is a little gentle humming followed by soft singing
(Coleman 63, p. 106).

If the chord is <u>forte</u>, sing it softly until it is in
tune ... (Wilson 450, p. 199).

F. Diction as a dependent factor

There is a very nice relationship between good
pitch and good diction. I have seldom noticed a
tendency to flat where every singer was pronunciation conscious. The flatters are usually the ones
who leave the consonants in their throats, unsaid
and incomplete.... Very often we freshen up the
pitch by freshening up the diction (Peterson 298).

It is astonishing how often flat singing can be corrected by drawing attention to slovenly enunciation
rather than to the notes concerned (Cashmore 46).

To avoid the bad habit called 'scooping,' careful
attention must be given to the pitch of initial con-

sonants. Accurate initial intonation (attack) will
result if singers always think in advance the pitch
of the first vowel and sing the preceding consonant
on that pitch. This device is a particularly helpful
aid to good intonation when the initial consonant is
a subvocal (b̲, d̲, g̲, or j̲) (Waring 420, p. 3).

MUSICIANSHIP AND THE MUSIC AS DEPENDENT
FACTORS IN CHORAL INTONATION

The musicianship of the singers and certain characteristics of the music are presented as dependent factors in
choral intonation. These are reported in Table 16 as: 1)
selection of singers, 2) development of listening skills, 3)
unaccompanied singing, 4) untempered tuning, 5) key of the
music, 6) tempo and rhythm, and 7) difficulty of the music.

Selection of Singers

Twenty-nine authors state that the development and
maintenance of good choral intonation is dependent upon the
careful selection of the singers. Gregg Smith laments the
severity of this problem:

> The singing profession is also plagued with too low
> a level of musicianship among many of its mem-
> bers. I have had to turn away 90 per cent of those
> who audition for me for this reason. Many aspir-
> ing singers will only work on vocal technique,
> avoiding solfege, theory, analysis and history,
> failing to see that vocal technique is a basic tool
> subservient in the long run to much more: phras-
> ing, intonation, rhythmic agility, interpretation
> (359).

Other authors state that most potential choristers, although
perhaps lacking in musicianship training, do not have defective hearing and are capable of singing with good intonation. It is the occasional "chronic flatter" who must be de-
tected and either denied choral membership or given special
training. "If there is continued trouble with intonation, the
cause will usually be found to be with one or two individuals
..." (Grace 140, p. 8). Dennis agrees that "one or two
voices in a large group may cause the entire organization to
adjust singing to the faults of the few" (89). Garretson

warns that when a strict tryout is not mandatory, there will
be "chronic flatters" (130, p. 135). Young declares, "The
war on out-of-tune singing starts at the audition of the individual singer" (473, p. 29). Van Bodegraven and Wilson
also express this viewpoint: "Certainly the ensemble which
admits many singers with defective hearing is inviting poor
intonation" (404, p. 82).

Development of Listening Skills

A very important part of choral training is the development of the listening skills needed for good intonation:
statements extracted from the writings of ninety authors may
be quoted as evidence. The present study did not include
the basic musicianship training of the singers; however, the
basic techniques for developing choral listening skills are
recorded. They are as follows:

1. Practice singing intervals and scales.
2. Practice singing chords and chord progressions.
3. Practice singing cadences and modulations.
4. Practice singing dissonances.
5. Practice deliberate sharping and flatting.
6. Develop the ability to "think high" or approach the
   notes from above.
7. Memorize a pitch.
8. Match pitches of individuals, rows, sections, or
   accompanying instruments.
9. Group the singers in quartets, circles, "scrambled," or change the location of various sections.
10. Hum or sing softly as an aid to hearing the other
   parts.

There is disagreement among the authors as to whether rehearsal time should be given to specific intonation
training or whether the problem should be solved within the
context of the music being studied. Although most of the
authors' opinions would have to be inferred from their
recommendations for developing listening skills, the varying
viewpoints are stated explicitly in the following quotations:

> ... the time spent in pitch training and interval
> recognition during a warm-up period might better
> be incorporated into the general rehearsal (Treggor
> 399).

Once the singers are selected, the work really begins. We drill on listening carefully and getting in
tune (O. C. Christiansen 52).

... the smart director says little about [pitch] in
rehearsal and never anything in concert (Swift 386).

Tune up your chorus before every rehearsal and
concert (James 186).

A choir that practices two hours a week should
spend at least 15 minutes out of the two hours in
learning to sing chords with perfect untempered
intonation (Williamson 442).

Unaccompanied Singing

It is the opinion of twenty-four authors that continuous
use of the piano as an accompanying instrument is detri-
mental to good choral intonation. The reasons for this viewpoint are expressed in the following representative statements:

Do a great deal of unaccompanied singing. It develops independent singers, and aids in the development of clean intonation. Many a muddy
chord has been hidden under a piano accompaniment (Rossel 341).

Singers listen more attentively, develop more self-
reliance, and sing with more accuracy and assurance
when they are not trying to follow their parts as
played on the piano (Smallman and Wilcox 358, p.
7).

... singing our phrases unaccompanied ... makes
for 'pitch mindedness' (Bach 6).

A chorus that cannot sing in tune without accompaniment is not likely to sing in tune when a piano
or organ plays the voice parts ... when the chorus
is singing without accompaniment, there is a chance
for some passages to be in tune ... (Wilson 450,
p. 84).

Nothing will develop pitch sense more quickly than

a cappella choir. Leaning on tones that come from
the piano tuned with sharp thirds and flat fifths
does not develop pitch sense in the singer ...
(Williamson 448).

The reason why this training should be done as far
as possible without piano, is, not only to favor in-
dependence but to achieve the beauty of just intonation (Pierce 301).

Untempered Tuning

Although it is not within the scope of this study to
present a detailed description of untempered tunings, a discussion of choral intonation should include this controversial
issue. Of the nineteen authors who discuss this subject,
fifteen advocate untempered tuning in choral singing. Cleall
and Dykema-Gehrkens call it the natural scale, Pierce advocates just intonation, and Norden identifies it as just intonation, pure intonation, and untempered tuning. The remaining
authors call it untempered tuning.

In the subsequent quotations by Norden, Earhart,
Ehmann, Williamson, Cleall, and Dykema-Gehrkens it may
be noted that each author infers, if he does not state explicitly, that unaccompanied choral singing will, as a matter
of course, tend to be in untempered tuning.

The authors' statements concerning untempered tuning
in choral singing include the following:

... chords as wholes should not be trued to the
piano, for the tempered scale of the piano will
make the thirds of the chords slightly dissonant.
(The pupils should find the third of the chord from
the root, which may be sounded on the piano.)
(Earhart 105, p. 13).

A good 'listening' choir does not sing with the
tempered tuning of a mechanical keyboard instrument; between the e as the tonic of E major and
the e as the leading note in the key of F and the
e as the third of the key of C, there is a distinct
difference which can be recognized by the ear
(Ehmann 113, p. 76).

The conductor will find that in unaccompanied singing the choir will gradually sing the third a little
lower and raise the fifth a little higher (Williamson
442).

... If one person sings C and another attempts to
sing E, the second will tune to the first so that
there are no beats. He does this 'by ear.' If a
third person sings G, this singer will tune to the
E, and C already in tune, so that there are no
beats, and so on. All Equal Temperament chords
have beats in them, and such chords can be produced only by means of an instrument previously
tuned (Norden 280).

If the singers have no accompaniment, their voices
are likely to return to the natural tuning of the
scale ... (Cleall 62, p. 37).

Most singing is accompanied by instrument--or instruments. This forces the voices always to
sound--or at least to approximate--intervals based
on the tempered scale, thus making impossible the
'smooth' effect of the natural scale (Dykema and
Gehrkens 104, p. 107).

... music of the Renaissance ... It is also necessary to have an understanding of untempered pitch,
so vital in the singing of these works, as the equal
temperament of the modern piano can be fatal to
them (Little 240, p. 121).

Finn, Klein, Barkley, and Apel express their doubts
concerning the use of untempered tuning. Finn avoids a
"debate" on the subject--"the value of the issues involved being academic rather than practical" (122, p. 72). Klein
says:

Intonation--is the one department of choral singing
that seems to make for the most heated conversa-
tion among people from different 'camps.' There
are the 'just' intoners and the 'tempered' intoners,
those that say the thirds and sevenths must be
sung a bit flat, and those that say they should be
sharped. ... I feel sure, however, that most of
this is 'talk' and could very well be eliminated
(212).

Berkley agrees, "If we can achieve the accuracy of the tempered scale we can safely relegate enharmonic discrepancies
to the realm of acoustics or physics" (7). Apel analyzes the
problems of performance in just intonation and concludes:

> Since harmonies including the supertonic (this chord
> is responsible for the lowering of pitch) are par-
> ticularly frequent in the Palestrina style, just in-
> tonation proves unsatisfactory for exactly that type
> of music for which it has frequently been recom-
> mended. The conclusion to be drawn from all
> these facts is that the interest of just intonation
> lies only in the theoretical field, and that the ap-
> plication to actual performance is limited to oc-
> casional chords (initial, final triads) in a cappella
> music (4, p. 385).

Although they do not explicitly recommend equal
temperament, some authors recommend singing the third,
sixth, and seventh degrees of the scale high. From their
recommendation it may be inferred that they reject the idea
of untempered tuning. Perhaps they are recommending
Pythagorean tuning, although it is never identified as such.

Key of the Music

According to twenty-eight authors, a frequent occurrence in choral singing is the realization of a relationship
between intonation problems and the key of the music being
sung. The following statements are representative of the
evidence found in the writings:

> Often a song is in the wrong key for your group.
> It may, for example, keep one or more parts sing-
> ing around a 'break' in their voices (Krone 225, p.
> 79).

> All else failing, a practically infallible cure [for
> flatting] is afforded by raising (or sometimes low-
> ering) the given pitch a half or a whole tone (Da-
> vison 85, p. 37).

> Most choral groups sing in better pitch in certain
> keys than in others. It is well to determine in
> which keys the group sings in pitch and cater to
> those keys (Archie Jones 191, p. 91).

For some reason--probably acoustic--certain keys
do not seem as comfortable in some rooms as
others (Young 473, p. 66).

... pitching the number a half-step higher than
written. This seems to call forth a brighter tone
and a certain emotional stimulation which react
favorably on the intonation (Rowles 344).

Unaccompanied numbers particularly should be sung
in a variety of keys. Repetition of a number in
the same key day after day leads to inertia and
poor intonation. Flatting may often be corrected
by raising the pitch of the song a half-step (Van
Bodegraven and Wilson 406, p. 82).

During the long process of preparing a choir for
concert appearances it is wise to change keys occasionally in order to prevent songs from getting
into a 'groove.' Ordinarily it is better to raise
the pitch a half step than to lower it, although
there are exceptions to this rule (Veld 407).

Tempo and Rhythm

The factors of rhythm and tempo are discussed by
seventeen authors with reference to choral intonation. Wilhousky says, "I let the singers understand ... that a fast
tempo tends to sharp tone while a slow tempo flats it" (431).
Archie Jones asserts that "tempo has much to do with pitch
also. Fast tempo is conducive to singing in pitch, while
slow tempo is inimical to it" (191, p. 91). Krone warns,
"If you take sustained music too slowly, you will have trouble
keeping up the pitch because of the inadequate breath support
of the singers and lack of rhythmic vitality in the song"
(225, p. 79). According to Finn, "Slow tempos and flatten-
ing are allies ..." (122, p. 79). Williamson makes the following observation:

It is the non-rhythmic individual who usually is the
poorest in tuning. When each member in a group
becomes rhythmic, good tuning seems to be the
natural result (445).

Difficulty of the Music

Seventeen authors state that a frequent cause of poor
choral intonation is that the music is too difficult for the
singers, or conversely, that the singers do not know their
parts. Fuhr declares, "Nine times in ten a group will sing
a thoroughly familiar tune in pitch." He emphasizes the
problems which are created by attempting to perform music
which is "over the heads in difficulty" and declares: "No
ensemble can be expected to sing with true intonation until
all sections can vocalize their individual parts accurately
without accompaniment" (128, pp. 65-66). Krone also expresses this viewpoint when he discusses "insufficient practice on the part as a melody" as a cause of poor intonation
(225, p. 73).

MENTAL AND PHYSICAL ATTITUDES AS DEPENDENT
FACTORS IN CHORAL INTONATION

An analysis of the authors' statements concerning the
role of mental and physical attitudes in the development and
maintenance of good choral intonation reveals the following
factors and author-coverage totals:

	Number of Authors
1. Poor mental attitudes or mood	36
2. Lack of concentration	23
3. Nervousness or excitement	23
4. Fatigue	27
5. Physical inertia or lack of vitality	21

The following are representative statements concerning mental and physical attitudes as dependent factors in
choral intonation:

When concentration is overly intense and the
chorus is nervous, as in a contest, the pitch tends
to rise; when concentration is weak and the chorus
tired, bored, or inattentive, the pitch tends to fall.
Flatting is by far the more common. It is chiefly

due to inertia, to a lack of physical and mental
alertness (Christy 58, p. 57).

Inability to hold the pitch is sometimes due to
fatigue resulting from unskillful rehearsing (Davison
85, p. 38).

A rehearsal immediately after lunch puts an addi-
tional strain on the conductor, who must be ever
alert in matters of sagging pitch and drooping
spirits (Cain 37, p. 47).

Why do choirs flat? Because they lack the ability
to concentrate! [Bergman quotes F. M. Christian-
sen] (Bergman 15, p. 160).

Sharping is rare: it is generally due to over-
anxiety and nervousness (Whittlesey 427, p. 112).

Fear, distaste, and mental fatigue frequently effect the timbre and pitch of a tone (Finn 125, p.
8).

Pitch is partly psychological in nature. If the
chorus believes it is singing in pitch, the chances
are better that it will (Archie Jones 191, p. 91).

Sharp singing is relatively rare, and generally occurs when the choir is trying too hard and forcing
the tone....
    The fundamental cause of flat singing is lack of
concentration, coupled with unawareness of danger
spots (Cashmore 46).

ENVIRONMENTAL FACTORS IN CHORAL INTONATION

    Three environmental or external factors are discussed
with reference to choral intonation: 1) ventilation of the rehearsal room or auditorium, 2) atmospheric conditions, and
3) acoustics and the audibility of the other voice parts or the
accompaniment.

Ventilation of the Rehearsal Room or Auditorium

    Of the thirty authors who discuss the ventilation of the

room as a factor in choral intonation, fifteen specify that
an over-heated room causes flatting.   Other authors point
out the need for an adequate amount of oxygen in the air or
make general reference to the need for proper ventilation.

Atmospheric Conditions

King reports a twelve-year study of English choral
performances in which it was determined that choral intonation is good when the barometric pressure is rising and poor
when it is falling (210).   Of the eleven authors who discuss
atmospheric conditions in relation to choral intonations, the
following statements are representative:

> ... in hot muggy weather or on cold, damp days,
> hearing is bound to be impaired in some degree;
> and the ideal hearing conditions may be found on
> cool, crisp days (Paul 293).

> Dark, depressing days often cause groups to flat
> (Swift 386).

> The change of keys and tempos to offset the de-
> pressing effect of heavy atmosphere of wet weather
> is frequently helpful, but generally, if the director
> be free to change the programme he is well ad-
> vised to eliminate polyphonic music on such days
> and all a cappella music in the minor mode (Finn
> 122, p. 78).

> Sometimes, a dry, cold invigorating day after a
> warm, humid spell will give a group excess ner-
> vous energy which will result in sharping (Krone
> 225, p. 80).

Acoustics and Audibility of Other Voice Parts
or Accompaniment

Thirty-two authors discuss the acoustics of the rehearsal room or auditorium and the need for the singers to
be able to hear the other parts in order to maintain good
choral intonation.   The following statements illustrate the
authors' viewpoints:

> ... it may be established with certainty that in

small halls or in larger halls with flat and low-
studded ceilings, the polyphony of the 15th, 16th,
and 17th centuries is difficult of performance, except by a small group of singers, proper attention
being given to the selection of the pitch, the tempos, the decibels of quantity used, and the dynamic
undulations.
... Polyphonic music needs headroom to assure
the floating about of the partial tones of many involved and interlaced lines ... (Finn 122, p. 78).

... a room with low ceilings and poor acoustical
properties, or an overheated auditorium may cause
the tone to flat, whereas a large, echoing auditorium is almost sure to produce sharpness (Fuhr 128,
p. 65).

... a thorough shuffling of all the sections, keeping
the stronger voices in the rear of the group, so
that there is no sectional or individual predomi-
nance.... Intonation benefits, moreover, because
each singer, surrounded by the other parts, is
aware of his relation to the total harmony, and is
therefore not so likely to stray in tonality (Waring
418).

We find it much easier to keep in tune if the
basses increase amplitude when they sing the low
tones, and the sopranos decrease amplitude as they
ascend (Williamson 443).

The entire male section will keep on the pitch when
enclosed on the sides by the higher voices of the
girls. It is a mistake to put the boys' voices behind the girls. It causes much of the flatting that
is so difficult at times (Cain 37, p. 58).

The commonest cause of choirs being out of tune
is failure to hear the root of the harmony, which
is generally in the bass (Steck 363).

CHAPTER 6

RANGE

In singing, as with other musical media, range denotes the extent of pitch variation between the high and low
tonal limits of the voice. However, since the voice is the
uniquely human instrument, one encounters several significant variables when attempting to define the limits or characteristics of that range. For example, the physical maturity of the singer--whether he is in high school or college
or is an older adult--may be a determining factor in the
range of his voice. Further, the amount of vocal training
and singing experience which he has had may be an influence
on the extent of his range. Finally, as conductors and teachers describe the range of the voices of choral singers they
may consciously or unconsciously be considering variables
such as: 1) the normal, approximate, or practical range,
2) the comfortable range, 3) the possible range, or 4) the
range required in the music. Each of these variables may
introduce an apparent lack of agreement to the published
writings and should therefore be kept in mind when studying
the evidence reported in this chapter.

Pitch Dimensions of the Voice Ranges

Thirty-two authors give specific pitch dimensions of
the range of choral voices. A tabulation of the pitches presented in Table 18 is divided into two sections: 1) the
range of choral voices when four voice classifications (SATB)
are designated, and 2) the range of choral voices when
eight parts (e.g., first soprano, second soprano) are designated.

Quality Changes Within the Range

Thirty-one authors discuss tone quality changes within
the range; these are referred to as changes of registers,

TABLE 17

Author-Coverage Table for Range Showing the Chapter Outline
Which was Evolved from the Data, the Number of Authors Who
Discussed Each Sub-Topic of the Outline, and the Page Number
of this Study's Presentation of the Data
89 Authors are Represented

	Number of Authors	Page
I. Characteristics of the range of choral voices		
A. Pitch dimensions of the voice ranges	32	89
B. Quality changes within the range	31	89
II. Recommendations for developing the range of choral voices		94
A. Through concept of tones	51	94
B. Through resonance sensation	27	103
C. Through concern with physiological factors	46	106
D. Through vowel study	32	108

lifts, change-of-color points, or breaks. The following
statements reveal the nature of this aspect of singing:

> In untrained voices there are several tones, usually
> a fourth or fifth apart, at which a new color or
> timbre is heard as the student sings up the scale.
> These change of color points are called by various
> names, 'breaks,' 'lifts,' or 'harmonics' (Krone
> 225, p. 56).

> The lift is a place in the range of the voice where
> it is necessary to use less breath. The lift is the
> place where the voice becomes easier to produce,
> and where the singer senses a spontaneous buoyancy
> in ascending scales (Williamson 440).

TABLE 18

Pitch Dimensions of the Range of Choral Voices with the
Number of Authors Recorded for Each Pitch

Four Parts Designated: SATB

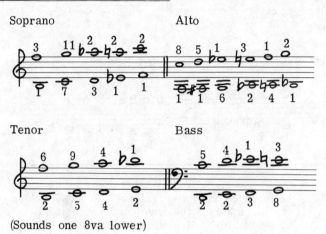

(Sounds one 8va lower)

Eight Parts Designated

TABLE 18 (continued)

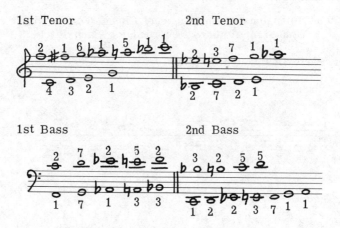

1st Tenor   2nd Tenor

1st Bass   2nd Bass

Resonances are often referred to as registers
(chest, middle, and head) and cause much trouble
to the singer. Registers should never be considered in voice development, for they do not exist
by nature.... Registers are produced when a singer forces a series of tones, when ascending, upon
one resonating point ... instead of remembering
that each tone requires a change of the vocal
organs (Tkach 398, p. 62).

... most present-day competent voice teachers
agree ... that the voice consists of two registers
only, the lower and the upper (falsetto) register.
... Isolation of these registers is necessary before
a full-voiced tone, without "thickening" can be produced (Loney 241).

There is disagreement about the number of registers
or quality changes. Fuhr agrees with Loney's designation
(op. cit.) of two registers for men's voices, although he
calls them head and chest register. He states, however,
that women's voices possess three registers: the chest,
middle, and head registers (128, p. 45). Pierce, Nitsche,
and Cain are among the authors who refer to head tones and
chest tones (Pierce 304; Nitsche 278; Cain 37, p. 51). Pitts,
Finn, Epstein, Hintz, and Sunderman refer in various ways
to three registers, calling them head or upper, middle (Ep-

stein refers to it as "mouth tone"), and lower or chest
(Pitts 315; Finn 122, p. 162; Epstein 119, p. 19; Hintz 164;
Sunderman 376, pp. 32-37). Krone presents three change-
of-color points for each voice, which suggests four registers
(225, p. 26). Wilson attempts to clarify the discrepancy as
to the number of registers:

> The most popular number is three registers: head,
> middle (or mouth), and chest.
> This latter conception of registers is based upon
> the sensations of resonance. The latest scientific
> findings indicate that there are two registers in
> every type of voice and that they are based upon
> muscular action, with a resultant difference in
> resonance between the two registers. These two
> registers are usually referred to as the lower and
> upper (or falsetto) registers.
> Briefly, the muscular adjustment for the lower
> register functions for low and loud tones; the ad-
> justment for the upper register functions for high
> and soft tones (450, p. 196).

There is general agreement that the soprano voice
may have a quality change around d" (fourth line of the
treble staff). Krone, Tkach, and Hintz recognize this
change of quality or color although their locations of the
change vary (Krone 225, p. 26; Tkach 398, p. 63; Hintz
164). Cain and Coleman state that sopranos sing pitches
above d" as "head tones" (Cain 42; Coleman 66, p. 59).
Fuhr designates c" or d" as the place where "the voice will
change quality and a lighter tone will emerge" (128, p. 53).
In addition to the quality change around d" for the sopranos,
Krone and Hintz also designate a change of quality at f♯'
(Krone Ibid. ; Hintz Ibid.).

Wilson notes that the soprano is written primarily in
the upper register. "The alto part lies in both registers.
That is the reason for the so-called break in the alto voice
usually around D above middle C" (450, p. 196). Fuhr
recognizes this change, noting that mezzo-sopranos and altos
may use a "heavy chest quality" below e' or f' (128, p. 55).
Tkach designates only one quality change which for the first
alto was b♭', while for the second alto, g' (Ibid.). Krone
recognizes quality changes for first alto at d♯', a♯', and
d♯"; for second alto the changes are at c♯', g♯', and c♯"
(Ibid.).

The problem of quality changes in men's voices is more complex because of the various descriptions of tone quality used for high notes; namely, head tones, falsetto tones, mezzo-voce or half-voice tones, and covered tones. Coleman declares that tenors should sing all notes above c' or d' "in the head" (63, p. 55). Tkach also designates c͞ and d' as quality change points for tenors (Ibid.). Steckel advocates the use of mezzo-voce tones and emphasizes that somewhere between c' and f' "the boy has to learn to adjust his vocal mechanism" (364). Barkley says that the changes to falsetto tones for tenors should be made between d' and f' (7). Grace, Wilson, and Winslow acknowledge the tenor pitches of e' and f' as points above which they should sing with what are called "covered tones" (Grace 140, p. 4; Wilson 456; Winslow 463). Krone's highest change-of-color for second tenor is e', for first tenor, f♯' (Ibid.).

For baritones, Tkach recognizes b as a quality change (Ibid.). Winslow recommends that for pitches above c' and d', baritones should sing with a forward tone (Ibid.). Wilson noted that baritones "cover" above d' (Ibid.). Krone's change-of-color points for baritone are d♯, a♯, and d♯' (Ibid.).

Grace declares that basses should "cover" tones above b or c' (Ibid.). Winslow asks for a forward tone above b for basses, and Coleman recommends that basses sing notes above a or b "in the head" (Winslow Ibid.; Coleman 63, p. 55). Tkach recommends a bass quality change at g (Ibid.). Krone advocates quality changes for basses at c♯, g♯, and c♯' (Ibid.).

RECOMMENDATIONS FOR DEVELOPING
THE RANGE OF CHORAL VOICES

The recommendations for developing the range of choral voices are organized into four sections: 1) through concept of tone, 2) through resonance sensation, 3) through concern with physiological factors, and 4) through vowel study.

Concept of Tone

The concepts of tone discussed in this section include light tone, falsetto tone, mezzo-voce or half-voice tone, and

covered tone. The use of imagery as an aid in the development of vocal range is also discussed. As reported in
Table 17, the writings of fifty-one authors are represented.

The actual characteristics which the various authors
associate with the quality concepts of a light tone, falsetto
tone, and mezzo-voce tone are difficult to ascertain. It is
clear that some authors use the terms interchangeably while
others make distinctions among them. The meaning and role
of these terms in the development of the range of choral
voices are presented in the following paragraphs.

The concept of a light tone in the development of
vocal range includes factors of dynamics, physical effort,
and tone color. Its meaning and use are illustrated in the
following quotations:

> [for blending the registers] Use a very light
> quality of tone, even though it may sound very thin
> or almost falsetto....
>   Be sure that the starting tone is always free,
> relaxed and of light, flute-like quality (Pitts 313).

> A light free tone is always to be employed in the
> upper voices (Fuhr 128, p. 16).

> Scales should generally be practiced downwards
> ... in order to develop the right light production
> of high notes and to smooth over 'breaks' ... tak-
> ing care that your tenors use light tone at the
> start of each scale. If they prefer to sing the
> top G sharp and A in falsetto, let them (Grace 140,
> p. 12).

> As sopranos and tenors sing higher their voices
> usually become lighter and more 'flute like' (Swift
> 384).

> This emphasis on light singing is important--so
> important that if a choir director had to choose
> just one thing to teach his choir, this should be
> it. And the way to do it. Teach them to yodel
> ... (Kortkamp 223).

> Weight, murkiness and thickness are other defects
> traceable, in a measure, to habitual loudness, but
> perhaps more directly to upward singing, that is,

bringing the heaviness of the low notes up through
the middle register and trying to force it into the
naturally lighter upper register (Finn 125, p. 5).

Falsetto tones are recommended for extending the
range of male choral voices. The following quotations illustrate the authors' recommendations:

> ... there is a wide use of falsetto in the upper
> register, but the question of whether falsetto sing-
> ing should be deliberately cultivated, whether it
> damages in any way the medium part of the sing-
> er's voice, whether--in fact--it is a legitimate
> device either in solo or choral singing, is a point
> so controversial that no basic statement can be
> made at this time supported by a substantial ma-
> jority of outstanding voice teachers (Bartholomew
> 9).

> The use of falsetto and mezzo-voce (while the sub-
> ject of dispute by the learned) should be taught in
> connection with good tone (Nitsche 278).

> ... the upper notes of male tenors are sometimes
> best sung falsetto, where the men are not genuine
> tenors. A hard, clear tone should be cultivated
> (Cleall 61, p. 104).

> ... we accept the use of the falsetto as a legitimate
> part of our vocal ensembles.... Although almost
> any true tenor can encompass it, falsetto is best
> attempted by an organ which is very light and lyric
> by nature. Its use must be based on perfect voice
> placement and depends entirely upon head resonance.
> One often hears it said that frequent use of falsetto
> 'ruins' the voice. This is not so.... The danger
> of the falsetto is--like everything else in vocal
> work--its forcing or abuse (Jaroff 187).

> The problem can be obviated through the use of the
> light adjustment or falsetto--bringing that voice
> down gradually and finally going into the 'light'
> male adjustment. Careful practice--that of start-
> ing in the 'light' adjustment or falsetto in the high
> voice and carrying the quality down until it 'cuts
> down' can cure our vocal ills in the high voice
> (Gilliland 134).

Falsetto, by the way, may be used for soft extreme notes by real tenors, provided the tone is
good and the change easily managed. Nobody pre-
tends that it is as good as the real tenor quality,
but it is better than forced ... tenor tone ... the
tone blends well (Grace 184, p. 66).

I tell the boys to go right on up into falsetto, and
I do it with them until they get over the strange-
ness of it (Howard 174).

Every choral director should pay a great deal of
attention to the development of a strong and resonant falsetto in all the men's voices of his chorus.
Otherwise they are inclined to shout or yell their
high notes in the lower register quality (Pierce
302).

Should the range or tessitura be insurmountable,
it is wise to suggest the use of the 'falsetto.'
This relieves the strain and forcing. If the
falsetto can be brightened and placed forward,
avoiding the dark 'hooty' quality, it becomes a useful and legitimate sound. The use of the falsetto
is a step toward the fine rich head tones found in
more mature singers (J. L. Jones 200).

   Wilson, Tritchler, Garretson and Winslow agree with
Jones (op. cit.) that falsetto tones are an aid in developing
a mature tenor's technique. Wilson and Tritchler explain
the technique:

[Singing an octave skip to g' or a♭' for baritones,
c" or d" for tenors.] Sing 'hoo' very softly with
rounded lips. The voice will automatically change
to falsetto. The sensation of highness will be useful in developing a high virile tone later (Wilson
456).

We encourage the use of falsetto in our male
voices. A high pitch will discover this register
for them. The tone is usually weak and breathy
when first used. This impractical tone is a means
to an end, and with encouragement by singing pure
falsetto tones as loudly as possible, progress to a
lower and better used register will result (Tritchler
400).

For developing the high tones of male singers, eleven
authors recommend the use of mezzo-voce or half-voice
tones. Some authors consider this to be the same as falsetto
tones, while others point out a distinction between these two
quality concepts. Hollis Dann emphasizes mezzo-voce singing; his instructions for its development are quoted by Krone,
Steckel and Burns. The following quotations describe its
nature and illustrate its use:

> Intelligent use of mezzo-voce singing has simplified
> the male voice problem in the senior high school,
> happily lessening the dangers of forcing, and re-
> sultant strain. Use of mezzo-voce has greatly
> widened the chorus repertoire, making practicable
> the use of music with wider compass and more
> strenuous type. Mezzo-voce singing has also
> helped to build up the first tenor part. A second
> tenor with a well-developed mezzo-voce can safely,
> and quitely effectively, sing the first tenor part....
>   The use of mezzo-voce largely removes the
> danger of forcing the upper tone of all voices
> (Dann 80).

> ... train the tenors to use what is sometimes
> called the 'half-voice.' Most tenors can use this
> voice naturally; those who cannot will learn to do
> so very readily. This voice is a sort of mixture
> of full voice and falsetto. It is easily produced,
> and has considerable resonance in spite of its
> lightness. With a little practice boys can learn to
> change from full-voice to this lighter half-voice at
> any point in their range (Burns 32).

> Careful cultivation of the half-voice and the falsetto
> in the upper register will ease the tenor problem
> considerably (Schuetz 349).

> Male singers in the post-change period must learn
> to use the mezzo-voce, or light voice, which is
> merely an exact carryover from the head voice
> focus of the properly used child voice. The sensa-
> tion for this is readily taught through soft humming
> exercises on descending scales, carrying the vocal-
> ization to the highest possible tones and into the
> 'falsetto' range (Winslow 463).

A great deal of strain and off-key singing heard

among the boys of high school choruses is due to
the attempt (especially among tenors) to force
heavy, chest register quality up into the high tones
of their parts. This can be eliminated in both
tenors and basses by the proper use of messa-
voce or 'half-voice' (Krone 225, p. 59).

... the use of the male mezza-voce, or light
voice, which is an indispensable feature of all
mature artistic singing.... All well-schooled male
choral sections use the mezza-voce on pianissimo
passages. There is no other means of producing
a really soft, pure tone, for the physical effort en-
tailed in attempting to squeeze down the full voice
to piano proportions brings the singer very swiftly
to a vocal 'dead end' (Fuhr 128, p. 57).

It is imperative that high school boys learn to use
half-voice proficiently and to use it on all upper
tones which would otherwise cause tension. Half-
voice utilizes what is left of the man's child voice
and is often called falsetto. It produces an effortless tone and can be developed to have good carrying power. A good way to rediscover this voice
is to sing the vowel oo in the middle register, say
G, mezzo-forte and then sing the G above, softly
(Van Bodegraven and Wilson 404, p. 80).

Dann's procedure for developing male mezzo-voce
tones is quoted by Steckel (364) and Krone (225, pp. 59-60).
It consists of a "la-la-la-la-la" pattern sung on g' or ab'
(actual pitch) quickly and lightly, without the slightest effort.
The next step is to sing a do, ti, la, sol, la, ti, do pattern
on "la" beginning on the high ab'. This pattern is repeated
each time a half-step lower, with the choristers singing
rapidly, very lightly, and with complete relaxation. According to Steckel, carrying the light voice all the way down is
the quickest way to eliminate the "break" into the full voice.
The tone may be weak and breathy at first, but as the singers get accustomed to the ease of production, the tone will
gradually gain in resonance, timbre and volume if correct
posture, breathing and breath support are applied.

Fuhr and Winslow recommend establishing the mezzo-
voce tone through effortless downward vocalizations beginning
pianissimo on a high pitched hum, followed by oo and ee
(Fuhr 128, pp. 57-58; Winslow 462).

In presenting a basic classification of male high voice
concepts, Wilson does not distinguish between falsetto, mezzo-
voce, and light or head tones. He states:

> Men can sing high tones in three different ways of
> physical adjustment: (1) falsetto--a light, effemi-
> nate tone, (2) yelling--a strident tone secured by
> lifting the position of the larynx, and (3) adding a
> sensation of nasality--a virile tone produced with
> the larynx in normal position, sometimes referred
> to as a covered tone.... Many times men use a
> mixed quality of tone on extremely high pitches,
> combining the various physical adjustments indicated
> above. Such adjustment is present in a soft, lyric
> tone on a high pitch with predominantly falsetto
> color, or a forte tone on a high pitch with an open
> quality, but enough cover to eliminate the strident
> edge of a yell (453).

The use of a light tone in dealing with the range problems of the choir receives the following criticisms:

> Let me summarize the ten points which I have just
> made in my attack against the use of the light head
> voice as a standard of vocalization in our public
> schools today. They are: (1) high and light are
> diametrically opposed considerations; (2) high and
> light singing requires more skill than the average
> child possesses; (3) high and light singing is wrong
> temporally; (4) high and light singing is poor aes-
> thetically; (5) high and light singing is repressive
> psychologically; (6) high and light singing sacrifices
> the lower range; (7) high and light singing is too
> greatly removed from the speech level; (8) high
> and light singing is arbitrarily dictated by the
> teacher and sacrifices the interest of the child;
> (9) high and light singing instills the baseless fear
> of self-inflicted injury; and (10) high and light sing-
> ing is not so much a protection to the child as it
> is to the teacher (Kwalwasswer 229).

> The easiest volume for singers in the upper half
> of the range is best vocalized mezzo-forte, and
> successful piano and pianissimo singing are more
> difficult and require training and guidance (Ameri-
> can Academy of Teachers of Singing 1).

> I have been filled with disgust at many concerts
> when I have heard fine, husky men of college age
> imitate the tones of women. It is just as revolting
> to hear women--altos, in particular--imitate the
> tones of men. Where is their taste? It is no
> wonder, then, that such organizations fail to re-
> ceive support from the student body.
> If boys are allowed to sing in a normal, healthy
> and oftentimes vigorous manner, more talent than
> is needed will be attracted to choral groups (Wil-
> housky 430).

> The hushed or restrained voice usually is resented
> by high school students, especially by boys. They
> resist the 'namby-pamby' type of effeminate singing
> so frequently heard in high schools (Loney 241).

Nine authors discuss the covered tone in the development of the range of male choral voices. Wilson describes
this type of tone, saying, "It is the stock in trade of all fine
male singers, for it enables them to sing high notes with a
virile, manlike tone without tension or forcing" (450, p. 208).
Grace asserts that basses should cover their tones around ḇ
or c̱' and tenors around e̱' or f̱', explaining that "the covered
tonē is also described as 'closed' and is sometimes called
the 'mixed voice' " (140, p. 4). He suggests only the teacher's demonstration as a procedure for teaching covered
tones. In cooperation with Davies he emphasizes that private
lessons for the choirmaster would enable him "to show his
basses how to 'cover' the tone ... and to demonstrate to
his tenors the use of the light or 'head' register" (83, p.
73). Epstein declares, "If the focus is placed right and the
tone kept 'covered', falsetto can be prevented" (119, p. 37).
Sunderman acknowledges that covered tones are difficult to attain. He states that both men and women use them but recognizes that with male voices they present more problems.
He recommends bringing the head resonance as far down into
the range as possible and dove-tailing the registers (376, p.
32). Wetzler says that the higher you sing, the more dark,
covered, rounded, and modified the vowel must be; conversely, the lower you sing the more open and brilliant the vowel
must be (423).

Ehret, Garretson and Winslow present techniques
adapted from Wilson's procedure for developing male covered
tones. Wilson recommends legato ascending and descending
octave skips beginning e̱♭--e̱♭'--e♭ and ascending by half-

steps to g' or a♭' for baritones and c" or d" for tenors.
The exercise begins pianissimo on "hoo," utilizing a falsetto
tone to establish a high resonance sensation and a hum to
add nasality to the tone. "Ing," "Ay," and "Ah" (hunh) are
then vocalized on the same pattern at a mezzo-forte dynamic
with two fingers in the mouth to keep it open. The objective
is a virile quality and a sensation of covering. These are
aided by having "a drawing in or 'drinking in' sensation in
skipping the octave with added nasal feeling of resonance
which seems to be concentrated behind the bridge of the
nose" (Wilson 453, also 456, 450, pp. 208-209; Ehret 114,
p. 44; Winslow 462 and 463; Garretson 130, p. 87). Ehret
and Winslow refer to this quality as "'cover' or post-nasal
resonance" (Winslow Ibid.; Ehret Ibid.).

Imagery in the Development of Vocal Range. According to Coleman, the "difficulty of the production of what are
called the high notes is to a large extent a mental difficulty
and not a physical one" (63, p. 31). He advises never to
speak of high notes "in such a way as to imply something
difficult or unusual." Other authors recommend a more
positive approach to solving the "mental difficulties" of vocal
range. The following statements illustrate the various ways
in which imagery is employed in range development:

> Think of vocal tone as being diamond shape: broad
> and ample in the middle; pointed and small scale
> at both extremities of pitch (Cleall 61, p. 103).

> As the pitch rises, the singers should think down-
> ward and widen the tone (Coleman 63, p. 29).

> ... imagine a large triangle, the apex of which is
> the top of the head with the base at the knees.
> ... ask the singers to continually think downward
> (down the legs of the triangle), especially when
> singing high tones (Dyer 103).

> The lines ascending the cone shaped diagram indi-
> cate the gradual lessening breadth of concept as
> the singer mentally approaches his higher tones....
>   It has been found very beneficial to have the
> singer move his forearm horizontally in front of
> him while singing ascending and descending pas-
> sages (Sunderman 376, pp. 30 and 34).

> Always sing down to a tone--never up to it....

Extend one or both arms straight forward, shoulder
high. Now sing the lower tone. Then, as you approach and sing the upper tone, lower the hands as
though you were using them to bear your weight
upon a table (Deardorff 87, p. 6).

If the singer and conductor can accept the fact that
music is horizontal flow, not vertical flow, they
will quickly find tensions leaving the singer's
throat, developing a new coordination between his
body and the voice that he gives forth (Williamson
440).

Make certain to seat voices on bottom tone. Voice
is like a pyramid. The wider the voice is at the
bottom, the higher one can go before getting to the
top (King 209).

To catch on to how to begin the phrase in high
gear so you're ready for the high note, occasionally
sing an added high note first, before the low note,
and then scoop down and commence the phrase in
that high, tenorish quality (Kortkamp 219, p. 28).

... you should look on the ascending scale, not so
much as an ascending scale, but as something that
is getting bigger in the same place, each note developing inevitably out of the preceding one (Rowland 343, p. 36).

Care must be taken to see that the ascending tones
do not lose the contact with the vocal cords which
they gained on the lowest tone (Archie Jones 191,
p. 26).

Resonance Sensation

Twenty-seven authors discuss the development of the
range of choral voices in terms of the proper resonance
sensation of the tones. The need for a forward, head or
high resonance for higher pitches and the use of downward
vocalizations for extending the range and blending the qualities of the upper and lower tones are the most frequent
recommendations.

Each of the quality concepts discussed in the previous

section (light tone, falsetto tone, mezzo-voce tone, and
covered tone) employ a sensation of high or head resonance.
A statement by a representative spokesman for each of these
quality concepts illustrates this point:

> [light tone] ... the students should be encouraged
> to concentrate on the light upper quality ... frankly
> call it 'head tone' (Fuhr 128, p. 53).

> [falsetto] No one without a perfect command of
> head resonance should attempt it (Jaroff 187).

> [mezzo-voce] With much head resonance, even
> nasal quality, sing 'la' quickly and lightly five
> times on g' or a' (actual pitch), without any effort
> (Krone 225, p. 60).

> [covered tone] ... these sounds [ING and UNG]
> serve to introduce 'cover' sensation or postnasal
> resonance (Ehret 114, p. 44).

Head resonance sensations are frequently associated
with high pitches and their development, while chest resonance is associated (although less frequently) with low
pitches. The following statements illustrate this viewpoint:

> The upper register is associated with the head
> voice and light, lyric resonance, the lower with
> the chest voice and strong, virile resonance (Wil-
> son 450, p. 196).

> Registers, head, middle, and chest, are just ways
> of thinking of the mental effect of notes. High
> notes as a rule should feel 'heady,' for it is the
> head which is the best resonator for high voice.
> Similarly with 'chest' notes, where the ribs can--
> and should--be felt vibrating sympathetically ...
> (Phillips 299, p. 110).

> By starting on a high tone and proceeding down-
> ward, at the same time cautioning the candidate to
> sing softly, the head voice quality will more often
> assert itself and will carry down into the chest
> register (Cain 37, p. 51).

> In low notes the concentration of resonance is
> more in the chest; in middle tones it is felt strong-

ly in the roof of the mouth; in upper notes the
sensation is felt in the head and in the facial cavities behind the nose (Fuhr 128, p. 45).

[Bass high notes] Pitch the voice forward into the
front of your head. To get the feel of it, yell
'yay' in a high, 'calling voice.' Sing tenorish on
high tones. Don't be mellow (Kortkamp 219, p. 34).

As one ascends the scale, more breath should be
directed toward the postnasal cavities, without letting the main resonating cavity collapse. When
descending the scale, the singer should carry the
upper voice down over the notes on which tension
occurs (Tkach 397, p. 30).

For the lower third to lower half of the voice
range, the main resonating area is in the chest.
... the middle range ... the tone focused forward
in the mouth.... The higher notes of the range
need a resonance mostly in the head (Epstein 119,
p. 16).

Each tenor needs individual attention in the attainment and use of the head tone (Barkley 7).

When he is able to utilize 'head resonance' in the
higher tones and at the same time to keep the
larynx relaxed, using proper breath support and
pure vowels, the young tenor is better qualified to
handle demanding tessitura and the higher range
(J. L. Jones 200).

The use of the 'head voice,' that is, a feeling
that the sound is coming from the front of the
forehead instead of from the chest, should be encouraged for all upper notes (Coleman 66, p. 59).

A frequent concern of the authors is the equalization
of resonance qualities within the overall range; an accepted
procedure for this problem is the use of downward vocalization patterns. The authors' recommendations are summarized in the following quotations:

It is the general opinion that, as a rule, as many
notes as possible should be made with dominantly
head resonance; that is, the head-notes should be

carried down as far as possible. This means that
downward scales are the best tone-production exercises for beginners (Phillips 299, p. 110).

... the smoothing out at any point in the voice
must be through downward vocalization through the
change-of-color tone (Krone 225, p. 56).

Downward vocalization, pianissimo, from a point
above the middle register, will gradually endow the
middle and lower registers with some of the lightness, elasticity and buoyancy of the upper notes
(Finn 122, p. 22).

Greater success with the training of the vocal registers seems to issue from a working with the head
register down instead of the chest register up to
and through the middle one (Sunderman 376, p. 38).

In developing low tones a five-tone descending scale
is sufficient for all voices. Sopranos and altos
should sing on an aw vowel so that the break between the two registers is reduced to a minimum.
... Tenors and basses should sing on an ah vowel
keeping the high, arched resonance (Wilson 450, p.
209).

Physiological Factors

Recommendations for developing the range of choral
voices which are concerned with the physiological aspects of
singing were extracted from the writing of forty-six authors.
The points of emphasis are freedom from tension, position
of the structure of the resonators, and breathing.

The discussion of freedom from tension in the chapter
on tone quality emphasizes two factors which are particularly
relevant to the development of vocal range. They are forward or head resonance sensations and soft singing. These
two factors and the resulting freedom of production which
they may elicit are primary considerations in the recommendations of a light, falsetto, or mezzo-voce tone for
higher pitches.

Recommended positions of the physical structure of
the resonators in vocal range development are stated in the

following quotations:

> Vocalize with two fingers between the teeth. This
> device facilitates the dropping of the jaw, which is
> an absolutely essential condition in singing the high
> tones (Garretson 130, pp. 86-87).

> The lowering of the chin in attacking high notes re-
> laxes the throat and thus gives the vocal cords
> greater facility to function freely (Finn 125, p. 8).

> Dip the forehead on high notes, and sing more
> quietly the higher you go ... (Cleall 62, Preface).

> In producing the upper notes the tendency to stiffen
> the throat and squeeze the tone must be counter-
> acted. This may be done by letting the class low-
> er their heads, with the chins nearly touching the
> chest. In this position the tone seems to float up-
> ward, which is as required (Coleman 63, p. 13).

> ... the habit of raising the chin and 'stretching the
> neck' for all high tones is fatal (Sanderson 345).

> On all vowels the mouth is open more on high
> notes than on low notes (Wilson 456; also 450, p.
> 180).

> Never change the shape of your mouth when you hit
> a high note (Young 474, p. 8).

> The arching or raising and lowering of the soft
> palate for high and low pitches, together with an
> open nasal port, is the key to nasalization and a
> uniform tone quality throughout the entire range.
> It is also the technique that permits range exten-
> sion without any 'break' or noticeable registers in
> the voice (Arnold Jones 193).

In an article discussing the problems of high school
tenor, J. L. Jones recommends that "tensions, usually found
in the young tenor's throat, tongue, neck and chin, should be
'transferred' to the diaphragmatic area" (200). Hjortsvang
agrees that "high tones can be helped immensely just by an
improvement in breathing." He continues, "they will often
be further helped by opening the mouth sufficiently wide"
(165, p. 80). "If we develop our diaphragm well and use it,

our range limit is a matter of time," says McCall (255).
Jacobs agrees that lack of range is usually caused by lazy
diaphragms (184, p. 37). Peterson would have us keep the
"throat freedom of the lower tones" and "add a slight lift of
abdominal support and relax the lower jaw and back of the
tongue when approaching the upper range (295, p. 45).
Christy acknowledges, "It is easy to overweight low tones
with too much breath-effort; it is difficult to get enough
strength and endurance of breath-support for extremely high
forte tones in sustained singing" (58, p. 43). Cleall suggests, "Waist squeezing is for your upper notes, and can be
relaxed for quiet sound, or for low notes" (61, p. 35).

Vowel Study

Recommendations which employ vowels as the point
of departure for range development were extracted from the
writings of thirty-two authors. Two points of emphasis are
made: 1) the use of particular vowels for developing the
range, and 2) vowel modification.

Although various authors recommend vocalizing on a
particular vowel for developing the range of the voices,
there is little agreement among the recommendations made.
For example, Pierce discusses the shortage of low basses
and suggests that one or two low basses of the choir develop
their lowest tones "using the vowel eh (e as in 'let') for the
exercise, and endeavoring to place the other vowel-sounds in
the same manner" (301). Garretson says, "In developing the
lower range of the voice, it is suggested that the singers
vocalize, using the vowel ah, on the descending five tone
scale" (130, p. 88).

Fuhr recommends equalizing the alto middle and
chest tones by vocalizing downward on oo, oh, and ee--later
using ah (128, p. 55). In contrast, Wilson recommends a
similar procedure on aw and oh (450, p. 212).

The following statements illustrate the nature of vowel
modification in the development of the range of choral voices:

Many throaty or strident upper tones will be eliminated if the director understands and teaches the
principle of vowel modification. As a soprano
sings an ascending scale on an oo vowel, for instance, she will find it necessary to begin to low-

er the jaw (open the mouth) as she comes about to
D (fourth line treble staff) if she wishes to sing
with good tone. As she continues to ascend, pass-
ing F♯ and G, the true character of the o͞o will be
lost, and the vowel will become about the sound of
u. Continuing the ascent, the vowel will brighten
and be opened until it closely resembles a͟h. Some
such modification takes place in all voices, though
chiefly noticed in sopranos, and on all vowels.
The vowels farthest away from u in the mouth and
throat shape (that is, o͞o, e, and a) will start their
modification lower than vowels which are near u
(such as a͟w, o, and i) (Whittlesey 427, pp. 91-92).

As the voice ascends in pitch, the various vowels
tend toward--and eventually, at the very high register, become--uh or o͞oh, the 'compromise' sound
of the human voice, and diction becomes unintelligi-
ble (Richards 322).

The ascent and descent of the scale calls for certain modifications of vowel forms to accommodate
the necessary adjustments in throat and larynx (Fuhr
128, p. 73).

On high pitches i and e should be darkened, u
should be more like o, and o more like a (Vennard
411).

The 'covered' tone is a neutral color like the high
notes of treble voices. In other words, on extreme high notes all male voices gravitate toward
this neutral color.... The neutral color in the
treble voice is a͟h, in the male voice it is u͟n͟h
(Wilson 450, p. 208).

Notice that e͟e at extremely high pitch tends to grow
hard and shrill. It may be darkened by mixing
some o͟o or o͟h with it (Bingham 17).

Do not try to sing words on very high notes. Sing
'uh' with a suggestion of the sound in the words
(Jacobs 184, p. 38).

The higher you sing, the more dark, covered,
rounded, and modified the vowel must be toward o̅
and o͞o. And its corollary: the lower you sing,

the more open and brilliant the vowel must be
toward ah or ee (Wetzler 423).

The passage containing higher pitches should be
practiced in connection with ee, oo and the umlaut
ü, while the lower passages could be practiced with
syllables using oh and the umlaut ö (Ehmann 112,
p. 189).

CHAPTER 7

DYNAMICS

In musical performance, dynamics is that characteristic of the tone which deals with its degree of loudness and
softness. Expressed in terms of physical vibrations, this
attribute of the tone is called intensity. The degrees of intensity denote the measured physical energy or pressure of
the vibrations.

TABLE 19

Author-Coverage Table for Dynamics Showing the Chapter
Outline Which was Evolved from the Data, the Number of
Authors Who Discussed Each Sub-Topic of the Outline, and
the Page Number of This Study's Presentation of the Data.
72 Authors are Represented

	Number of Authors	Page
I. The role of dynamics in the development of choral voices		112
A. Soft singing should be the basis of vocal development	23	112
B. Mezzo-voce or forte singing should be the basis of vocal development	19	114
II. Recommendations for singing various dynamic levels		116
A. Through concept of tone	32	116
B. Through resonance sensation	22	118
C. Through concern with physiological factors	27	119
D. Through vowel study	6	121

111

THE ROLE OF DYNAMICS IN THE
DEVELOPMENT OF CHORAL VOICES

The statements extracted from the forty years of published writings reveal the controversial nature of dynamics
in the development of choral voices. The evidence is considered in two sections: 1) soft singing should be the basis
of vocal development, and 2) mezzo-voce or forte singing
should be the basis of vocal development.

Soft Singing Should Be the Basis of Vocal Development

As reported in Table 19, twenty-three authors emphasize the values of soft singing in the vocal development
of the choral ensemble. In an article entitled "Legitimate
Soft Tone in Choral Singing," published in 1932, Beach set
forth the soft tone's values for 1) encouraging freedom from
strain and tension, 2) developing accurate intonation, 3) re-
vealing defects in vowel color and enunciation, 4) affording
a safe procedure in the development of upper tones, and 5)
developing a uniform type of production throughout the dynamic range of the singing voice (11). He states, "The soft
tone is, above all, safe. This cannot be said of the fortissimo and mezzo-forte tone which is heard in some high
school choruses" (Ibid.). He also expresses the view that
"the full resonant vocal tone, which is rightly produced ...
can be none other than the soft tone increased in resonance
and power" (Ibid.).

Finn repeatedly emphasizes the role of soft singing in
his writings: "Pianissimo practice is the keynote of all
choral technique expounded in these pages" (122, p. 19). In
his later book, The Conductor Raises His Baton, he reviews
his thinking concerning the role of dynamics in choral training:

> I confess that for some years, fearing various and
> insidiously destructive aspects of quantity, I led a
> narrow and eremitical musical life in the quietness
> of panels No. 1 and 2 (pp and p), with an occa-
> sional bold adventure in No. 3 (mf). Blaming even
> well-behaved loudness (there probably is this kind
> of loudness) for every choral dereliction ... Life
> in the pianissimo hermitage having become too
> monotonous and some control of dynamic strength
> having accrued, I began eventually to appreciate

the importance of the upper panels in the aesthetic
scheme. I have no regrets for the 'days in the
desert,' for I learned then what later decades in
the dramatic fortes has confirmed, viz.: That
loudness is not only fiercely hostile to choral technique, but that in interpretative musicianship it is
the principal and ubiquitous peril to artistry (124,
p. 106).

Further evidence of the values of soft singing or the
dangers of loud singing is found in the following representative statements:

Soft singing promotes ease of tone production,
flexibility, smoothness, cleanness of enunciation,
and tone quality (Smallman and Wilcox 358, p. 164).

Throughout all this preliminary work, all singing
should be soft. Power will come automatically as
the voices develop, but it cannot be impressed too
strongly that the basis of all good singing is soft
tone and easy production (Coleman 63, p. 30).

... power and refined vocal quality are rarely
wedded. If they are mated at all, they approach
the marriage altar rather late in choral life (Fuhr
128, p. 90).

The combination of assurance and lightness of tone
production is the most important consideration of
all choral singing (K. Thomas 393).

... a choir that has been trained to sing softly and
without forcing is more likely to be under control
when, later on, matters of nuance and interpretation generally are being worked over. In choral
work as in any kind of ensemble work, a lightness
of voice in the early rehearsals can do much to
maintain and develop a good over-all quality of
tone (Bowles 24, p. 192).

There should be a general concern for much more
soft (piano not mezzo-forte) singing (Young 474,
p. 126).

Singing softly tends to make a natural blend, ...
Another reason for training the group to sing softly

is the fact that when an amateur sings loudly, he
is likely to produce a strained tone which not only
sounds bad, but which probably will be off pitch
and also will give off a distorted vowel (Eisenkramer 116).

So much of the faulty vocal production I hear today
comes from what I like to call 'over-singing'--try-
ing so hard to 'make' a tone, that what finally results is an artificial voice nobody could possibly
keep on pitch (Rodby 330).

Good (i.e., vital) soft singing should be made the
basis of a choir's work in the matter of tone
(Grace 140, p. 35).

Always practice new numbers piano. In fact most
of the rehearsal singing should be done piano.
Singers will frequently sing so loudly that they
can't hear the effect. Intonation problems are almost sure to be reduced if the 'piano' plan is followed (Barkley 7).

Mezzo-Forte or Forte Singing Should Be the Basis of Vocal Development

Nineteen authors express the conviction that mezzo-
forte or forte singing should be the basis of vocal development. As reported earlier, Kwalwasser presents a sharp
criticism of soft singing in the 1933 Yearbook of the Music
Supervisors National Conference. He particularly criticizes
the use of the light head voice as the standard of vocalization which was used in the schools (229). In 1937, Wilhousky
and R. Peterson continued the criticism of soft singing, as
reported in the Music Educators National Conference Yearbook:

Since choral singing as an art form is an expression of the thoughts, feelings, and impressions of
life, I am wondering how we can justify the constant overuse of soft singing on the grounds that
any tone will be beautiful if it is soft.... Too
long we have worshipped at the shrine of soft singing as a voice builder. Healthy voices develop
with normal and intelligent exercises, and should
of course occasionally venture into the extremes

of both loud and soft dynamics. To suppose however, that great good will come from staying constantly in the one extreme is a fallacy, both from
the standpoint of voice building and from that of
sincere speech expression. It is at variance with
the thesis that fine choral singing arises out of
rich, round tone, clean articulation, and alertness
and sincerity on the part of both the conductor and
the choir (R. Peterson 298).

This theory of soft singing properly belongs in the
lower grades, and, with reservations, occasionally
applies to the training of tenor voices in high
school (Wilhousky 430).

Dunham refers to the overuse of soft singing as the
"style of subdued choralism often prevalent in high school
choirs" (99). P. Peterson criticizes the "'hush-hush' type
of directing that devitalizes the choral tone" (296). Loney
discusses the over-emphasis upon soft singing, explaining,

To say that good pianissimo singing is more difficult than singing at any other dynamic level is an
understatement. True, it is possible to sing with
little or no vocal technique but the result is a
hushed, restrained and breathy pianissimo that
lacks carrying power and quality (241).

Loney also quotes Stanley's book, Your Voice: "There is
nothing so technically destructive as illegitimate, soft singing" (Ibid.). Van Bodegraven and Wilson warn that "There
is no doubt that very loud strained singing will hurt voices,
but the anaemic singing of the a cappella choirs in many of
our high schools will equally impair voices for expressive
singing" (404, p. 79). Wilson also states:

... I am willing to go on record as saying that
we teachers of singing are 'ruining' many more
voices by the perpetual use of light, devitalized
type of tone with our students than we are in the
attempts we make to have them produce a correct,
full-bodied, vital tone (460).

Ward says:

Many experienced school music teachers agree that
the way to secure a lovely, light tone is to acquire

first the full, solid voice--a good vital beautiful
tone, bodily supported--rather than to develop the
larger tone from the lighter (414, p. 69).

Jacobs claims that "it is better to get raucous tone
and then refine it, than to tolerate a nondescript merely
nice tone. Fight against thin, pinched tones" (184, p. 58).
King seems to agree as he suggests, "Loud singing helps to
open the voice" (209). Vennard declares, "Mezzo-forte and
forte are the most healthful dynamic levels" (411). Jones,
Rhea and Rhea state that "the safe dynamic level for singing,
consequently the level at which most practice is done, is
mezzo-forte" (192, p. 21; also Ehret 114, p. 23; Van Bodegraven and Wilson 404, p. 79).

RECOMMENDATIONS FOR SINGING
VARIOUS DYNAMIC LEVELS

The recommendations for singing the various dynamic
levels are grouped into four sections: 1) through concept of
tone, 2) through resonance sensation, 3) through concern
with physiological factors, and 4) through vowel study.

Concept of Tone

Recommendations for singing various dynamic levels
through attention to tonal concepts were extracted from the
writings of thirty-two authors. The points of emphasis are
concepts of pianissimo, concepts of forte, and concepts of
dynamic variations.

The authors' statements indicate that pianissimo tones
should have a quality of energy, vitality, and intensity. It
should be noted that the use of the word intensity when dealing with dynamics has two different meanings. In acoustics,
intensity refers to the strength or pressure of the sound
wave, and is the physical counterpart of the psychological
attribute of the tone, loudness. However, it also is used in
referring to a more subjective quality of the sound. It may
carry no connotation of loudness as it refers to a vibrant,
energetic, or concentrated quality of tone. Such a concept
of choral tone is recommended for soft singing:

A pianissimo chord should be sung with the same
intensity as a fortissimo chord. If a chord is

sung without this vibrant feeling it sounds slack
and lifeless (Woodgate 456, p. 22).

... soft singing should never be feeble, nor loud
singing noisy. Vitalize and intensify your pp; en-
rich and beautify your ff (Grace 140, p. 37).

The difficulty here is to keep the tone pointed,
energetic, vital and spinning although it is soft.
Avoid a flabby, mushy, muffled or devitalized tone.
The perfect pp will have a concentrated, spinning
quality which gives great carrying power, and makes
a tone sound almost as loud in the farthest balcony
as it sounds on the stage (Smallman and Wilcox
358, p. 182).

... insist on an aliveness of tone, even, or should
I say especially, in pianissimo singing (Fischer
127).

Tell them to sing very softly, but with the preparation and control they would use for a fortissimo
phrase. Pianissimo is big tone, intensely com-
pressed (Jacobs 184, p. 37).

Softer passages require a really greater expendi-
ture of physical and psychological energy than
louder ... (Green 143).

... most singers do not intensify and vitalize their
soft tones enough....
    To correct this condition, have the choristers
sing their tones loudly and then repeat softly while
retaining the same mental and physical sensations....
(Ehret 114, p. 19).

    A variety of concepts are recommended for singing
forte tones. Wilson asks for a tone which is "full and vigorous for forte singing and rich and vital for pianissimo singing" (456). Woodgate suggests an exercise for practicing
crescendos on long notes with the instruction to "commence
softly, and gradually press into the note, with a warm feeling
of sound ..." (466, p. 8). According to Coleman,

    ... let increased power be thought of as bigger,
    wider tone rather than as more intense tone. The
    idea of loudness too often suggests tight and harsh

tone, whereas bigness suggests wideness and freedom (63, p. 46).

Davison acknowledges that subjective tone is not conducive to
real fortissimo but explains that it does permit a degree of
pianissimo which is unattainable with a more objective quality.
He adds that "by opening the tone slightly when volume is required the resulting contrast in tone color ... supplies a dynamic range as wide as that possessed by objective tone"
(85, p. 70).

Fuhr, Sunderman, Finn, Rowles, Cain, Coleman,
Kortkamp and Smallman and Wilcox emphasize the concentration necessary to control dynamics and recommend exercises
for developing control of a series of dynamic gradations.
Sunderman presents a diagram of dynamic markings which is
an aid in "building a mental concept for proper dynamic
range ..." (376, p. 35). Finn recommends a diagram for
practicing five different dynamic levels (pp, p, mf, f, ff);
he calls it a "listening eye" (122, p. 224). Kortkamp calls
such a diagram a "dynameter" (219, p. 44). For developing
dynamic control, Fuhr recommends the concept of a circle
with the circumference representing the maximum tone volume (128, p. 90).

Resonance Sensation

Recommendations taken from the writings of twenty-
two authors were tabulated as approaches to the singing of
various dynamic levels through resonance sensations of the
tone. The points of emphasis were forward resonance and
humming. For example:

By proper placing one can obtain power without
forcing....
The first essential of pp singing is 'forward
tone' (Staples 361, pp. 38 and 44).

A pianissimo tone should be sung well forward to
the front teeth and lips of a nearly closed mouth
... (Christy 58, p. 43).

To establish a fine pp ...
1. Hum the passage. This establishes the standard
of softness for a spinning pp.
2. Sing the passage in 'hummy' style which

means to sing words with a relatively closed mouth
and to pronounce these words with very little movement of the articulatory organs. As the words are
produced there should be a continuous feeling of
hum and nasal resonance (Ehret 114, p. 25).

Humming is also a ... good way of training a
choir to sing p or pp (Edeson 109, p. 33).

... an application of certain well-known principles
is essential in securing a singing tone that is a
true pianissimo. In developing this tone with
groups, whether large or small, the employment
of the light and properly sustained hum as a preparation for open and closed vowels, followed by the
development of a natural, easy diction, is not only
possible but practical (Beach 11).

Ask the chorus to sing a fortissimo chord on the
word 'Lord!' Let them almost shout with enthusi-
asm, and point out the harshness of the sound.
Then tell them to sing the same word on the same
chord, pressing the sound to the front of the face
(the mask) and thinking of a round warm quality.
The difference is remarkable, the first example
being ugly because it is uncontrolled, the second
being rounder and fuller, and indeed louder because of concentrated resonance (Woodgate 466, p.
20).

Fulltone--considers sonority, resonance, and depth
above power.... The fullness of tone is secured
by tone placement, breath support and correct
vowel equalization (Woods 467, p. 10).

Physiological Factors

In tabulating statements by twenty-seven authors on
physiological factors in singing various dynamic levels, body
intensity or physical energy and breathing emerge as the
points of emphasis.

The more subjective meaning of the word intensity,
as explained earlier, applies to physiological as well as conceptual factors. Ehret advises that the intensity level of
p and pp be watched, explaining that "most groups lose body

intensity and become sluggish as they sing softly" (114, p.
23). Wilson agrees: "Singers have a tendency to energize
themselves insufficiently when singing softly ..." (450, p.
201). Kortkamp admonishes his singers not to relax when
they diminish a tone or before the last note is ended (219,
p. 13). Loney, Christy, and Green refer to the "physical
and psychological energy" which is required for soft singing"
(Loney 241; Christy 58, p. 57; Green 143). "Ringing crescendos and climaxes can be attained in only one way--by intensity, and intensity is the result of expansion," according
to Jacobs. She further recommends, "The director who
knows voices will keep his arm movements virile but quiet,
while his chest will become broad and firm" (184, p. 31).

The following authors' statements are representative
of the attention given to breathing in singing various dynamic
levels:

> All crescendos must be built by action of the
> breath. Be sure the rib cage and waist are well
> expanded at all times, the control of the dynamic
> coming largely from the abdominal muscles (Pitts
> 313).

> The secret of both delicate pianissimo and robust
> forte singing lies largely in a steady and adequate
> supply of breath. Fortissimo singing must come
> as a gradual result of growing strength and control
> of the muscles which govern breathing....
>   Fine pianissimo singing demands an even steadi-
> er control of the breath than does fortissimo ...
> (Christy 58, p. 43).

> A fine pianissimo which is maintained at pitch re-
> quires mainly a controlled tone and full breathing
> ... (Davison 85, p. 70).

> A true pianissimo cannot be sung from the throat;
> it must come from the diaphragm, and thus the
> tone must necessarily be of good quality (Archie
> Jones 191, p. 53).

> I believe every group should strive for a well-
> controlled pianissimo, but it cannot be accom-
> plished by practicing only pianissimo. The activity
> of the diaphragm can best be observed under
> vigorous exercises of the fortissimo ... (Erdman

118).

> These two principles of quality and power involve
> increasing the size or diameter of the resonating
> chamber and compressing the air which agitates
> the vocal cords. I usually start with the later
> first. It involved unusual energizing of the breath-
> ing muscles at the waist ... here the idea of
> quantity is added ... the lowered jaw and open
> throat cause a bigger resonance ... (Evanson 120).

> If the thought of 'breath support' is confined to the
> front breathing muscles of the body, you will have
> control of the tone, but to get volume, you must
> call into action the side and back muscles (Tkach
> 398, p. 6).

> In regard to soft singing (mezzo-voce) it is com-
> mon for singers to fail to understand that as a
> person diminishes the volume of dynamics his
> breath support should increase proportionately
> (Sunderman 376, p. 28).

> A sustained fortissimo is well-nigh impossible to
> amateur singers unless costal breathing is em-
> ployed: power is obtained through breath pressure,
> and breath pressure depends largely on capacity
> (Staples 361, p. 49).

Vowel Study

Six authors' recommendations for singing various dynamic levels are centered upon the vowel and its qualities.
These recommendations are:

> The author always instructs a chorus to line the
> forte singing on an aw form. This vowel elimi-
> nates the tendency for strident voices to be promi-
> nent without causing the other voices to become too
> dark and colorless....
> ... Line piano or pianissimo singing on an ooh
> or ah (not uh) vowel, depending upon the basic
> color desired ... (Wilson 450, pp. 138-139).

> 'ah' ... soft, is just--ah ... loud, has some--oh
> (Kortkamp 215, p. 58).

It would be difficult to picture tone of a more
'heroic nakedness' than that of short o̲ centered in
N; it has no cloak of softness; it is a̅l̅l metallic
core, nothing else. It represents the authentic
choral f̲o̲r̲t̲e̲, not voluminous, but lean and spare
(Cleall 6̅2̅, p. 30).

Once having established the soft tone pattern [oo]
of the initial phases of the procedure, the director
should lead his singers out into the more open,
resonant vowel country of e̲e̲, a̲h̲, [a̲y̲], o̲h̲, and a̲h̲
(Fuhr 128, p. 59).

U̲n̲c̲a̲l̲l̲e̲d̲ ̲f̲o̲r̲ ̲a̲c̲c̲e̲n̲t̲s̲ ̲w̲i̲l̲l̲ ̲s̲o̲m̲e̲t̲i̲m̲e̲s̲ ̲o̲c̲c̲u̲r̲ ̲w̲h̲e̲n̲
s̲h̲i̲f̲t̲i̲n̲g̲ ̲f̲r̲o̲m̲ ̲a̲ ̲d̲a̲r̲k̲ ̲v̲o̲w̲e̲l̲ ̲(̲a̲w̲)̲ ̲t̲o̲ ̲a̲ ̲b̲r̲i̲g̲h̲t̲ ̲v̲o̲w̲e̲l̲
(̲e̲)̲ (Ehret 114, p. 28).

The vowel o̅ favors this big resonance and makes
a good starting point in working for volume and
power ... (Evanson 120).

CHAPTER 8

DICTION

In singing, diction refers to the three cognate and overlapping processes of pronunciation, enunciation, and articulation. In common usage, these terms are frequently used interchangeably; however, five authors of writings on choral training give the following definitions:

> Pronunciation is the utterance of words with regard to sound and accent. Enunciation is the manner of that utterance as regards fullness and clearness. Articulation is the action of the speech organs in the formation of consonants, vowels, syllables, and words. (Maybee 251, p. 8; also Lindsay 239; Mowe 269; Tkach 398, p. 26; Krone 225, p. 61).

A composite definition of diction as given by Lindsay (Ibid.), Krone (Ibid.), and Maybee (Ibid.) may be stated as follows: Correct pronunciation, clean enunciation, and distinct articulation in singing constitute good diction.

COMPARATIVE IMPORTANCE AND TREATMENT OF VOWELS AND CONSONANTS

Eighty-nine authors consider the comparative importance and treatment of vowels and consonants in regard to good choral diction. The main points of their discussion are: 1) the vowel is the tone, 2) the importance of the consonants, and 3) the "closing in" of consonants.

In chapter two, it was reported that 180 authors approach the development of choral tone quality through a consideration of the vowels. To some of these authors the development of good choral diction is also approached from the overriding premise that the vowel is the tone. The following quotations present this point of view and its implications

TABLE 20

Author-Coverage Table for Diction Showing the Chapter
Outline Which was Evolved from the Data, the Number of
Authors Who Discussed Each Sub-Topic of the Outline, and
the Page Number of This Study's Presentation of the Data.
140 Authors are Presented

	Number of Authors	Page
I. Comparative importance and treatment of vowels and consonants	89	123
II. Vowels		129
A. Classification of vowels	30	129
B. Treatment of vowels	78	131
1. Compound vowels	60	131
2. Vowel attacks	38	133
III. Consonants		135
A. Classification of consonants	40	135
B. Treatment of consonants	95	137
1. Attention to the physical location of articulation	23	137
2. Voiced consonants	39	138
3. The special problem of r	41	140
4. Explosives	31	141
5. Sibilants	28	143
IV. Pronunciation		144
A. Contiguous vowels and consonants	59	146
B. Common errors of pronunciation	27	150
V. Influence of the musical context	35	151

for choral diction:

> Every consonant interrupts the breath current in
> some form. Since beauty of tone depends upon the
> vowel sounds this interruption should be very brief.
> Try to articulate with as little change of the vowel
> position as possible (Tkach 398, p. 27).

> Consonants are spoken; vowels are sung (Archie
> Jones 191, p. 40).

> Consonants must never interfere with tone. They
> must be made so crisply and articulated so quickly
> that the flow of tone is not impaired (Pitts 304).

> ... unification of the vowels and minimization of
> consonants.... For a better unification of the
> vowels Christiansen instructed his singers to place
> the sounds back in the throat, breaking the vowel
> stream as little as possible with intervening con-
> sonants. For instance, in the opening phrase of
> Gretchaninoff's 'Our Father,' the l in the words,
> 'Holy, holy, holy,' was given scant attention,
> while the transition from the o to a dark-toned e
> was made with an almost imperceptible mouth
> movement (Bergman 15, p. 154).

> Consonants should be uttered plainly but rapidly.
> They should never be prolonged to the extent that
> they interfere with the flow of tone on the vowel
> (except humming consonants, for unusual interpre-
> tative effects) (Christy 58, p. 44).

> The vowels should be held as long as possible in
> the time allotted to a syllable without interference
> with the consonants. Care should be taken to
> avoid anticipation or over-emphasis of consonants
> (Deardorff 87, p. 5).

> Consonants must be pronounced in the mouth, with
> light, free action of the lips and tongue. The
> vowel that follows or precedes is made by the
> stream of breath from the body ... articulation
> need not and should not be connected with the pro-
> duction of singing tone, but must rather be carried
> on separately in such a manner as not to engage
> or impede the production of the singing tone. If

pronunciation is kept as far forward as possible,
on the tip of the tongue and the lips, the dissocia-
tion from the breath-supported tone may be accomplished more easily (Earhart 105, p. 24).

... function of the consonant and vowel must be
kept strictly separate. Any encroachment on a
vowel by a consonant causes adulteration of the
vowel. It is the failure completely to separate
the two functions which creates so much havoc in
the diction of singers and of speakers (Fuhr 128, p.
71).

The consonant interrupts the steady flow of the
vowel sound and, therefore, of the tone (Green 142,
p. 187).

In the study of words remember that it is the
vowels that are sung while the consonants are
short and really are only interruptions of the
steady flow of tone in order to separate the vowels
into words (Hjortsvang 165, p. 119).

The strongest conviction of the viewpoint that "the
vowel is the tone" is expressed by Cain. In his book,
Choral Music and Its Practice, and in a series of articles,
he criticizes the emphasis upon voiced consonants, humming,
and the secondary sounds of diphthongs. The following statements from his later publications reveal what is his con-
sistent viewpoint:

... each word in every language has a tone and a
noise. Each syllable of each word has a tone and
a noise! The tone is the vowel; the noise is the
consonant! Even the double vowel or diphthong has
one part of itself on which the tone is fuller than
on the other part (42).

... the vowel is the ONLY vehicle for tone. The
secondary vowel in a diphthong, and similarly the
consonant, is for release of tone.... Lingering
on such secondary vowels and consonants not only
cuts off tone but distorts language (39).

Viewpoints which differ from those stated above may
be found in the following quotations:

The impression I receive from a good deal of
choral singing is that conductors lay almost exclu-
sive emphasis on vowels. As a matter of fact, it
is consonants that are of overwhelming importance.
Once a tonal method has been established, the vowels will, save for occasional special treatment,
take care of themselves (Davison 85, p. 49).

If more attention were paid to the great importance
of consonant articulation, much of the muddiness of
diction would be eliminated, for contrary to wide-
spread opinion the consonants are of equal if not
greater importance than the vowels (Strickling 372).

Important as the correct formation of vowels is
for intelligibility and elegance in speech and song,
the articulation of consonants must be stressed as
of greater importance (Finn 122, p. 231).

Our treatment of speech ... vigorous and rhythmic
singing of the consonants which have pitch, M, N,
and NG ... and exploitation (for intonation's sake)
. of the beginning pitches of 'subvocal' consonants,
V, L, G, J, D, B, Z, and TH (Shaw 353).

L is a singing consonant ... and should be so
treated. Its singing quality if beautifully demonstrated in the word 'alleluia.' A safe slogan is,
'Linger on the l's' (Wilson 450, p. 149).

Do not stop the tone as consonants and vowels are
formed. Press the tone through the consonant, letting the vowel spring forth after a quick execution
of the consonant (Ehret 114, p. 41).

Perhaps the most influential spokesman for the approach to choral diction which Cain so sharply criticizes is
Waring, who, through his choral performances, workshops,
choral editions, and writings promotes his phonetic system
of choral diction. The following are representative quotations:

To achieve absolute clarity, we have developed a
method of enunciation, the essence of which is a
rough and practical system of phonetics. We break
down each word into its simplest units of sound.
Each of these units is called a 'tone syllable.'

Our enunciation technique is the process of sounding these individual tone-syllables.

... Vowels make up the main body of tone in singing; consonants are stressed only to the extent
necessary to bring out the meaning and beauty of
the poetry....

Vowels and consonants must 'melt' together. If
the chorus will carefully and intensively practice
stressing all tuned consonants, they will find that
use of this technique will become habitual and auto-
matic.

Give subsidiary vowel and tuned consonant sounds a
proportionate, rhythmic amount of the full time
value....

The amount of time allotted to these subsidiary
sounds is governed by considerations of tempo and
taste (420, pp. 2, 3, 5 and 6).

According to Davison, "A deep-rooted fault, so common among chorus singers that it might almost be called the
'original sin' of amateur vocalists, is 'closing in' on consonants" (85, p. 55). Howerton devotes nearly five pages of
one publication to discussing the problem of maintaining the
pure vowel and avoiding the closing in or over-extension of
consonants (178, pp. 28-32). The following statements are
further illustrations of this concept:

Unless the consonants are hard, clean and rhythmic,
we have no articulation. Unless the vowels are
well-formed, well-focused, and maintain their shape
throughout the full dynamic range as well as the
full length of a note value (whether long or short),
we have no sonority (Hillis 162).

The conductor must determine how much time is
given to diphthongization and consonant formation,
and achieve perfect ensemble of articulation. An-
ticipation of consonants can spoil vowel color (Vennard 411).

... the singer must be able to produce and sustain
a pure vowel sound, unchanged throughout the duration of the note.... Another common fault, that of

sounding the consonants too soon, intensifies the distortion (Mowe 270).

It is, therefore, of utmost importance that choristers have a clean, mental concept of the phonetic sound of every vowel.... Not only must a vowel be pure at the beginning of a tone, but its purity must be sustained for the full musical value of any given note (Veld 409).

The form or shape of the vowel must be held without the slightest change for the full value of the note (Tkach 397, p. 10).

... sustain the vowels, not the consonants ... sustained, unchanging in the slightest degree, for as long as the note is supposed to last--the mouth in the same shape when you finish as when you began the vowel (Kortkamp 219, p. 23).

... the necessity for keeping them (vowels) a constant shape during the holding of long notes (Staples 361, p. 39).

Vowels should retain the same quality throughout their duration (Jacobs 184, p. 38).

VOWELS

Classification of Vowels

Thirty authors present classifications of vowels as a part of their discussion of choral diction. Although these classifications vary from four to thirty vowels, two basic groupings are reported in this chapter. The first classification contains from four to six vowel sounds; the second, twelve or more.

The first classification is the attention given to oo, oh, ah, ay, ee. The role of these basic vowels in the development of choral tone quality was presented in chapter two. The following statements indicate their bearing upon the problem of choral diction:

For good diction, simplify the basic vowel sounds to five: AYE (a); EE (e); AH (a); OH (o); and OO

(u). All other vowels may be called sympathetic
to one or more of these basic sounds ... (Vail
403).

First of all, we should reduce to a minimum the
number of vowel sounds which we employ in singing.
... five prime sounds of ah, ay, ee, oh, and oo.
Through the correct articulation of the consonants
he can make practically any English text crystal
clear to the hearer with only a minimum use of
the partials (Fuhr 128, p. 72).

To help in analyzing the vowel sounds ... Each
word is taken apart, and the vowel sounds are related to the primary sounds used in our vocalization plan. (Oo, Oh, Aw, Ah, Ay, Ee). I have the
students try singing just the vowel sounds without
the consonants. This concentrates attention on
what the vowel sounds are and how they feel (Gilley
133).

The second classification of vowels includes twelve or
more sounds. Cleall recommends the following sentence as
an aid to remembering thirteem basic vowels: "You should
go for top marks son; perhaps then they'd increase" (62, p.
6). Fourteen words for developing the proper concept of
the vowels are recommended by Williamson: soon, so, saw,
psalm, say, see, soot, sod, sung, sat, set, sit, swirl, and
fast (441). The following statements clarify the use of these
classifications:

These ideas must be in the minds of your choir;
till they are, there can be no unanimity of production, and hence no unanimity of tone; there cannot
be intelligibility; there cannot even by rhythm, for
vowels that are not well founded urge the singer
to conclude them ... (Cleall 61, p. 60).

Too often in directing a choir or in teaching an individual to sing, we go on the assumption that
there is one 'ah' vowel as in psalm, one 'e' vowel
as in see, one 'oo' vowel as in soon, one 'o' vowel as in sew, one 'a' vowel as in say, and one 'i'
vowel as in sigh. This faulty assumption ... makes
the singer's diction clouded because it limits the
vowels used to these few vowel sounds (Williamson
447).

The singer who has developed his power of directed
concentration to the point where he is aware of the
fundamental qualities of these classifications [13
basic vowel sounds] and who knows as he sings
which of these classifications is proper for the
text of the moment will have acquired considerable
knowledge of good singing diction (Howerton 177,
p. 28).

... thirty some [vowel sounds] we have in English.
... it becomes abvious that the singers in the
chorus will have to pattern their articulation of the
letters and syllables after that of the director
(Strickling 372).

The foregoing [three pages of classifications and
descriptions of vowels and consonants] has been
introduced as a handy table of reference. It should
be carefully studied by the teacher or director and
used, without comment, whenever a vowel or consonant sound is being mispronounced (Archie Jones
191, p. 42).

Waring presents a list of fourteen pure vowel sounds
and six compound vowel sounds or diphthongs, and advises
that after the correct sound for each of these is learned,
"they should not present any further problem to pronunciation
or to blended tone" (420, p. 6).

Treatment of Vowels

Recommendations concerning the treatment of vowels
in choral diction extracted from the writings of seventy-eight
authors are concerned with two aspects of vowel production:
1) compound vowels, and 2) vowel attacks.

Compound Vowels. Statements taken from the writings of sixty authors are concerned with the problems of
compound vowels, or diphthongs and triphthongs, in choral
singing. Examples of these compound vowels are found in
the following words: so, say, vow, night, voice, new,
your, wear, way, and wide. Regarding these compound
vowel sounds, the viewpoint expressed by a majority of the
authors is that the secondary sounds should be minimized.
The following are representative statements:

Diphthongs require a quick change of shape either at the beginning or the end of the syllable, the emphasis being on the shortness of the subsidiary vowel (Cashmore 49).

When sustaining a diphthong, the first vowel is held for the duration of the tone--the last vowel is not heard until the final release (Bellows 14).

English ... has many diphthongs, or combinations of vowel sounds, which are unpleasant in singing. ... 'sky,' we pronounce 'skah--ee,' which sounds unpleasant in singing unless the final 'ee' is tacked on at the very end of the sound (Jones, Rhea and Rhea 192, p. 10).

... the pure sound of the vowel, that is, its principal element, should be extended, while any secondary element should receive properly subordinate and inconspicuous treatment (Howerton 177, p. 21).

The ending sound in double vowel combinations ... should be articulated as rapidly as a consonant (Christy 58, p. 45).

In singing, each syllable must have only 'one basic' vowel sound. In the case of diphthongs ... only one of these vowels can be basic (fundamental). The other secondary vowel (vanish) must be treated as a consonant and clipped off crisply and precisely. This rule applies whether the diphthong is sung on one note or many notes (Ehret 114, p. 45).

I: as in might. This is a diphthong consisting of the vowel ah which is sustained for practically all of the length of the tone, and the vowel ee which is a vanish sound and added just before the tone is ended (Krone 225, p. 64).

Statements which indicate that each component of compound vowels should receive a degree of emphasis are given below:

Diphthongs are simply compound vowels and should be sounded distinctly, especially in legato singing. Normal pronunciation is the best rule to follow in this matter (Wilson 453).

We sing, not words, but all the sounds of every
word, which we call 'tone syllables.' Compound
vowels (diphthongs and triphthongs) receive exaggerated treatment of their component vowel sounds.
For example: say is 'seh--ee,' bow is 'bo-oo,'
bite is 'baheet' ... (Waring 418).

Our treatment of speech has ... clear and vigorous
voweling, with emphasis upon compound vowels ...
(Shaw 353).

I note an ignoring of the diphthongs. They are the
sounds we have in the words: so, say, vow, vie,
voice, and view. Each one of those words has two
vowel sounds. We must clearly differentiate between those vowel sounds. For example, the vowel in so; the English language demands that the oo
sound follow it ... the vanish-sound ... (Williamson 447).

Fred Waring's contribution to choral art ... included the intelligible sounding of all the vowels
with diphthongal vanishes (ayee, ahee, ohoo) as
well as the pure vowels which are not composite
(ah, ee, oo). Revolutionary as his influence has
been, this is nothing more than clearly articulate
speech (J. W. Jones 203).

Vowel Attacks. Thirty-eight writers discuss vowel
attacks in their publications. Nine authors warn of the
glottis stroke as a deterrent to good vowel attack. Ehret
expresses this admonition:

When singing a word beginning with a vowel, avoid
making an introductory sound in the throat. This
objectionable glottis stroke is caused by the coming
together of the vocal chords (sic.) before the start
of a tone (114, p. 37).

Fuhr writes about this "clucking sound" which occurs
"when the cords actually come into contact with each other
before the start of the tone and must be forced apart by the
breath." He warns that the glottis stroke is "both unpleasant
and harmful, for the error easily becomes a habit and is ir-
ritating to the edges of the vocal bands" (128, p. 74).

In contrast to the glottis stroke, Fuhr, Becker, Sunderman, Krone, Peterson, and Coleman warn of a breathy attack in which "air is allowed to escape before the vocal bands assume their correct approximation ..." (Fuhr Ibid.; also Becker 13; Sunderman 376, p. 28; Krone 225, p. 46; Peterson 295, p. 16; Coleman 63, p. 37).

Seven authors recommend prefixing vowel attacks with a silent h in order that a smooth attack may be accomplished. Wilson, Davison, and Jones, Rhea and Rhea describe this device as follows:

> Even with a well-trained chorus it is difficult to obtain a uniform attack on a word beginning with a vowel. Such words require a glottis attack of the vocal action, and this is almost impossible for several singers to do simultaneously. Therefore it is wise procedure to use an unobtrusive, aspirate h to introduce attacks on these words, especially on soft attacks (Wilson 450, p. 154).

> If the attack is forte the difficulty is less great, though the h materially strengthens the impact, but where the beginning is pianissimo as, perhaps in Adoramus, the following method will make a ragged attack less audible; the chorus, as always, will breathe in with your warning-beat; as your hand begins the indication of the singing-beat the chorus breathes out soundlessly on the letter h; and as you reach the customary point in your motion where the attack is to occur, the singers slide gently from the h into the vowel sound (Davison 85, p. 51).

> Generally, it may be said that all vowels begin with an aspiration or a 'h' sound. The 'h' is almost inaudible, but is present nevertheless (Jones, Rhea and Rhea 192, p. 16).

For singing several notes on one vowel sound (roulades or florid passages), thirteen authors recommend a staccato or semi-staccato style. Hjortsvang, Krone, and Wilson recommend prefixing the letter h to each note for eliciting clarity and precision of attack. Green makes the following statement concerning this device:

> Since the choral profession is apparently sharply

divided on the next point, we shall state the two
views in brief without urging the acceptance of
either. The problem concerns the vowel which is
slurred over several notes.

One hears, at times, the articulation of a soft
'h' attack in the slurred vowel as the pitch changes.
Certain very fine teachers argue against the use of
this device for two reasons: 1) It tends to inter-
rupt the legato line which is the main reason for
the writing of the slur; and 2) It tends to build
breathiness into the tone. Other very fine teachers sanction its use to prevent the glissando which
often mars slurred runs in vocal execution (E.
Green 142, p. 187).

CONSONANTS

Classification of Consonants

In the writings analyzed for this study it was found
that forty authors group or classify consonants as a part of
their consideration of choral diction. Although there are
various groupings and terms used in classifying the consonants, they may be incorporated into three modes of classification. The following is a presentation of the three types
of classifications with representative quotations given for
each type:

I. Classification according to the degree to which the
consonants receive voice:

Generally the consonants may be classified into two
types--the voiced and voiceless (non-voiced). The
voiceless consonants include k, p, t, f, h, s, and
sh, whereas the voiced consonants include b, d,
v, z, zh, l, g, j, w, r, y, m, n, and ng. The
consonants th is voiced in some words and voiceless in others (Garretson 130, p. 97).

The consonants fall into three groups:
1. Vocals--l, m, n, ng, y, and r when followed
   by a vowel.
2. Semi-vocals--b, d, g, j,
3. Non-vocal--the rest (Tkach 398, p. 28).

... consonants are classified as vocal or pitch

consonants (m̲, n̲, ng, l̲, v̲, and z̲); partial pitch
(d̲, g̲); and non-pitch or surds (t̲, h̲, s̲, f̲, p̲, sh̲,
and others) (Jones, Rhea and Rhea 192, p. 6).

II. Classification according to the physiological location of production:

    Dentals: d, t, n, l, th
    Labials: b, p, m, w
    Labio-dentals: f, v
    Sibilants: s, soft c, z, soft g, j, sh, soft ch
    Palatals: r, y
    Aspirate: h
    Gutturals: hard c, hard ch, k, hard g, q, x
    (Howerton 177, p. 45).

... classified according to the articulators used
in the stoppage or replacement of sound.
Labial or lip consonants ... b, f, p, w, and v.
Dental consonants ... d, l, t, and th.
Palatal consonants ... g (gem), j, r, y (yes), ch
    (chin), sh (she), and zh (vision).
Nasal consonants ... m, n, and ng.
Guttural consonants ... g, k, and qu.
Aspirate consonants ... h.
Sibilant consonants ... s, z, sh, ch, and soft c ...
(Wilson 450, pp. 149-150).

Consonants in voice training are divided into three
classifications:
Labials ... (B, F, M, P, V)
Dentals ... (C, D, L, N, R, S)
Gutturals ... (G, K, Q) (McCall 255).

III. Classification according to the manner in which
the sound is produced.

The four kinds of consonants in the English language
... Resonant ... M, N, V, TH (thou), W (oo), R
(trilled or smooth), Y (ee), NG ... Explosives ...
B, K, D, G, J, P, T, Ch ... Fricatives ...
S, SH, F, Z, ZH (azure), TH (thought) ... As-
pirates ... H, Wh (Nordin 283).

According to manner of formation:
1. Oral, or mouth consonants, c, h, q, x.
2. Nasals, m, n, ng.

3. Stopped, or occlusive, b, d, g, p, t, k.
4. Partly stopped, or fricative, w, v, th, l, r, z,
   zh, j, y, f, s.
5. Voiced, or sonants, r, m, n, l, z, sh.
6. Voiceless, or surds, p, t, k, f, s, h, sh, ch.
   (Archie Jones 191, p. 40).

Treatment of Consonants

Recommendations from the writings of ninety authors for the treatment of consonants in choral diction are presented in the following sections: 1) attention to the physical location of articulation; 2) voiced consonants; 3) the special problem of r; 4) explosives; and 5) sibilants.

Attention to the Physical Location of Articulation. Twenty-three authors focus attention upon the articulating organs and the precision of their movement in the formation of consonants. The following statements represent this point of view:

To attain perfection of tone the singer must know the exact spot where each consonant is made, the sensation it produces, and the effect it has upon the vowels and other consonants in the word. Each click, hum, buzz, hiss, or aspirate should be so clear and definite that it can be traced to the source of action (Peterson 295, pp. 34-35).

With consonants, directly controlled action can and should be cultivated.... If consonants are to accomplish their part in promoting good diction, they must be articulated deftly and disposed of quickly (Finn 122, p. 233).

To secure diction which is clear, clean, and precise, the singer must be aware of the exact point at which the articulation of the tongue, lips, and teeth must take place in order to sound the various consonants. He must be able to direct his attention to the point of articulation so that when a certain consonant is desired he knows what activity is necessary in order to sound it properly (Howerton 178, p. 11).

In order to let the class discover for themselves

where the consonant machinery is situated, and
consequently where the attention must be focused,
considerable practice in whispered words is necessary and frequent returns to this whispering will
always be found of great value as a corrective to
careless consonant articulation (Coleman 63, p. 40).

Ask the singers to imagine that they are speaking
to a deaf person, so that it is necessary to make
themselves understood completely through lip movement (Wilson 450, p. 147).

... good diction takes muscular strength and will
power (Nordin 283).

Exaggeration will have to be employed at first,
getting muscles of the face to give more than the
usual effort.... Words should actually be seen
upon the lips and in the face of the singer ...
(Strickling 372).

It is very difficult to exaggerate facial movements
to the point of ridiculousness. In fact the author
has yet to encounter this situation (Hammermeyer
283).

Voiced Consonants. There are two basic considerations regarding the treatment of voiced consonants in choral
diction: 1) their pitch, and 2) their duration and timing.
Thirty-nine authors are represented in this discussion. The
following quotations are representative of the viewpoint that
the pitch of voiced consonants should be the same as the
vowel with which it is associated:

All resonant consonants have a definite pitch.
When such a consonant precedes the vowel sound
of a syllable, the pitch of consonant and vowel
must be the same (Blauvelt 19).

Briefly, as to consonants, all such as can be sung
should be sung, and on the pitch allotted to the
vowel in the syllable (Wodell 464).

If the song starts with a consonant, it must be
articulated quickly and right on pitch (Krone 225,
p. 46).

Voiced consonants are usually pitched on the same
note as the ensuing vowel; but at the end of a word
they take the note of the preceding vowel (Cleall
62, p. 13).

Since singing is exaggerated speech, all sung consonants will require more emphasis than spoken
ones. ... some consonants should be over-done.
The sounds m, n, l, and ng can be, and should be,
put on a singing tone, just as the vowels are, and
they should be given extra time as well (Urang 402,
p. 137).

In his criticism of the use of voiced consonants, Cain
declares that "of themselves they have not pitch" and the
practice of sustaining them is a "perversion of the language
in singing" which has grown out of radio techniques (41).
Krone, Veld, Vail, Pitts, Dykema-Gehrkens, P. Peterson,
and Cain criticize the overemphasis upon m's and n's, especially the final m, such as in "Amen."

Waring acknowledges that because his choir had emphasized the singing quality of m, n, and ng, it had "often
been referred to as the 'M and M Choir'" (418). The first
of four basic rules which he presents in his booklet, Tone
Syllables, is: "Be conscious of all consonants which have
pitch and sing them with exaggerated intensity and duration"
(415, p. 2).

It has been stated that the vowel makes the rhythm in
vocal music and therefore, consonants which have duration,
notably the voiced consonants, m, n, l, and r should precede the actual point of attack. Although this procedure is
attacked by Cashmore, who said it "seems to be an unneces-
sary complication" (48), it is endorsed by the following authors:

When attacking words which begin with a consonant,
care must be taken that the vowel coincides exactly
with the downbeat. It follows that the consonants
must precede the bottom of the downbeat. Singing
consonants such as m, n, l, and rolled r should
start at the top of the downbeat. The entrance of
the other consonants will vary depending upon the
effect desired (Wilson 450, p. 135).

Since tone and pitch are sung only on vowels, it is

clear that rhythmic beats must begin with vowel
sound (Swarm 380, p. D3).

Begin every pulse or beat of music with a vowel
sound.... The enunciation of all initial consonants
must be completed prior to the instant the beat (or
its subdivision) occurs (Waring 420, p. 5).

The consonant should precede the time-value for
the note written, so that the vowel sound will begin at the time indicated for the note (Smallman
and Wilcox 358, p. 16; also Blauvelt 19).

Explodent consonants are so vigorous that there is
no perceptible interval between them and their vowels. Accordingly, they can be sung on the beat.
But any consonant combined with R at the beginning
of a word, or R itself in that position, should be
sounded half a beat early, or even a full beat--as
in the great word PRAISE ... (Cleall 62, p. 17).

... the tone should start on the beat, unless for
purposes of interpretation it is delayed or advanced. This can be accomplished where the word
begins with a consonant, especially the first word
in a phrase by sounding the consonant before the
beat ... (Mowe 269).

Most consonants come actually before the time of
the note.... The only consonants which come
exactly with the time of the note are the Explosives
and Aspirates (Nordin 283).

The Special Problem of "R". Forty-one authors discuss the special problems created by the consonant r in
choral singing. The controversial nature of the authors'
recommendations is indicated in the following statements:

The letter r should almost always be rolled; less
often, perhaps, in the case of the final r, but even
then it must be clearly heard, especially if the
sense of the word is in some degree dramatic ...
unless that letter is rolled it invariably gives the
effect of w, especially if the chorus is sizeable
(Davison 85, p. 49).

R demands particular attention because it requires

various treatments, depending upon the position it occupies in the word. When r̲ is followed by the vowel it may be rolled. When r̲ is at the begin-ning of a word, it is rolled with great strength. If it is in the middle of the word, it has less strength, and if it is at the end of the word, it is eliminated almost entirely (Smallman and Wilcox 358, p. 16).

The word 'lord' is not sounded l-o-r-d, but is sounded with the sustained vocal sound given to the letter 'l,' the vowel as in 'saw,' the r silent, and a quick 'du' ending the word (Williamson 439).

Yet, we find a certain authority in school music, printing the assertion that 'water,' 'river,' and 'winter' should be pronounced as if spelled w̲a̲t̲a̲h̲, r̲i̲v̲a̲h̲, and w̲i̲n̲t̲a̲h̲, which leads to the inquiry as to whether t̲h̲i̲s̲ authority ever heard of the sound e̲r̲ in the word j̲e̲r̲k̲ (Wodell 464).

An analysis and tabulation of the authors' statements concerning the treatment of r̲ revealed three recommenda-tions:

1. Initial r̲ and r̲ following an initial consonant (e.g., praise, drum bright) should be rolled or trilled. (19 authors)

2. Final r̲ (e.g., ever, father, Lord, heart) should be controlled by concentrating on the accompanying vowel with r̲ only at the point of release. (16 authors)

3. Eliminate final r̲ or sing 'er' as a pure vowel sound. (12 authors)

Explosive Consonants. Statements extracted from the writings of thirty-one authors include recommendations for performing the consonant sounds which are produced by stop-ping and subsequently releasing the air stream: the explo-sives. The pure or unvoiced explosives are p̲, t̲, and k̲, while their voiced (or sub-vocal) counterparts are b̲, d̲, and hard g̲. The attention which explosive consonants require in choral singing is indicated in Williamson's statement that p̲, t̲, and k̲ "are the curses of the choral conductor; they are the sounds that break legato; and they are the sounds that

people want to omit altogether" (447). The most frequent
recommendation concerning explosive consonants is that
voiced and unvoiced explosives should be carefully differenti-
ated. The following statements convey the varying viewpoints concerning the voiced and unvoiced nature of these
consonants:

> Unless time is given to voice d̲ at the beginning
> and end of words, it will sound like t̲ (Wilson 450,
> p. 149).

> T̲: as in fate.... The common tendency is to
> place the tongue as for d and to move it sluggish-
> ly. Fate thus sounds like fade, and greater like
> grader (Krone 225, p. 67).

> The 'd' can be made to come through if we imagine
> that we are singing 'Lorduh.' Although this
> might seem to be an exaggeration effect to the
> choir, it will sound to the congregation like 'Lord'
> (Mead 259).

> As final consonants (B, D, hard G) their release
> is made cleaner by a vocalized vowel, hardly
> more than a breath, 'ih.' It should never be 'uh'
> or 'ah' as is too frequently heard. It must be so
> thin that one is not conscious of the vowel but
> only the distinctness of the final consonant (Norton
> 285).

> For additional clarity, release all final consonants
> with a vocalized, added 'ih' (Ehret 114, p. 42).

> At the beginning of a word, b̲ is a subvocal con-
> sonant having pitch. (Boy is pronounced uh-boy
> with uh being sung on pitch.) At the end of a
> word, it is only a voiced explosive. (Rub is pro-
> nounced ruh-bub and the bub has no pitch.)
> (Richards 322).

> Henry Coward teaches his singers to vocalize--
> very softly and deftly--the release of the con-
> sonants with the sound of uh. For example,
> 'Help Lord' is sung 'Help (uh) Lord;' the uh
> naturally being timed exactly to synchronize with
> the release of the p̲ (Fuhr 128, p. 80).

... following b, d, and g you may and you must
have the sound uh as in sung, but only following
those three sounds. The sound uh must not follow
p, t, or k (Williamson 447).

Final explosive consonants should not be emphasized with an 'uh' sound after them (Vail 403).

When a short consonant [k, p, ch, t, b, d, g,
and j] ends a syllable which is followed by any
consonant, the short consonant is stopped. [to
avoid 'do it (uh) now']....
    When a doubled short consonant occurs within a
word, only the second of the two is sounded and
its 'soft' form is used (Waring 420, pp. 4-5).

Sibilants. Twenty-eight authors give suggestions for
dealing with the hissing consonants or sibilants: s, z, sh,
zh, j, ch. The basic problem with these sounds in choral
singing is gaining precision of articulation which avoids a
prolonged hissing sound. The common recommendations are
to: 1) de-emphasize the sibilants, and 2) articulate sibilants
in relation to the sustained vowel. The following quotations
illustrate these two points of emphasis:

    ... sibilants, the 's' sounds.... About all we can
    do is look out for such snares and then de-empha-
    size the sibilants (Urang 402, p. 164).

    Sibilants require general curtailment ... the effect
    often is as of frying sausages ... (Young 473, p.
    28).

    ... pronounce s's as short as possible ... es-
    pecially for s's that end words (Epstein 119).

    Attention must be directed also to an unhurried
    pronouncement of sibilants, postponing the hissing
    element to the last fraction of the second (Finn
    122, p. 53).

    Some directors have found it particularly helpful
    in dealing with the hissing s's to assign the singing
    of the consonant to only a particular portion of the
    chorus ... (Garretson 130, p. 105).

In the case of an initial s followed by a vowel, the

chorus should be urged to pass to the vowel as
quickly as possible (Davison 85, p. 54).

S̲: as in hi̲s--as z̲.... The problem is to secure
unanimous attack and release of the consonant....
   If the letter occurs between syllables, the hissing effect can usually be eliminated by pronouncing
it with the second syllable, e.g., wa̲--sti̲ng; not
wa̲s--ting, or wa̲st--ing. If some of your singers
have dental trouble that makes him whistle his s̲'s̲,
have him lisp, or drop them altogether (Krone 2̲25,
p. 66).

Attach these consonants (sibilants), and most consonants for that matter, to the second syllable of
a word; not ma̲s--ter, but ma̲--ster. This avoids
the danger of ma̲s-s̲-ter (Wilson 4̲50, p. 152).

PRONUNCIATION

   Pronunciation has been defined as the utterance of
words with regard to sound and accent. A logical point of
departure for a discussion of pronunciation would seem to
be Cain's dictum: "A general rule to follow is to sing as
one would properly speak" (32, p. 113). However, several
of the factors discussed in this study (e.g., vowel modification, pitch of voiced consonants, duration of secondary
sounds of diphthongs) indicate why such a speaking approach
to choral diction is difficult to maintain. The following
authors' statements set forth the various viewpoints concerning the relationship between choral diction and the spoken
word:

   Every artist should learn to speak clearly and distinctly, and when singing, not to distort his speech
   because he is adding music to the words (Woodgate
   466, p. 12).

   'Pronounce well and you will sing well' is a truism
   of voice culture.... Since student speech is so
   slovenly, the vocal teacher must first make the
   necessary corrections and then apply the resulting
   beautiful English to singing. The personal example
   of the teacher is of paramount importance....
   Stress should also be laid on the natural pronunciation of words, so that the thought is not distorted

(Nitsche 278).

When in doubt, sing the word as you would say it.
This will not work 100 percent of the time, but
generally should eliminate some of the odd, and
often amusing, pronunciations I have heard (Whaley
424).

It is well to practice on pure vowels, but this is
only part of the trick ... the wise director will not
permit pronunciation of words to become a <u>fetish</u>
(Klein 212).

Almost as important as knowing what to do in the
matter of good diction, is knowing what not to do.
Bad taste makes itself evident in diction more
quickly than in any other phase of singing (Archie
Jones 191, p. 45).

... there are NOT two ways to articulate words;
one for speaking and one for singing. We do not
speak of sailing 'sheeps' so why sing it that way?
(Strickling 373).

For choruses that are mastering the fundamentals
of singing, two general rules can be given for diction:
    1. Sing the words with the sounds and style of
everyday (spoken) speech.
    2. Exaggerate the pronunciation slightly to make
it more clear (Epstein 119, p. 33).

An absolutely intelligible and impressive rendering
of the text is obtained only by 'meticulous' pronunciation which involves the singer in frank exag-
gerations (Davison 85, p. 48).

The ideal of pronunciation which should be held before every singer is that of speech which shall be
dignified and natural, cultured and unaffected. 'The
best language is one's own,' but it should be one's
own language dignified by study and polished by education (Howerton 178, p. 20).

Contiguous Vowels and Consonants

Fifty-nine authors make recommendations concerning the relationship of contiguous vowels and consonants. One viewpoint is that words and syllables must be cleanly articulated without linking to adjacent sounds; the other is that the sounds should be smoothly joined. Representative quotations are given below:

> The insertion of y or w between adjacent vowels as in 'me(y)only,' or 'do(w)open' is very common and easily corrected by insisting on a momentary suspension of breath between them. The same momentary suspensions between adjacent consonants as 'Drink to' or 'with thine' will allow the release of the first consonant before the next is taken on, and so prevent the half-articulation and distortion of the initial consonant as well as the prolonged stoppage of the voice ... (Fuhr 128, p. 80).

> The habit of running words together is perhaps one of the most difficult to eliminate. 'O Blest Are They' is usually sung 'O Bless Star They'; 'Guide us on our way' is usually sung 'Guy duh sah nour way.' ... The teacher should study these lines, anticipating every possible place where this can happen, and then drill the chorus in correct separation of the words (Cain 37, p. 113).

> God of God ... Go dof God ... make a distinct break between the two words and so avoid running them together; then the gap must be reduced gradually until it is imperceptible. Some slight sacrifice of true legato may be necessary, but we will console ourselves with the thought that the words are more important than the music (Cashmore 49).

> Iamalpha andomega. The separation of such words is a necessity, and should be insisted upon at every sign of carelessness (Staples 361, p. 62).

> The aspirated 'h' which is suffixed to many words and prefixed to sequential words in phrases such as: 'Many (h) and Many' can be eliminated if the singers are careful to sing the voiced consonants and use a mental hesitancy between words as in the process of stringing pearls on a string....

They are closely approximated to each other, yet each bead (word) retains its identity (Sunderman 376, p. 23).

To eradicate the fusion of the last sound of one word with the vowel sound that opens the next, a slight break or stop is necessary. This stop should be but the completed pronunciation of the first sound and should in no way break the phrase line (Whittlesey 427, p. 95).

When an important word might be mistaken for another word when sung in a legato manner, it must be slightly separated from the preceding consonant sound and the second word slightly emphasized. For example, 'but I' ... 'and ear' ... 'your eyes' ... (Peterson 295, p. 41).

The concluding consonant of a word should be clearly terminated before the initial sound of the following one is produced except in the situation involving identical or similar consonants (Howerton 177, p. 57).

The following express a different point of view:

Establish continuity of tone from word to word and from syllable to syllable....
    ... the end of each word or syllable is joined to the beginning of the following word or syllable ... (Waring 420, p. 4).

Unanimous phonation of the explosive and sibilant consonants always as though they began syllables, never as though they ended them (thus: Thi-si-zuh-luh-vlee-daee) (Shaw 353).

So that continuous tone may be achieved, consonants are often attached to the vowels in preceding and following words (Swarm 380, p. D3).

Carry the consonant of the first word over to the second unless it changes the meaning (Wilson 450, p. 152).

Linking over the consonants to the following word is common, e.g., 'Let us now pray' sounds like

'Le tus snow pray' ... (Christy 58, p. 44).

When you have a word ending in a consonant and
it is followed with a word beginning with a vowel,
sing the consonant with the vowel (Young 474).

... remember that for smooth, continuous vocal
tone, the singer should carry a final consonant of
one word over to the initial vowel of the next
(Urang 402, p. 167).

In legato singing, the final consonant of a word and
the initial consonant of the succeeding word are
connected and sounded without a break.... In dramatic singing the consonants are sounded separately
and distinctly (Peterson 295, p. 38).

For choral purposes, it has been found useful to
attach final consonants to the next word. This not
only allows a better legato but insures more precision and unification in articulation (King 208).

Two special problems of contiguous vowels and consonants receive attention: contiguous vowels, and double
consonants. Although Waring declares that in dealing with
a vowel sound followed by a vowel sound there should be
'no break in the flow of tone between the vowels, unless a
staccato effect is desired' (420, p. 4), other authors differ.
Fuhr, Ehret, Wilson, Davison, Howerton, and Strickling
warn of the insertion of a y or w sound between the two
vowels: examples such as 'to(w) all,' 'go(w)on,' 'who(w)are,'
'the(y)arm,' and 'we(y)are' are given to illustrate the error.
Cain, Fuhr, Staples, Lewis, Peterson, and Sunderman recommend a slight separation of the vowels, while Davison,
Wilson, Urang, Epstein, Krone, and Sunderman suggest the
insertion of the aspirate, h. Davison and Wilson comment
on this technique:

The letter h is most valuable, however, when it
is introduced between two adjacent vowels; and the
common neglect of this device leads, first, to
rhythmlessness and, second, to unintelligibility
and an occasional effect of word-scrambling sug-
gestive of James Joyce's later prose style. 'Dow-
open' (do open), 'myyeye' (my eye), and 'whowis'
(who is) both look and sound confusing. If, however, they are sung 'do (h) open,' 'my (h) eye,'

and 'who (h) is,' their meaning is instantly clear
(Davison 85, p. 52).

Probably the most frequent use of the ever-service-
able h̲ is its introduction between two adjacent vowels i̲n̲ such concoctions as 'gowon' for 'go on,' 'too-
wold' for 'too old,' and 'myyown' for 'my own.' If
these words are sung by inserting an unobtrusive h̲
between them, the meaning becomes clear and the̅
rhythm is preserved.... Admittedly, this is a
mechanical method, but it is the kind of device to
which a choral conductor must resort to obtain
clarity of diction. If at first it appears overdone,
by habitual use it becomes a tool and natural as any
other technique in artistic singing (Wilson 450, p.
151).

According to Staples, "another bad habit to avoid is
the running together of consonants, when the same sound
ends one word, commences the next, thus: 'that t̲ellest,'
'Come m̲y way,' and 'I̲n̲ nearness'" (361, p. 63)̅. ̅Cleall
agre̅e̅s t̅hat such combina̅t̅ions as "that took" and "did deliver,"
involving double consonants, "should be articulated with a
vehemence foreign to speech. The essence of their articulation is the inevitable silence between them" (62, p. 13).
Seven authors express an opposing view, stating that when
double consonants occur, one should be omitted. Their
statements follow:

Where two s̲'s occur together, one may be omitted;
and it is ge̅nerally the second of the two that is
sounded. 'Creatures share' may be sung 'creature
share,' 'his soul' as 'hi soul' ... (Davison 85, p.
55).

In most cases, when dealing with double consonants,
the first of the two should be eliminated (Garretson
130, p. 106).

When the same consonants occur together between
words, usually omit one of them (Wilson 450, p.
152).

When a doubled short consonant occurs [k̲, p̲, ch̲,
t̲, b̲, d̲, g̲, and j̲] within a word, only the second
of the two is sounded and its 'soft' form is used
(Waring 420, p. 5).

When one word ends with a consonant and the next
one begins with the same consonant, as 'and
dream,' only one is articulated. The same applies
to double consonants like, 'with that,' etc. (Tkach
398, p. 28).

In the case of a double s between syllables, or of
one word ending with an s and the next word beginning with one, pronounce the second one only,
e.g., pa-(s) sing; thy soul' (s) supreme endeavor
(Krone 225, p. 66).

In the case of double consonants of identical character, the first should be omitted altogether, and
the second sounded particularly clearly (Howerton
177, p. 43).

Common Errors of Pronunciation

Twenty-seven authors list specific errors of pronunciation which are commonly found in choral singing. Whittlesey
proposes that these "most common errors in pronunciation
may be catalogued as: substitution, omission, addition of
sounds in syllables, and the overlapping of words in sentences" (427, p. 95). Pitts classifies "faults in diction"
under three headings: 1) complete omission of sounds; 2)
careless or partial utterance of sounds; and 3) faulty link
or liaison of sounds (258). For the purpose of presenting the
recommendations of the twenty-seven authors, I have added
one further grouping to the four proposed by Whittlesey:
namely, the occurrence of improper accents. The resulting
five groupings are given below with representative examples
of each type of error.

Substitution of sounds

Consonants: medal for metal, bower for power, vine
for fine, ach for age, lizen for listen, nachure for
nature, meetchew for meet you.

Vowels: dearuhst for dearest, trinuty for trinity,
beauteeful for beautiful, Bethleham for Bethlehem,
git for get.

Omission of sounds

> Consonants: hos for hosts, wen for when, an the for
> and the, umble for humble, moutain for mountain,
> La'n for Latin, chil for child, lif for lift.
>
> Vowels: noo for new, reely for really, jewl for
> jewel, covring for covering.

Addition of sounds

> from(uh), song(uh), soon(uh), hum(uh), live(uh),
> goal(uh), coat(uh), hope(uh), back(uh), me(y)only,
> do(w)open

Liaison of sounds

> fee tof for feet of, bless star for blessed are, sen
> dout for send out, hel pus for help us, thi sour
> for this our, an die for and I, bla kiz for black
> eyes, its stew for it's too, a pup for up, up

Improper accents

> tor-rents for torrents, govern-ment for government,
> ho-ly for holy, pre-pare for prepare, dee-vine for
> divine, high-est for highest, dark-ness for dark-
> ness, un-fold for unfold.

INFLUENCE OF THE MUSICAL CONTEXT

The interrelationships which make up the dynamic act
of singing are evidenced in various ways throughout this
study. Monson's statement indicates the influence of these
relationships upon the problems of diction:

> When sectional and group unity in quality, color,
> intonation, pitch, and rhythm have been achieved,
> the director will be pleasantly surprised to find
> that his chorus has also greatly improved its dic-
> tion without any particular mention being made of
> the matter (288).

Thirty-five authors acknowledge the importance of the
total musical context in their consideration of choral diction.
Three factors are given particular attention: 1) the style of

the music; 2) the musical phrase; and 3) the expressive intent of the singers.

Finn, Davison and Strickling discuss the relationship of diction problems to the musical style and state that contrapuntal music requires a greater effort for diction clarity than does homophonic music (Finn 122, p. 225; Davison 85, p. 56; Strickling 372). Klein and Ehmann make the following observations:

> The necessity for clear enunciation varies with the style of music and text to be sung. If the choir is presenting a song that tells a story, each word should be clear enough so that the audience will not be left guessing at the meaning. If, however, the composition is contrapuntal and depends for its effectiveness on a smooth rendition of melodic line, or the fusion of subtle harmonic details, time will be wasted in working for an overdone enunciation (Klein 212).

> The singing tradition of different epochs has treated the relationship of consonants and vowels in a variety of ways.... The treatment of language has always been influenced by the character and style of the music (Ehmann 112, pp. 60-61).

Wilson, Ehret, and Garretson discuss legato, staccato, and marcato styles of diction (Wilson 450, pp. 124-125, and 153; Ehret 114, p. 36; Garretson 130, p. 100). P. Peterson proposes two classifications: legato and dramatic (295, pp. 38-41). Of the legato, staccato, and marcato styles, Wilson says:

> In legato singing much use is made of all diphthongs and the singing consonants--l, m, n, ng, and r. Final consonants, especially those just referred to, are carried over to the next word. In articulating these consonants in a legato style they are doubled....
> To attain marcato style there is a 'bounce' to the diction. Diphthongs and ending consonants are sounded immediately....
> Staccato diction employs the abrupt beginning and ending of words with a definite feeling of a rest between each syllable (450, p. 125).

Williamson makes the following assertion concerning
the style of diction and expressive intent:

> Style in diction can be achieved through the expres-
> sion of mood. If I speak to you with irritation, I
> do not use the same style as when I speak to you
> with tenderness, contemplation, or calm poise.
> The instant the idea is realized, mood, pronuncia-
> tion, enunciation, articulation and style in diction
> become simplicities rather than fears (448).

Helvey agrees that "there is no one right pronunciation or
one interpretation for any given vowel sound, since each has
many shadings of pronunciation and quality to fit the dramatic
requirements of the music" (159). Lindroth states that "the
most vital ingredient in good diction is the strong determina-
tion to express a thought" (238). "The required energy must
of course be prompted by the imagination and the will to express," declares Coleman in reference to articulation (63,
p. 40). Sydnor suggests:

> The starting point towards craftmanship in diction
> is singing with understanding which means that the
> individual singer must have a clear conception of
> the intellectual and emotional meaning of the text
> (389, p. 57).

According to Richards, "Good diction is in the phrase-
line ..." (322). Woodgate explains this point, saying that
the most important words should be stressed. The choir
should be asked to think in sentences, with each word leading to the most important word, as for instance, "Blessing
and honor, glory and power be unto Him" (465, p. 34). R.
Peterson asserts,

> There is form and design in every word, every
> phrase, every sentence, and true directness and
> sincerity will aid in securing that smoothness and
> flow, that true melodic line, that elegant rise and
> fall which is characteristic of all expressive
> speech and all expressive singing (298).

Cain proposes that "the secret of clarity and distinct-
ness lies in the correct use of that neglected thing called
Inflection" (39). According to Ehret, "Key word emphasis--
Stressing, not to mention coloring, of key words within the
phrase results in better text communication to the listener"
(114, p. 37).

ANNOTATED BIBLIOGRAPHY

1. American Academy of Teachers of Singing. "Problems of Tessitura in Relation to Choral Music," Music Publishers Journal, 2:28-29, September, 1944.
A presentation of the range and best tessitura for amateur choral singers with suggestions for voice classifications and development of the upper range.

2. Angell, W. M. Choir Clinic Manual. Nashville: Broadman Press, 1952.
Tone quality, intonation, auditions, vocal techniques and drills are among the topics discussed.

3. _____. "Vocal Musicianship," Music Journal, 7:9 ff., March, 1949.
A review of the demands which are made of the professional choral singer.

4. Apel, Willi. Harvard Dictionary of Music. Cambridge, Mass.: Harvard University Press, 1944.
The article on Just Intonation states that its application to actual performance is limited to occasional chords in a cappella singing.

5. Aschenbrenner, Walter. "What Is Symphonic Singing?" Music Teachers National Association Proceedings for 1936. Vol. 31. Oberlin, Ohio, 1937, pp. 181-182.
A description of the style of singing of the Chicago Symphonic Choir.

6. Bach, Ida E. "Training the A Cappella Choir," Music Educators National Conference Yearbook. Vol. 28. Chicago, 1935, pp. 308 ff.
A brief statement regarding intonation, using altos for tenor high notes, and the "psychic" experience of a cappella style.

7. Barkley, Robert C. "Tuning Up the A Cappella Choir, "
    Educational Music Magazine, 18:35, September, 1938.
        Points of emphasis include posture, dynamics,
    and the tenor shortage.

8. Bartholomew, Marshall. "Benefits of Choral Singing, "
    Music Educators National Conference Yearbook. Vol.
    27. Chicago, 1934, pp. 142-144.
        The benefits of choral singing are presented and
    the need for highly trained teachers is emphasized
    by referring to incorrect methods.

9. _____ . "Problems of Tessitura in Relation to
    Choral Music, " Music Teachers National Association
    Proceedings for 1944. Vol. 39. Pittsburgh, 1945,
    pp. 325-328.
        A plea for choral music and singing which will
    train rather than strain young voices.

10. Bartholomew, Wilmer. "The Role of Imagery in Voice
    Teaching, " Music Teachers National Association Pro-
    ceedings for 1935. Vol. 30. Oberlin, Ohio, 1936,
    pp. 78-94.
        The article includes the author's famous definition
    and discussion of tone quality.

11. Beach, Frank A. "Legitimate Soft Tone in Choral
    Singing, " Music Supervisors National Conference
    Yearbook. Vol. 25. Chicago, 1932, pp. 110-113.
        The legitimate soft tone is the vocal basis of all
    beautiful singing; it is the foundation for vocal de-
    velopment.

12. Beachy, Morris. "Are Choral and Vocal Studio Re-
    hearsal Techniques Compatible?" Choral Journal,
    10:24-28, September, 1969.
        A summary of a questionnaire answered by choral
    directors, voice teachers, choral/vocal teachers,
    professional singers, and conductors.

13. Becker, Arthur C. "Choral Training, " Specialized
    Activities in Music Education. Richard Werder,
    editor. Washington: Catholic University of America
    Press, 1956, pp. 35-51.
        Basic approaches to tone quality and intonation
    are taken from Cain's Choral Music and Its Practice.
    Generalizations for interpretation are included.

14. Bellows, E. L. "Suggestions to Choral Directors,"
    Music Journal, 18:54 ff., March, 1960.
        From the viewpoint of the voice teacher the author
    discusses the problems of tone and range as they af-
    fect the voice student in choral singing.

15. Bergman, Leola M. Music Master of the Middle West,
    the Story of F. Melius Christiansen and the St. Olaf
    Choir. Minneapolis: University of Minnesota Press,
    1944.
        The history of Christiansen and the St. Olaf Choir
    including descriptions of choral procedures, an ap-
    pendix of programs from 1912 to 1944, and many
    interesting personal experiences.

16. Best, Florence. "Mastering Skills," Educational Music
    Magazine, 18:16 ff., March, 1939.
        The procedure for demonstrating the mastery of
    vocal skills. Emphasis is placed upon exercises for
    posture, breathing, and mouth formations.

17. Bingham, S. "Vocal Exercises for Choristers Can Pay
    Rich Dividends," Diapason, 47:12, August, 1956.
        Why do certain choirs have a fine, homogeneous,
    ringing tone? The author gives exercises for the
    development of posture, breathing, tone, and diction.

18. Bird, C. "He's Got Everybody Singing," Saturday
    Evening Post, 221:34 ff., December 25, 1948.
        An article on Robert Shaw, his activities and
    singers.

19. Blauvelt, Velma. "A Few Corrections for Flat Sing-
    ing," Etude, 56:787, December, 1943.
        The principal causes of flat singing are bad
    ventilation, fatigue, inertia, indistinct consonants,
    faulty chording, not knowing or understanding the
    music and word, and the tremolo.

20. Boette, Marie. "Training the A Cappella Choir,"
    Music Educators National Conference Yearbook.
    Vol. 28. Chicago, 1935, pp. 309 ff.
        Brief recommendations concerning intonation,
    breathing, blend, humming, and singing with pure
    vowels.

21. Borchers, Orville. "The Development of Sectional

Tone Quality in the Chorus," Music Publishers
Journal, 2:13, July, 1944.
    The fetish of some choral organizations to develop
a certain type of uniform tone quality throughout the
chorus in order to achieve choral blend is denounced
and a plan for developing the individual quality of
each section is prescribed.

22. Bostock, Donald. Choirmastery. London: Epworth,
    1966.
        A survey of choral teaching including organiza-
    tion, conducting, voice production, repertoire and
    rehearsal techniques.

23. Bowen, G. O. "Voice Training in Ensemble Groups,"
    Music Teachers National Association Proceedings for
    1939. Vol. 34. Pittsburgh, 1940, pp. 326-333.
        Observations concerning range and tone quality in
    the school choir.

24. Bowles, M. A. The Art of Conducting. New York:
    Doubleday, 1959.
        An interpretive and historical approach to or-
    chestral conducting which includes a discussion of
    choral works with orchestra.

25. Boyd, C. N. Organist and Choirmaster. New York:
    Abingdon Press, 1936.
        The chapters of this book include the opening
    voluntary, the doxology, the anthem, the offertory,
    the various hymns, vocal solos, and choir re-
    hearsals. The emphasis is upon organ playing.

26. Brainerd, Jessie L. "How to Improve the Enunciation
    of Choir Singers," Etude, 62:258, May, 1944.
        Problem words are discussed and basic principles
    are given.

27. _____. "Points for the Choir Director," Etude, 56:
    259, April, 1938.
        Eight points are given which range from having
    a dictionary at hand to unity of tone.

28. Brigham, Forest. "When Singers Disagree Who Shall
    Decide?" School Musician, 13:14 ff., January, 1942.
        There are fads and extremes which have values,
    but to the student and director alike, it is safest to

avoid them.

29.   Buckley, William. "Distinct Choral Diction," Etude,
        58:669, October, 1940.
            Assign definite time values to consonants and
        components of a diphthong to gain unity of execution.

30.   Burnau, J. "Building and Balancing Choral Blend,"
        Music Journal Annual, p. 68 ff., 1967.
            A discussion of tonal balance, intonation, and
        pronunciation as the major elements of choral
        blend.

31.   Burns, Samuel T. "Problems of the Choral Conductor
        in Small High Schools," Music Supervisors National
        Conference Yearbook. Vol. 25. Chicago, 1932,
        pp. 129-132.
            The report of a demonstration of possible solu-
        tions for the problem of a shortage of tenors.

32.   _____. "Securing Tonal Balance in the Small High
        School Chorus," Supervisor's Service Bulletin, 12:
        13 ff., November, 1932.
            Various voice-part arrangements, and the aug-
        mentation of the tenor part with alto-tenors, altos,
        and baritones singing "half-voice" are the main
        points of this article.

33.   Busche, H. E. "College Treble Chorus: Women's
        Choirs," Etude, 73:17 ff., September, 1955.
            Special problems of balance, dynamics, intona-
        tion, accompaniment and literature for the treble
        chorus are discussed.

34.   Butler, Eugene. "Choral Technics (The Rehearsal),"
        Music Ministry, 1:38, April, 1969.
            Brief suggestions for choral warm up and re-
        hearsal procedure.

35.   Cain, Noble. "Broadcast Pickup," Music Educators
        National Conference Yearbook. Vol. 32, Chicago,
        1939-1940, pp. 335-358.
            Observations concerning choral blend and the
        factor of chorus size are of special interest.

36.   _____. "Choral Fads and Jitterbug Fancies,"
        Music Educators Journal, 26:26-27, September,

1939.
   The author warns that the a cappella movement
may be absorbing other kinds of good choral music,
but strongly opposes the inclusion of popular, swing
or jitterbug music in the educational program.

37. _____ . Choral Music and Its Practice. New York:
M. Witmark and Sons, 1932.
   This discussion of choral music ranges from
aesthetics and educational values to programming
and seating charts. Chapters on vocal technique include intonation, tone quality, and the rehearsal.

38. _____ . "Church Music After the War--and Now,"
Music Educators Journal, 31:23 ff., November, 1944.
   The church should eliminate special effects in its
music such as humming choirs, elaborate, over-
arrangements of chordal progressions which sound
secular and theatrical, secular melodies, concertiz-
ing, disregard for texts, and an over-all tendency
to entertain the congregation.

39. _____ . "Classical Versus 'Popular' Effects,"
Choral and Organ Guide, 6:15-17, May, 1953.
   A sizzling statement against H. R. Wilson's edit-
ing of anthems in the magazine by pointing out what
Cain called "popular" effects: the lingering upon
vanish elements of a diphthong and final consonants.

40. _____ . "Observations and Comment," Educational
Music Magazine, 30:16-17 ff., November, 1950.
   A casual, personal article with many interesting
viewpoints including the function of vowels and consonants in the Hawaiian language.

41. _____ . "This Is Not an Article," Educational Music
Magazine, 25:27 ff., March, 1946.
   Of special interest is the strong statement against
the stress of consonants.

42. _____ . "Treatment of Words," Music Journal, 5:13
ff., January, 1947.
   The author sets forth his views on some aspects
of choral diction and his objection to the practices
of prolonging the consonants in a "microphone technique."

43.   Calvers, F. Leslie. "How to Succeed with Your First
        Choir," Etude, 56:610-611, September, 1938.
        Open throat, diction, vowels and phrasing are dis-
        cussed.

44.   Cappadonia, Anthony and Herrick, George. "Some
        Psychological Aspects of Intonation," School Musician,
        34:44-45, January; 44-45, February; 34-35, March,
        1963.
        The authors list twenty-nine factors which seem
        to have a direct relationship to poor intonation and
        then discuss some of the psychological implications
        of those factors.

45.   Carr, Raymond. "Off the Record," Educational Music
        Magazine, 17:48 ff., January, 1938.
        The recording machine is a great aid in improving
        tone, intonation, diction, ensemble precision, and
        blend.

46.   Cashmore, D. "Choral Intonation," Musical Times,
        103:118-119, February, 1962.
        The fundamental cause of flat singing is lack of
        concentration.

47.   _____. "A Good Performance," Musical Times,
        105:56-57, January, 1964.
        A discussion of the measures of good performance
        ranging from intonation and blend to selection of ap-
        propriate music.

48.   _____. "More Words About Words," Musical Times,
        102:791-792, December, 1961.
        Some differing opinions involving the author,
        Charles Cleall, and L. E. Crabb are discussed.
        The topic is diction.

49.   _____. "Some Practical Observations," Musical
        Times, 102:514-515, August, 1961.
        Observations concerning the mouth-shape of vow-
        els, the execution of diphthongs and consonants, com-
        mon errors of diction, and sounds which require
        special care.

50.   Christian, Palmer. "Report of the Committee in Organ
        and Choral Music," Musical Teachers National As-
        sociation Proceedings for 1933. Vol. 28. Oberlin,

1934, pp. 235-243.
This annual report is very uncomplimentary to
choral music and "church-choir" men. Special point
is made of the woeful sagging from pitch.

51. Christiansen, F. Melius. "Ensemble Singing," Music
Supervisors National Conference Yearbook. Vol. 25.
Chicago, 1932, pp. 121-124.
The author discusses the importance of intonation
in ensemble blend and lists fourteen points on which
potential choir singers should be tested.

52. Christiansen, Olaf C. "Choral Tradition Lives On,"
Music Journal, 26:36 ff., March, 1968.
A summary statement of the philosophy, principles of programming, selection of singers and rehearsal procedures of the St. Olaf Choir.

53. _____. "Solo and Ensemble Singing," National Association of Teachers of Singing Bulletin, 21:16 ff.,
February, 1965.
A discussion of the vibrato and straight tone concepts in choral singing.

54. _____. Voice Builder. Park Ridge, Illinois: Neil
A. Kjos Music Company, 1959.
This fifteen-page booklet of vocalization and warm-
up exercises for rehearsal and concert has a few
basic statements concerning the requirements of
artistic singing.

55. Christy, Van A. "Balance and Blending," Supervisors
Service Bulletin, 12:18-19, January, 1933.
A good discussion of these two factors, including
teaching procedures.

56. _____. "Developing Choral Technique," Supervisors
Service Bulletin, 13:9 ff., January, 1934.
Vocal exercises with their objectives and detailed
directions of procedure.

57. _____. Evaluation of Choral Music. New York:
Bureau of Publications, Teachers College, Columbia
University, 1948.
The results of a detailed study in which choral
music was evaluated by students, experienced di-
rectors and audiences.

58.   . Glee Club and Chorus. New York: G. Schirmer, Inc., 1940.
      A handbook of organizing, conducting, and main-
taining choral organizations, with selected, graded,
and classified lists of octavo music.

59.   . "How to Prepare for Choral Contests and
Festivals," Supervisors Service Bulletin, 12:7-8,
January, 1933.
      Selection of voices and music precede an outline
of suggested rehearsal steps.

60. Cleall, Charles. "The Master of the Choir," Musical
Opinion and Music Trade Review, 80:683, August
1957 through 83:275 ff., January, 1960.
      A monthly column discussing matters of general
interest to choirmasters.

61.   . The Selection and Training of Mixed Choirs
in Churches. London: Independent Press, 1960.
      Outstanding points of this choral method include a
choir master's alphabet, achieving tone color through
the use of "breath notes," and the selection of the
singers.

62.   . Voice Production in Choral Technique.
London: Novello and Company, 1954.
      A detailed discussion of choral vocal training with
emphasis upon tone and diction problems.

63. Coleman, Henry. Amateur Choir Trainer. London:
Oxford University Press, 1932.
      A practical book which is addressed to the vocal
training of young voices with the statement that in
training adults, the same procedure will be effective.

64.   . Choral Conducting for Women's Institutes.
London: Oxford University Press, 1933.
      A brief book dealing with the female choir from
choice of conductor, accompanist and music, to
tone, blend, and enunciation.

65.   . Conducting for Church Musicians. Croydon,
England: Royal School of Church Music, 1962.
      One of a series of nine in a "Study Note Series"
published by the RSCM, this twenty-three page booklet contains conducting patterns, phrasing, expression,

dynamics, use of left hand, and useful related ideas.

66. _____ . Youth Club Choirs. London: Oxford University Press, 1950.
A fine, small book addressed to the organization and direction of youth choirs.

67. "A College Concert Choir," Choir Guide, 3:8-9, June, 1950.
A review of the activities, basic philosophy and rehearsal procedures of the Concert Choir of Teachers College, Columbia University, under the direction of Harry Robert Wilson.

68. "Collegiate Chorale Rehearses," Choir Guide, 1:9, December, 1949.
A brief article in the first issue of Choir Guide telling how Robert Shaw emphasizes rhythm and groups his singers so that they may hear better the parts of the total structure.

69. Colness, R. C. "On the Need for 'Soul' in Choral Singing," American Music Teacher, 19:30 ff., September, 1969.
Choral singing should possess more variety and meaning through careful attention to the interpretation of the music's deeper values.

70. _____ . "Tone Quality; a Pragmatic Approach for High School Choirs," American Music Teacher, 17: 21-22, November, 1967.

71. Conway, Marmaduke P. The Self-Taught Country Organist and Choirmaster. London: Canterbury Press, 1956.
The book is in two parts. Part one is for the organist and part two is concerned with basic points on the training and management of small church choirs.

72. Craig, Don. "Say Something When You Sing," Music Journal, 12:31 ff., March, 1954.
A discussion of expressing the music through emphasis on the rhythm, tempo, and clarity of poetic communication.

73. _____ . "Watch Those Unaccented Notes," Musical

Journal, 14:20 ff., February, 1956.
Interpretation of choral music needs more well-
connected legato phrases, with every note and every
syllable important.

74. Crawford, H. R. "Choral Devices or Vocal Techniques," American Music Teacher, 16:17 ff., February, 1967.
Choral devices should not be contrary to correct
basic vocal techniques. The author discusses singing consonants, vowel attacks and distorted pronunciations.

75. Cushing, H. Caleb. "Fundamentals for Choirs," Music
Ministry, 2:12-13, September, 1969; 2:41-42, October, 1969; 2:41-42, November, 1969.
Procedures for choral warm-ups, correct posture,
breathing, and diction.

76. Dann, Hollis. "A Personal Letter to Each Member of
the Supervisors Chorus," Music Supervisors National
Conference Yearbook, Vol. 25, Chicago, 1932, pp.
156-157.
A brief letter to the chorus stressing key factors
in the success of their performances.

77. _____. "Choral Club Organization," Etude, 50:175,
March, 1932.
The author gives points of advice on recruitment,
organization, and first year activities and states the
vocal guidelines for a new choral organization.

78. _____. "Essential Factors of Good Choral Singing,"
Music Educators Journal, 22:17, November, 1935.
The essential factors are: (1) beautiful tone, (2)
superior diction, (3) greatly increased and refined
reading power, (4) emotional element developed and
made vital, (5) perfect attack, release and dynamics,
and (6) artistic interpretation.

79. _____. "Some Essentials of Choral Singing," Music
Educators Journal, 24:27 ff., September, 1937.
A sharp criticism of technically proficient choirs
with mechanical perfection of tone, blend, phrasing,
diction and intonation, but whose singing lacks spir-
itual, emotional, imaginative, and inspirational elements.

80. _____ . "Voice Classification in Junior and Senior
     High Schools," Music Educators National Conference
     Yearbook, 1937, pp. 267-269.
          A copy of the paper distributed by the author at
     the Southern, Southwestern, North Central and Eastern
     MENC Conferences. Characteristics of girls' and
     boys' voices are given and comments made in ref-
     erence to range problems.

81. Darr, Guthrie. "Choral Technics (Hummed Consonants),"
     Music Ministry, 7:39, December, 1965.
          Improve diction through attention to vocal and sub-
     vocal consonants.

82. _____ . "Choral Technics (What's the Message?),"
     Music Ministry, 7:39, November, 1965.
          Improve diction through emphasis upon each vowel
     sound with special attention to compound vowels.

83. Davies, Walford and Grace, Harvey. Music and Wor-
     ship. London: Eyre and Spottiswoode, 1935.
          Two spokesmen for the English choral tradition
     discuss all aspects of music in the worship service
     including music as a means of worship, the part of
     the clergy, solos and soloist, congregational singing,
     chants, hymns, and anthems.

84. Davidson, Roy. "Choral Technics (Maintaining Vital
     Posture)," Music Ministry, 5:33, August, 1964.
          A discussion of the importance of good posture in
     choral singing.

85. Davison, Archibald. Choral Conducting. Cambridge:
     Harvard University Press, 1940.
          The five chapters of this fine book are the con-
     ductor, the beat, the chorus, rehearsals, and choral
     technique.

86. Day, George H. "Trials of a Choir Director," New
     Music Review, 31:212-213, April, 1932.
          The problem areas range from recruitment to
     choice of music and special services.

87. Deardorff, June B. Voice Production for Choirs. Day-
     ton: Lorenz Publishing Company, 1953.
          A twelve-page manual of instruction and exercises
     which accompanies a phonograph record of musical

illustrations. Breathing, vowels, consonants, and
range procedures are emphasized.

88. Decker, Harold. "Choosing Music for Performance,"
    Choral Director's Guide, Kenneth Neidig and John
    Jennings, editors. West Nyack, New York: Parker,
    1967, pp. 77-114.
    Guidelines for selecting literature and a list of
    literature selected by members of the American
    Choral Directors Association.

89. De Jonge, James. "Are You Guilty?" Educational
    Music Magazine, 25:39, March, 1946.
    Sometimes we get so close to the mechanics and
    techniques of our work that we accept singing that
    is lacking in warmth of tone, rhythmic freshness
    and spirited animation.

90. Dennis, C. M. "High School A Cappella Choir,"
    School Music, 32:3 ff., May, 1932.
    A brief background of the a cappella choir is
    given. Some key points of a cappella work are the
    size of the choir, selection of singers and its edu-
    cational values.

91. Diercks, Louis. "The Detection, Care and Preserva-
    tion of the Young Tenor," Music Educators Journal,
    51:135-136 ff., February, 1965.
    Guidelines for classifying, and developing the
    young tenor voice.

92. _____. "The Individual in the Choral Situation,"
    National Association of Teachers of Singing Bulletin,
    17:6 ff., May, 1961.
    An explanation of "scrambled" seating arrange-
    ments and their favorable effect on tone quality,
    blend and intonation.

93. _____. "The Individual in the Choral Situation,"
    Choral Journal, 7:25-29, March, 1967.
    A discussion of the values of "scrambled" choral
    seating with mathematical justifications by E. Milton
    Boone.

94. _____. "Two Wrongs Won't Make a Right," Choral
    Journal, 9:25-26, July, 1968.
    Criticism of darkening the vowel to improve

choral tone rather than working for vowel accuracy.

95. Dorr, William Ripley. "The Influence of Pitch Upon
    Intonation, " New Music Review, 31:197-199, April,
    1932.
        The necessity of changing the key of a selection
    to fit the "whole vocal pitch of the choir, the tes-
    situra, so to speak" is the point emphasized.

96. Douglas, Ruth. "How Good Is Your Choir?" Choral
    and Organ Guide, 6:20-21, June, 1953.
        A brief article which judges a choir by its "one-
    ness" of appearance, movement, sound, and spirit.

97. Draper, Dallas. "Choir Auditions, " Music Education
    in Action, Archie Jones, editor. Boston: Allyn
    and Bacon, 1960, pp. 169-172.
        The audition must reveal the (1) range, (2) voice
    quality, (3) evenness of vibrato, (4) basic musician-
    ship, and (5) sight-reading ability of the individual
    singer. Audition technique, tone quality, and in-
    tonation are given special emphasis.

98. Dryden, H. R. "The Camera and Chorus, " Music
    Educator's Journal, 42:28-31, January, 1956.
        By use of a Polaroid Land Camera, pictures
    can be taken in the rehearsal to reveal defects in
    posture, mouth formation of vowels, diphthongs and
    consonants, and the lack of unanimity in attacks
    and releases.

99. Dunham, Rowland W. "Choir Work, " American Or-
    ganist, 36:264, August, 1953.
        Basic points for church choir work including
    views on tone, humming, dynamics, and unaccom-
    panied singing.

100. _____. "Organist as Choirmaster, " American Or-
    ganist, 44:11-12, July, 1961.
        If the organist is also the choirmaster he must
    have knowledge of the art of singing.

101. _____. "Vocal Tone, " American Organist, 36:411-
    412, December, 1953.
        A plea for more consideration of vocal resonance
    in the church choir.

102. _____. "Vocal Tone," American Organist, 37:52,
     February, 1954.
     A brief description of correct tone production
     proceeding from the "oo" sound with lips pursed
     to "ah" with mouth open.

103. Dyer, Harold S. "Effective Rehearsal Technic that
     Builds Better Choirs," Educational Music Magazine,
     14:31, January, 1935.
     A procedure for warming-up the choir is given;
     the objective is a mental and physical loosening
     and the development of a "soft, covered quality of
     tone."

104. Dykems, Peter and Gehrkens, Karl. The Teaching
     and Administration of High School Music. Boston:
     C. C. Birchard and Co., 1941.
     This extensive volume on high school music in-
     cludes chapters on "The Vocal Program: Intro-
     duction," "The High School Chorus," "Glee Club,"
     "The Voice Class," and "Unaccompanied Singing."
     The role of blend in a cappella singing is empha-
     sized.

105. Earhart, Will. Choral Technique. New York: M.
     Witmark and Sons, 1937.
     A study course which includes vocal training,
     musicianship training and examples of music.

106. _____. Teachers' Manual for Choral Technics.
     New York: M. Witmark, 1938.
     A companion work to the author's Choral Tech-
     nics, giving instructions for using the text.

107. _____. "The Educational Values of A Cappella
     Singing," Supervisors Service Bulletin, 12:13 ff.,
     March, 1933.
     The refined ear training and tonal reflectiveness
     that are required in a cappella singing are at the
     very roots of training for musical taste, discrimina-
     tion and culture.

108. Eddy, Clark. "Save the Church Choir," Music Jour-
     nal, 20:38 ff., April, 1962.
     A description of a struggling church choir and
     a list of suggestions for making the choir better.

109. Edeson, D. J. S. Training of Catholic Choirs. London: Cary and Company, 1934.
A book which is primarily addressed to the training of the boys' voices in the choir.

110. Edwards, Frederick. "Choral Technics," Music Ministry, 3:43-44, August, 1962.
A review of many dependent factors in good choral intonation.

111. Ehlert, J. K. "Choral Suggestions," Music Educators Journal, 35:47, April, 1949.
The importance of the text in choral interpretation is discussed and a few guidelines to good diction are presented.

112. Ehmann, Wilhelm. Choral Directing. Translated by G. D. Wiebe. Minneapolis: Augsburg, 1968.
An extensive discussion of the choral training process including posture, breathing, voice training, diction, ear training, body movement, conducting and rehearsal procedures.

113. _____. "The Artistic Unison," Music Journal, 26: 81-82, September, 1968.
The most basic and vital aspects of the choral art are to be learned from unison singing. The author describes these basics and illustrates his approach with a musical example.

114. Ehret, Walter. Choral Director's Handbook. New York: Edward Marks Music Corp., 1959.
A collection of choral ideas, procedures, and rehearsal devices presented in outline form.

115. _____, and Wilson, Harry Robert, arranged and edited by. Salute to Music. New York: Boosey and Hawkes, Inc., 1953.
A few instructions concerning the improvement of singing through work on tone and diction are included with these arrangements of choral music of several styles and periods.

116. Eisenkramer, H. E. "Techniques in Voice Blending," Music Educators Journal, 35:48-49, February, 1949.
Exact pitch, soft singing, and clean, clear vowel

sounds are the principle factors in achieving good blend. Other techniques are given.

117. Engelstad, Paul. "C-Day: Are You Ready?" Choral Journal, 6:17-18, January, 1966.
   A review of factors and rehearsal sequences which assure a good performance.

118. Erdman, Howard. "Vocal Music in a Class 'C' High School," School Musician, 24:13, May, 1953.
   The Wautoma, Wisconsin, vocal program is described with emphasis upon the methods of vocal training.

119. Epstein, David (Leonard Stone). Belwin Chorus Builder. 2 vols. Rockville Centre, New York: Belwin, 1961-1962.
   Book One deals with fundamentals of choral singing: rhythm, tone, pitch, diction, dynamics and phrasing, and warm-up exercises. Book Two is a little more advanced, covering the topics in Book One and adding harmony, blend and special effects. Each volume has a student book and teacher's manual.

120. Evanson, J. A. "Classroom Choral Technique," Music Supervisors National Conference Yearbook. Vol. 25. Chicago, 1932, pp. 140-149.
   The author outlines his procedure for developing a chorus. The three primary points are reading music, correct vocal technique, and interpretation.

121. _____. "Essentials of Better Choral Singing," Music Supervisors Journal, 17:40, February, 1931.
   A statement of the objective of the school choral program and an outline of the procedure for developing a fundamental choral technique.

122. Finn, William J. The Art of the Choral Conductor. Boston: C. C. Birchard and Co., 1939.
   Father Finn's wealth of experience and understanding of choral and vocal problems are presented in a comprehensive and colorful style.

123. _____. "The Building of the Paulist Choristers," Etude, 65:615 ff., November, 1947.
   The history of the Paulist Choristers is followed

by the author's basic choral procedures, including
the importance of pianissimo singing, downward
vocalization, and the development of the alto and
tenor lines.

124. _____. The Conductor Raises His Baton. New
York: Harper and Brothers, 1944.
A discussion of the role of the conductor as in-
terpreter. Primary emphasis is upon the importance of quantity as "the chief trustee of quality."

125. _____. Epitome of Some Principles of Choral Technique. Boston: C. C. Birchard Company, 1935.
A concise statement of basic philosophy and rehearsal procedures.

126. Fischer, C. M. "Church Choir 'bel canto'," Choral
and Organ Guide, 8:27-28, March, 1955.
Imagination, intelligent listening and concentration are presented as three points to improve
choral singing.

127. _____. "The Four Freedoms in Singing," Choral
and Organ Guide, 6:14-16, November, 1953.
Good singing demands freedom from constriction,
slump, technique, and intonation.

128. Fuhr, H. M. Fundamentals of Choral Expression.
Lincoln, Nebraska: University of Nebraska, 1944.
A book of choral techniques with good coverage
of tone quality, intonation, diction, and ensemble.

129. Fuller, Esther Mary and Atkinson, Thelma. Handbook
for Choir Directors. New York: Pro Art Publications, 1953.
Practical suggestions for organizing and developing children's and adult choirs.

130. Garretson, Robert L. Conducting Choral Music.
Boston: Allyn and Bacon, 1961.
The job of the choral conductor is discussed
from planning and organization, to programming,
concerts, and budgets.

131. _____. Helpful Hints for the Choir Director.
Champaign, Illinois: Collegiate Cap and Gown Company, 1956.

A twenty-page booklet on organizing the church choir, improving the choir rehearsal, and selecting the choir robes.

132. Gilbert, Harold. "Organize Your Choir Rehearsal," Journal of Church Music, 1:2, July, 1959.
The tenor shortage, the strong soprano, the rehearsal room, seating plans, and basic rehearsal procedures are some of the points of emphasis.

133. Gilley, Donald. "Choir Directing Problems," American Music Teacher, 1:8-9 ff., May, 1952.
The author sketches his methods for handling choral problems. Rehearsal procedure, tone quality, diction, and intonation are the principle topics covered.

134. Gilliland, Dale V. "Fundamentals of Voice Education for the Choral Program," Choral Journal, 10:12-13, November, 1969.
Fundamental guidelines for good choral voice technique including discussions of posture, breathing, tone and range.

135. Goetz, Esther and Christiansen, F. M. "The Choral Director's Round Table," Educational Music Magazine, 15:48, March, 1936.
F. M. Christiansen answers questions for church choir directors concerning organizing the choir, the music committee, blending the solo quartette, and rehearsal planning.

136. Goetz, Esther (compiler). "The Choral Director's Round Table," Educational Music Magazine, 15:52, September, 1935.
The report of a round-table held at the Christiansen Choir School. The topic was how to overcome flatting.

137. _____. (compiler). "The Choral Director's Round-Table," Educational Music Magazine, 15:48, November, 1935.
The outstanding feature of this round table was F. M. Christiansen's response to the question, "Dr. Christiansen, will you tell us the method and procedure you use in testing voices?"

138. _____. (compiler). "The Choral Director's Round-Table," Educational Music Magazine, 15:51, January, 1936.
The high-light of this Christiansen Choir School round-table was the answer to the question, "What can be done to correct tremolo habit?"

139. _____. "A Summer Master Course," School Music, 35:18-19, September, 1935.
The Christiansen Choral School at Winona Lake, Indiana, is described from organization to class procedures.

140. Grace, Harvey. The Training and Conducting of Choral Societies. London: Novello and Company, 1938.
A good discussion of choral training. Choral tone is discussed by considering its quality, quantity, control, colour, naturalness, blend, and balance.

141. Grant, Richard W. "How Voice Training Classes Benefit the School Chorus," Supervisors Service Bulletin, 12:43-44, January, 1933.
Observations of the interrelated voice class and vocal ensemble.

142. Green, Elizabeth. The Modern Conductor. Englewood Cliffs, New Jersey: Prentice-Hall, 1961.
The emphasis is upon instrumental conducting; however, a few points are given on choral diction, intonation, and tone quality.

143. Green, Spencer. "Effective Use of the Large Chorus," Educational Music Magazine, 22:32 ff., March, 1943.
The advice here may be applied to all choral groups, not just the large chorus. Diction, dynamics, and interpretation are points of emphasis.

144. _____. "Furthering the Vocal Ideal," Educational Music Magazine, 16:29, November, 1939.
By teaching basic fundamentals we can best achieve our aim. Good quality is achieved by appropriate suggestion, and by teaching the group to listen.

145. Guadnola, P. "Let Them Sing," School Musician, 24:

13-14, February, 1953.
Both philosophy and rehearsal techniques are included in this discussion of the choir.

146. Gustafson, Anna Marie. "Vitalized Tone," Educational Music Magazine, 19:44 ff., September, 1939.
The personality and attitude of the teacher, breathing technique of the singers, and emphasis upon text and phrasing are a few of the factors which make up a vitalized tone.

147. Halfvarson, Sten. "Experiments in Ear Training for Vocal Groups," Educational Music Magazine, 19:9 ff., March, 1940.
Scales and chord progressions are recommended as a means to improve intonation and sight reading.

148. Hamilton, W. "Musicians for the Choir," Etude, 69:24 ff., July, 1951.
A description of how a church choir developed ability to read and improved tone quality in a series of weekly lessons.

149. Hammer, R. A. "Achieving Choral Balance through the Vowel," Music Journal, 23:62 ff., March, 1965.
A description of a choral method based upon vowel production.

150. Hammermeyer, Jonathan. "The Conductor's Preparation," School Musician, 12:28-29, December, 1940.
A step-wise procedure for the conductor's preparation of a composition from learning the notes to determining the fine points of interpretation.

151. _____. "Intonation and the Piano," School Musician, 12:3, June, 1941.
The tempered tuning of the piano places limitations on its use for the choir which hopes to perform true a cappella music.

152. _____. "Pronunciation in Choral Music," School Musician, 12:35 ff., October, 1940.
The fundamentals of pronunciation involve concepts of breathing, proper use of consonants and vowels, enunciation, word accent and emotional quality.

153. _____. "Sing, America! Sing!" School Musician,
      11:27, May, 1940.
          Points discussed include tone, diction, dis-
      sonances, phrasing, and dynamics.

154. Hansen, C. "Tuning the Choir," Music Educators
      Journal, 51:85-89, November, 1964.
          A comprehensive discussion of intonation prob-
      lems and corrective techniques.

155. Hartman, B. "Bodily Movement: A Choral Aid,"
      Music Educators Journal, 51:123-124 ff., February,
      1965.
          Body movement can aid the singer in solving
      vocal problems as well as heighten his awareness
      of the creative process.

156. Heaton, C. H. How to Build a Church Choir. St.
      Louis: Bethany Press, 1958.
          Practical ideas and suggestions for recruitment,
      choir rooms, rehearsals, recognition, and other
      problems.

157. Heim, Norman. "Choral Technics (Text and Pronunci-
      ation)," Music Ministry, 1:40, January, 1969.
          Inflection in the text line and clear pronunciation
      of words is necessary for good choral performances.

158. _____. "Choral Technics (Tone Quality, Pitch, and
      Range)," Music Ministry, 1:40, December, 1968.
          Brief recommendations for a warm, pleasant
      tone, good intonation and choral warm-ups.

159. Helvey, Kenneth W. "Methods of Choral Tone Pro-
      duction," Music Educators Journal, 41:56, Febru-
      ary, 1955.
          A report of an M.M. thesis at the University
      of Southern California.

160. Henson, B. R. "Posture and Breathing," Music Edu-
      cation in Action, Archie Jones, editor. Boston:
      Allyn and Bacon, 1960, pp. 154-156.
          A description of breathing and the role of the
      diaphragm and intercostal and abdominal muscles
      is given with a few points on good posture.

161. Hilbish, Thomas. "Establishing a Program of Per-

manent Value," Choral Director's Guide, Kenneth
Neidig and John Jennings, editors. West Nyack,
New York: Parker, 1967, pp. 287-299.
   A description of the structure of the Princeton,
New Jersey, high school choir program which in-
cluded performances of compositions by Webern,
Stravinsky and Sessions.

162.   Hillis, Margaret. At Rehearsals. New York: Ameri-
       can Choral Foundation, Inc., 1961.
          The brochure which is given each member of the
       Chicago Symphony Orchestra Chorus contains "a
       few of the cornerstones of choral practice." In-
       cluded are points of listening, watching, counting,
       good singing, good diction, phrasing, studying,
       knowing the music, marking the music, definitions
       of musical terms, and the chorus membership
       rules.

163.   Hinrichsen, M. (editor). Organ and Choral Aspects
       and Prospects. Music Book, Vol. X. London:
       Hinrichsen, 1957.
          A collection of lectures and papers most of
       which were given at the International Organ Con-
       gress in London, 1957.

164.   Hintz, Elmer M. "Selecting Voices for the Special
       Chorus," Music Educators National Conference
       Yearbook. Vol. 30. Chicago, 1937, pp. 290-
       291.
          Musicianship, vocal range, and balance and
       blend of the tone are the items discussed as the
       basis for selecting the voices.

165.   Hjortsvang, C. Amateur Choir Director. New York:
       Abingdon-Cokesbury, 1941.
          A book for the church choir director which
       covers baton technique, vocal technique, types of
       church music positions and recommended anthems
       for the volunteer choir.

166.   Holcomb, Clifford A. Methods and Materials for
       Graded Choirs. Nashville: Broadman Press, 1948.
          One of the series of books on church music
       developed by the Department of Church Music of
       the Baptist Sunday School Board, Nashville, Ten-
       nessee, this practical book presents many useful

ideas related to the graded choir program.

167. Holden, D. L. "A Survey of Attempts to Solve Vocal
     Problems in the High School Chorus," Music Edu-
     cators Journal, 41:52-53, April, 1955.
        The author reports his survey of the recom-
     mendations by outstanding choral directors.

168. Holley, Kay. "Building the Glee Club," Etude, 66:
     461 ff., August, 1948.
        The associate director of the Radio City Music
     Hall Glee Clubs discusses the philosophy and pro-
     cedures of the organization.

169. Hooper, William. "Try Singing A Cappella," Music
     Ministry, 6:11, August, 1965.
        The experience of unaccompanied singing can be
     a great aid in developing intonation, blend, balance,
     interpretative nuances and an expanded repertoire.

170. Horton, Lewis Henry. The A Cappella Primer. Cin-
     cinnati: Willis Music Co., 1935.
        A collection of easier numbers for a cappella
     choir with brief "hints and suggestions."

171. Hosmer, Helen. "As the Adjudicator Hears It!" Etude,
     67:224 ff., April, 1949.
        Any conductor who intends to submit his chorus
     for adjudication must have: (1) an ideal, (2) a
     power to analyze, and (3) an ability to act re-
     medially. A list of comments which were made by
     the author in judging vocal events is given.

172. _____. "Down to Earth with Ideals," National As-
     sociation of Teachers of Singing Bulletin, 10:13 ff.,
     May, 1954.
        Practical suggestions dealing with posture,
     breathing, tone rhythmic flow, and the meaning of
     the song.

173. _____. "Technics of Choral Conducting," Etude, 67:
     18, January, 1949.
        A good conductor, plus the right kind of re-
     hearsals, equals a good chorus and a good choral
     program.

174. Howard, C. H. "Anyone Can Sing," School Musician,

26:22 ff., November, 1954.
An optimistic statement by a director who takes
singers from where they are and has not yet found
a student who absolutely could not sing.

175. Howerton, George. "Music Education through Choral
      Experience," Music Educators National Conference
      Yearbook. Vol. 32. Chicago, 1939-1940, pp.
      330-335.
      Educational values such as the relationship to
      other humanities, the emotional essence of art,
      knowledge of choral literature and the learning of
      desirable attitudes are discussed.

176. _____. "Organizational Practices in School Choral
      Programs," Etude, 73:17 ff., November, 1955.
      An outline of the procedures developed by lead-
      ing choral educators including try-outs, balance of
      parts, the high school tenor, student officers, seat-
      ing of the group, organization of the rehearsal, and
      repertoire.

177. _____. Technique and Style in Choral Singing.
      New York: C. Fischer, 1957.
      The first half of the book is addressed to choral
      technique and the second half to generalizations
      concerning choral styles and interpretation.

178. _____. The Use of Victor Records in the High
      School Choral Training Program. Camden, New
      Jersey: RCA Victor, 1944.
      Breath control, phrasing, diction, legato and
      non-legato tone, and interpretation are the topics
      of this fifty-eight page book. Record lists are in-
      cluded.

179. Howes, Arthur. "A Joyful Noise: Plainsong, the
      Ideal Vocal Method," Organ Institute Quarterly, 4:
      16, Spring, 1954.
      The use of melismatic chants to develop pure
      vowel resonance are recommended for choral
      training.

180. _____. "A Joyful Noise: Selection of Voices,"
      Organ Institute Quarterly, 3:5, Winter, 1953.
      A discussion of tone quality, blend and balance
      of parts.

181. _____ . "A Joyful Noise: Vibrato," Organ Institute
Quarterly, 4:9-10, Autumn, 1954.
Correct, natural singing possesses a mild,
scarcely noticeable vibrato which is preferred over
the excessive vibrato or the "straight" tone.

182. Hume, Paul. Catholic Church Music. Toronto: Dodd,
1956.
A good book for the Catholic Choir director
which includes helpful discussions of recruitment,
wedding music, boys' choirs, music in school,
selection of music, personnel relations, and other
areas. Encyclical letters by the Pope and lists of
graded music complete the coverage.

183. Ibbotson, Ernest M. "Guideposts for a Choir Director,"
Etude, 53: 426-427, July, 1935.
A brief outline of a warm-up procedure is fol-
lowed by some ideas on interpretation of anthems.

184. Jacobs, Ruth Krehbiel. The Practical Choirmaster.
Los Angeles: Choir Publications.
A book of techniques for the director of adult
church choirs.

185. Jacobsen, O. Irving. "The Tempered Scale in Instrumental and Choral Ensemble Work," School
Music, 35:3 ff., March, 1935.
The tempered and natural scales are explained
and applications made for ensemble singing.

186. James, Milton. "Do They Sing in Tune?" School
Musician, 13:9, December, 1941.
Make your chorus pitch-conscious and watch
your problems of intonation disappear. Warm-up
exercises and causes of poor intonation are given.

187. Jaroff, Serge. "The Original Don Cossacks and the
Music of the Don," Etude, 61:706 ff., November,
1943.
The history of the Cossack choir, its musical
traditions and special points of their technique are
presented by their founder and conductor.

188. Jeffers, E. V. "Integration of Vocal Class Work with
Choral Activities," Music Educators National Conference Yearbook. Vol. 28. Chicago, 1935, pp.

298-300.
        The five main points of this discussion are: (1)
        the proportion of voice class time to regular re-
        hearsal, (2) the voice class as a time-saver for
        rehearsals, (3) blending voices, (4) progress through
        solo voice work, and (5) the decrescendo.

189.   Jeffries, Arthur.   "For the Untrained Singer, " Etude,
        51:544-555, August, 1933.
        Open throat, diction, vowels, phrasing, range,
        volume, care of the voice, and vocal exercises are
        discussed.

190.   Jones, Archie, editor.   Music Education in Action.
        Boston: Allyn and Bacon, 1960.
        This book is an extensive compilation of writings
        of 130 music educators.   It includes articles on
        choral tone, posture, breathing, diction, intonation,
        and the high school tenor.

191.   _____.   Techniques in Choral Conducting.   New
        York: Carl Fischer, 1948.
        Chapters on conducting technique, tone quality,
        diction, interpretation, program building, and or-
        ganization precede appendix lists of terms, songs,
        recordings, and an interpretative analysis of se-
        lected anthems.

192.   _____, and Rhea, Lois and Raymond.   First Steps
        to Choral Music.   New York: Bourne, Inc., 1957.
        Twenty-four pages of basic techniques and 134
        pages of easy choral music.

193.   Jones, Arnold.   "Choral Director as Voice Teacher, "
        Music Education in Action.   Archie Jones, editor.
        Boston: Allyn and Bacon, 1960, pp. 150-154.
        The techniques of Kenneth Westerman are offered
        as a method for building the voice through attention
        to posture, respiration, phonation, resonation, and
        articulation.

194.   Jones, Donald.   "Let's Sing! How?"   Choral Journal,
        10:15, July, 1969.
        Improve choral singing by attention to the proper
        sounds of the English language.

195.   _____.   "Scrambled Singing, " Choral Journal, 8:8-9,

September, 1967.
The values of mixed choral seating plans are discussed with diagrams of various arrangements.

196. Jones, Edwin W. "Awaken! Analyze! Adjust! (Preparation for Contests)," Educational Music Magazine,
34:29-32, January, 1955.
Some final check-ups before contest time include
intonation, beauty of tone, enunciation, blend and
interpretation.

197. _____. "Choral Balance and Blend," American
Music Teacher, 5:2 ff., November, 1955.
A discussion and list of techniques for balancing
and blending choral voices.

198. _____. "Emotion, Enemy of Ennui," Educational
Music Magazine, 34:21 ff., November, 1954.
Nuance, controlled tempo, clarity, vocal quantity,
intonation, and diction are important; there is something more-emotion.

199. _____. "Tuning Tips for Teensters," School Musician, 26:25 ff., October, 1954.
A list of ideas to solve intonation problems.

200. Jones, John Loren. "Problems of the High School
Tenor," Music Education in Action. Archie Jones,
editor. Boston: Allyn and Bacon, 1960, pp. 140-
142.
The choral director should encourage as much as
possible the development of a well-supported tone
production depending upon the diaphragm as the
main power supply. Should the range or tessitura
be insurmountable, it is wise to suggest the use of
the falsetto.

201. Jones, John Paul. The Director of School Music.
Kansas City, Missouri: Jenkins Music Co., 1949.
The director's background, his personality, his
plans, and various procedures for planning, organizing, rehearsing, and performing school music.

202. Jones, J. W. "An Examination of Basic Choral Con-
struction," Choir Guide, 3:10-11, September, 1950.
The author speaks against the selection of particular voice types, such as a soprano section of a

few "very light, colorless, flutelike voices," and
recommends a basically lyric tone in contrast to
"aw" or "dark, rich" tone.

203.   . "Tone Production in Choral Art," Choral
and Organ Guide, 10:10-18, April, 1957.
    The description of a method of tone production
based upon natural singing which grows out of
natural speech and is devoid of any imposed method.

204. Kaltrider, W. D. "Let's Begin by Being in Earnest,"
American Organist, 36:371-373, November, 1953.
    A down-to-earth approach to the volunteer choir
which stresses basic motivation of the group.

205. Kettering, Charles. "Some Practical Vocal Helps for
Supervisor and Choral Director," Supervisors Service Bulletin, 12:39 ff., November, 1932.
    Tone, diction, and range problems are the main
topics of this article.

206. Kettring, Donald D. Steps Toward a Singing Church.
Philadelphia: Westminster Press, 1948.
    A complete discussion of the church choir pro-
gram including philosophy, organization, rehearsal
procedures, and repertory.

207. Kindig, A. "Choral Rehearsal Techniques," School
Musician, 33:32-33, January, 1962.
    Techniques and exercises for the development
of breathing.

208. King, C. B. "Essence of Things Choral," Educational
Music Magazine, 25:23 ff., March, 1946.
    Diction, blend, breathing, placement and range
are all dependent upon the vowel.

209.   . "Suggestions and Drills for the A Cappella
Choir," Educational Music Magazine, 21:40-43 ff.,
September, 1941.
    A mimeographed form which was given to each
choir member includes procedures for tone, intonation, blending, diction, breathing, and general re-
sponsiveness.

210. King, Robert J. "Choirs and the Weather," Musical
Times, 103:841-843, December, 1962.

The report of a twelve-year investigation which
revealed that choral performances were better when
the barometric pressure was rising and poorer when
it was falling.

211. Kirk, Theron Wilford. Choral Tone and Technic.
Westbury, New York: Pro Art Publications, 1956.
. Twenty pages of exercises with brief comments.

212. Klein, Maynard. "Choral Cultism," Etude, 65:618,
November, 1947.
Beware of being known as a "straight toner," an
"a cappella fadist," or a "phonetic fiend." The
author gives his basic choral technique in ten
points, which are tone, rhythm, phrasing, pronunciation, intonation, breathing, text, styles, spirit,
and ensemble.

213. Kolb, D. "Something More Than Singing," Educational
Music Magazine, 22:8-9 ff., November, 1942.
Personal, emotional, expressive, and aesthetic
development are some of the true long range values
of choral singing.

214. Koontz, J. E. "An Approach to Choral Tone," Educational Music Magazine, 33:19 ff., September,
1953.
Subjective versus objective tone is described.
Subjective tone is that which gives emotional coloring and essential reality to the underlying meaning
of the word. Objective tone is a result of unity
and "oneness" of vowel shape and color of sound.

215. Kortkamp, Ivan. The Advanced Choir. Decorah,
Iowa: Decorah Publishing, 1956.
An illustrated book of choral-vocal techniques
covering breath, posture, intonation, tone quality,
tone-color, blending, articulation and other choral
factors.

216. _____. "Compensation ... for Flatting," Educational Music Magazine, 20:46 ff., September, 1940.
Rehearsal devices for correcting flatting.

217. _____. "Give Your Choir a Checklist," Educational
Music Magazine, 28:29 ff., November, 1948.
Several sample items from the author's personal

checklist of choral technique.

218. _____. "Graded Breathing Exercises," Choir Guide,
3:26 ff., October, 1950.
Unusual exercises are given for application in
three yearly stages of development.

219. _____. 100 Things a Choir Should Know. Nevado,
Iowa: Ivan Kortkamp, 1949.
A checklist of the author's choral techniques.

220. _____. "Power of Mind over Voice," Educational
Music Magazine, 22:15 ff., September, 1942.
A choir must discipline itself to control pitch,
intervals, vowel shapes, and rhythms.

221. _____. "Tone Color," Choir Guide, 2:9-10 ff.,
November, 1949.
A description of the role of overtone in tone
color by referring to the Hammond electric organ.

222. _____. "Tone Color Artistry," Choir Guide, 2:10,
May, 1949.
By careful awareness of the mood, emotion
and meanings of the text, a great variety of tone
colors may be found. Some are achieved through
a conscious modification of the vowel and others
by indirect suggestion and imagining the tone color
which is desired.

223. _____. "Yodel Up to a Better Register," Music
Educators Journal, 55:50-52, April, 1969.
Vocal technique must be built on a light style
of singing, which can be developed through use of
the yodel.

224. Kroeker, Esther. "Harmony in the Choir," Etude,
63:497, September, 1945.
Basic points for achieving harmony of voices
and harmony of personalities in the volunteer
church choir.

225. Krone, Max T. The Chorus and Its Conductor.
Chicago: Neil A. Kjos, 1945.
A comprehensive text on choral technique from
organization to rehearsal procedures and performance.

226. _____. "Conducting the College Choir," Music Education National Conference Yearbook. Vol. 31.
Chicago, 1938, pp. 119-123.
     Choice of music, functions of the choir, knowl-
edge of choral literature, choice of personnel,
scheduling rehearsals, seating the choir, use of
rehearsal time, technique of conducting, and cre-
ativity in performance are the topics discussed.

227. _____. "The Secret of Singing in Tune," Educational Music Magazine, 14:8, November, 1934.
     The author recommends extensive work in tuning
the major triad as the basis for singing in tune.

228. _____. "Silver Anniversary Resumé," Music Supervisors Journal, 14:8, November, 1934.
     A review of the convention with pertinent ob-
servations concerning the variety of tone quality
that had been developed by the various choruses.

229. Kwalwasser, Jacob. "Voice Problems in Public
Schools," Music Supervisors National Conference
Yearbook. Vol. 26. Chicago, 1933, pp. 105-110.
     This strong criticism of the following of "fears,
superstitions, taboos and questionable devices" by
the public school music teacher includes an objection to the use of the light, head voice as a standard of vocal production.

230. Kyes, J. F. "Simple Approaches to Choral Conducting," Etude, 72:20 ff., October, 1954.
     A choral director speaks plainly about the re-
sponsibilities and procedures of his work.

231. Landau, Irving. "Better Results in Choral Group
Work," Etude, 59:661 ff., October, 1941.
     The advice given ranges from conducting tech-
nique and good enunciation to rehearsal psychology.

232. Lawson, Warner. "Practical Rehearsal Techniques,"
Choral Director's Guide. Kenneth Neidig and John
Jennings, editors. West Nyack, New York: Parker, 1967, pp. 243-267.
     The practical techniques include time-saving
devices, rehearsal procedures, seating plans and
approaches to tone, diction and intonation.

233. Leeder and Haynie. Music Education in the High
      School. Englewood Cliffs, New Jersey: Prentice-
      Hall, 1958.
          This book discusses the entire secondary school
      music program with a few statements of procedure
      concerning the development of choral voices.

234. Legeman, Mary. "A Short Cut to Choral Directing, "
      Educational Music Magazine, 23:19 ff., January,
      1943.
          Tone quality, diction, attacks and releases,
      rhythm, and blend are among the improvements
      which can be made by giving attention to the con-
      sonants.

235. "Let the People Sing (Poor Diction in Choral Singing), "
      Musical Opinion and Trade Review, 80:389-390,
      April, 1957.
          Good diction has been sacrificed for vocal tone,
      vocal colour, and vocal blend. Too many choral
      niceties of the over-cultured tone are apparent.

236. Lewis, Joseph. Conducting Without Fears, Part II.
      Choral and Orchestral Conducting. London:
      Ascherberg, Hopwood, and Crew, Ltd., 1945.
          The chapter on choral conducting includes lis-
      tening technique, balance and blend, word produc-
      tion, phrasing, and attack.

237. Liemohn, E. "Intonation and Blend in the A Cappella
      Choir, " Music Educators Journal, 44:50, June,
      1958.
          Good intonation and blend are interrelated in
      the a cappella ensemble. The author discusses the
      selection of members, quality of the voices, the
      musical ear, the vibrato, and rehearsal techniques
      for achieving good intonation and blend.

238. Lindroth, R. K. "Does the Music in Your Church
      Express or Impress?" Music Journal, 12:24 ff.,
      February, 1954.
          An organist gives a strong plea for expressive
      music in the church.

239. Lindsay, Charles. "Importance of Diction, " Music
      Educating in Action. Archie Jones, editor.
      Boston: Allyn and Bacon, 1960, pp. 160-161.

A brief statement concerning the need for good
diction and a diction exercise which adds words
and syllables to the basic oo-ee-ay-ah-oh exercise.

240. Little, George. "Choral Aspects and Prospects,"
Organ and Choral Aspects and Prospects. London:
Hinrichsen Edition Ltd., 1958, pp. 113-125.
A history of choral music covered by major
style periods and discussion of the contemporary
scene, its problems and potential.

241. Loney, Andres, Jr. "Problems of A Cappella Choir,"
Music Education in Action. Archie Jones, editor.
Boston: Allyn and Bacon, 1960, pp. 172-177.
Schedule conflicts, voice production, falsetto,
breath control, posture, intonation, pianissimo,
and the rehearsal are topics discussed.

242. Lovelace, Austin. The Youth Choir. Nashville:
Abingdon, 1964.
A brief book covering the essentials of youth
choir development from motivation and discipline
to rehearsal procedures and repertoire.

243. _____ and Rice, W. Music and Worship in the
Church. Nashville: Abingdon, 1960.
A discussion of church music for the non-
specialist. Chapters include the music committee,
the director, the organist, the adult choir, children's and youth choir, the choir's music, and the
soloist.

244. Lukken, Albert. "Vibrato and Its Use," Music Education in Action. Archie Jones, editor. Boston:
Allyn and Bacon, 1960, pp. 158-160.
A brief report of attempts to control the vibrato
by use of a "straight-line tone" and the synchroniz-
ing of vibratos. The author reports that fortunately,
both of these theories are "pretty much in the limbo of the past."

245. Lynch, Frances Hill. "Blow Your Own Horn and
Sing," School Musician, 22:15-16, April, 1951.
The strongest plea is for an open throat, although there are techniques for range, quality, and
posture.

246. Mack, G. R. "Vocal Training in the High School,"
      Music Educators Journal, 50:95-96, February,
      1964.
          The true potential of the choral art can be re-
      alized only through work with breathing, diction,
      range and flexibility.

247. Maloney, Grace. "Vocal Perfecting," Supervisors
      Service Bulletin, 12:19, November, 1932.
          A basic outline for teaching good ensemble tone
      and blending.

248. Manson, J. L. Interpretative Choral Singing. Nash-
      ville: Broadman, 1961.
          A discussion of choral interpretation with em-
      phasis upon mood, beat, muscular suggestions,
      facial expression, dynamics, tone color, individual
      voice parts, dramatic factors, and intensity.

249. Marier, Theodore N. "On Basic Choral Techniques
      at the Secondary School Level," Specialized Activi-
      ties in Music Education, Richard Werder, editor.
      Washington: Catholic University of America Press,
      1956, pp. 135-137.
          A summary of the 1955 choral workshop at the
      Catholic University of America.

250. Maybee, Harper C. "The Technique of the Choral
      Ensemble," Supervisors Service Bulletin, 12:16-17,
      January, 1933.
          Basic points concerning warm-ups, attacks,
      tone, and diction.

251. _____. Tuning-up Exercises for Ensemble Singing
      and the Development of a Fundamental Technique.
      Boston: Ditson, 1930.
          A collection of exercises and comments in four
      volumes; mixed voices, men's voices, women's
      voices, and junior high school.

252. _____. Vocal Ensemble Exercises. New York:
      G. Schirmer, 1936.
          Twelve vocal exercises with a few suggestions.

253. Mayer, Fred. "The Relationship of Blend and Intona-
      tion in the Choral Art," Music Educators Journal,
      51:109-110, September, 1964.

The author discusses the blending of voice
qualities and the establishment of non-tempered
tuning through chord-building exercises.

254. McCall, Harlo. "Teaching the Winds," Educational
Music Magazine, 18:23 ff., November, 1938.
After a general survey of the relationship between vocal and instrumental teaching, the author
presents a discussion of breathing with many
teaching techniques.

255. _____. "Teaching the Winds, II," Educational
Music Magazine, 18:8-9 ff., January, 1939.
The discussion of similarities in instructing
vocalists and instrumentalists continues with articulation, intonation, range, and flexibility.

256. McChesney, R. "Some Thoughts on Choral Vocalizing," American Choral Review, 11:23-25, No. 1,
1968.
A discussion of choral warm-ups with emphasis
upon ear training.

257. McCollin, Paul. "Training for Life--The Objective of
the A Cappella Choir," Educational Music Magazine, 15:60 ff., September, 1935.
The a cappella choir offers its members the
unique concomitant values of training in concentration, co-operation, expression, and persistence.

258. McCutchin, Robert. "How I Conduct a Choir Rehearsal," Educational Music Magazine, 17:39, September, 1937.
A discussion of rehearsal procedures by a director who is not an "a cappella addict."

259. Mead, E. G. "Enunciation for Choir Singers," Etude,
52:276, June, 1934.
A brief article calling for the separation of
words with adjoining consonance, such as, "voice
shall."

260. Mielenz, Otto. "The Individual Placement and Baroque
Phrasing of Weston Noble," Choral Journal, 7:13-
14, September, 1966.
The author describes Noble's techniques used in
a California workshop.

261.   Miido, Maimu, "The Art of Conducting," Journal of
        Church Music, 10:2 ff., February, 1968.
            A philosophy of the choral art with emphasis
        upon unifying and beautifying the choir through the
        imagination and expressive intent of the conductor
        and singers.

262.   Miller, McClurg. "The Choral Conductor and the
        Singing Voice," National Association of Teachers
        of Singing Bulletin, 11:19 ff., May, 1955.
            The need for knowledge of singing is emphasized
        through brief discussions of diction, vowel-tone,
        blend, and range.

263.   Modisett, K. C. "Bibliography of Sources: 1930-1952,
        Relating to the Teaching of Choral Music in Sec-
        ondary Schools," Journal of Research, 3:51-60,
        Spring, 1955.
            The title correctly describes the contents of this
        article.

264.   Molner, J. W. "Choral Placement," Music Journal,
        20:118-119, January, 1962.
            The author describes a quick way to get choral
        blend by classifying the voices in three groups:
        flute, string, and reed.

265.   _____. "The Selection and Placement of Choir
        Voices," Choir Guide, 4:38 ff., March, 1951.
            A plan for the selection, placement and blending
        of choir voices based upon the identification of the
        basic quality of the voice: flute type, string type,
        or reed type.

266.   _____. "The Selection and Placement of Choir
        Voices," Music Educators Journal, 36:48-49, June,
        1950.
            Place voices by classifying them as flute, string,
        or reed quality to secure good blend.

267.   Monson, Herman. "Faulty Diction," Educational
        Music Magazine, 16:9, September, 1936.
            When sectional and group unity in quality, color,
        intonation, pitch, and rhythm have been achieved,
        the director will be pleasantly surprised to find
        that his chorus has also greatly improved its dic-
        tion.

268. Morgan, H. "Keep in the Middle of the Choral Road,"
      Etude, 67:474 ff., August, 1949.
           Examples of the "keep in the middle of the road"
      policy are given in such areas as tone quality, dic-
      tion, conducting movements, and programming.

269. Mowe, Homer G. "Voice Fundamentals and the Choir
      Loft," American Guild of Organists Quarterly, 3:
      149-152, October, 1958.
           Basic principles concerning posture, attitude of
      the mind, position of the vocal organs, and co-
      ordination of the body precede a brief discussion of
      vocal attack, tone, and diction.

270. _____. "Voice Fundamentals in Relation to Choral
      Singing," Organ Institute Quarterly, 4:10-12, Sum-
      mer, 1954.
           The unchanging principles of singing, and the
      methods and devices which are used to lead the
      singer into comformity with these principles.

271. Murphy, J. F. "For the Chorus," Music Journal, 14:
      33-34, November, 1956.
           Suggestions which the author has found effective
      in the development of choral musicianship.

272. Murray, Lyn. Choral Technique Handbook. Great
      Neck, New York: The Staff Music Publishing Com-
      pany, 1956.
           A few exercises and suggestions for choral de-
      velopment.

273. Music Education Source Book. Chicago: Music Educa-
      tors National Conference, 1947.
           An extensive compilation of objectives, proce-
      dures and related material for music education
      programs from elementary school through the col-
      lege.

274. Music in American Education. Chicago: Music Edu-
      cators National Conference, 1955.
           This second music education source book includes
      statements of basic principles concerning vocal mu-
      sic in the schools.

275. Music in the Senior High School. Washington, D.C.:
      Music Educators National Conference, 1959.

The report of six committees within the MENC
Commission on "Music in the Senior High School."
The committee on vocal instruction and ensembles
in the senior high school presents the broad objectives and guiding principles of the vocal program.

276. Neidig, Kenneth and Jennings, John, editors. Choral
      Director's Guide. West Nyack, New York: Parker
      1967.
          A compilation of writings on choral development,
      literature, performance and related subjects by
      well-known choral specialists.

277. Nicholson, Sydney H. Quires and Places Where They
      Sing. London: G. Bell and Sons, 1932.
          The history, traditions, and methods of cathe-
      dral choirs.

278. Nitsche, Theodore H. "Vocal Ensembles--Small and
      Large," Music Educators National Conference Year-
      book. Vol. 30. Chicago, 1937, pp. 275-278.
          Voice classification, good tone, breathing, pos-
      ture, diction, and intonation are some of the points
      discussed.

279. Norden, N. Lindsay. "A New Theory of Untempered
      Music," (a few important features with special
      reference to a cappella music), Musical Quarterly,
      22:217-233, April, 1936.
          A discussion of just intonation and equal tem-
      perament with the conclusion that a cappella music
      must be sung in just intonation.

280. _____. "Untempered Intonation," Organ Institute
      Quarterly, 3:16-23, August, 1953.
          "A Cappella music can be sung only in un-
      tempered intonation and has always been so sung."
      The author presents a detailed comparison of Just
      Intonation and Equal Temperament. Procedures are
      given for the development of untempered intonation.

281. Nordin, D. W., editor. The Choirmaster's Workbook.
      Rock Island, Illinois: Augustana, 1947-1962.
          A workbook (volume one was printed in 1947,
      volume eight in 1962) containing articles, anthem
      lists, rehearsal schedules, attendance reports,

and other practical aids for the choir director.

282. _____. "Two Types--Which Is Your Choir?"
Choirmaster's Workbook, 3:25 ff., 1952.
   Basic suggestions for improving a choir.

283. _____. "Consonants in Singing," Choirmaster's
Workbook, 3:40 ff., 1952.
   The author classifies the consonants and illustrates graphically how many initial consonants come
   before the time of the note.

284. _____. "Developing Good Choral Tone," The Choirmaster's Workbook, 2:30, 1949.
   A brief article with positive suggestions for tone
   quality, intonation, and blend.

285. Norton, William. "Consonants and Combinations of
Vowels," Educational Music Magazine, 21:19 ff.,
January, 1942.
   Consonants are classified and described. The
   role of tone colors in expression is discussed.

286. _____. "Principles Involved in Vocal Tone Production," Educational Music Magazine, 21:14 ff.,
September, 1941.
   Head resonance and breath control are basic
   principles of good singing; develop them with
   vocalizes derived from actual music.

287. _____. "Vowels and the Singer," Educational Music
Magazine, 21:29 ff., November, 1941.
   By starting on long "E" and proceeding to the
   other vowel sounds, good projection and ring may
   be developed in the voice.

288. Oakland, L. "Live the Music Together," Educational
Music Magazine, 32:15 ff., September, 1952.
   Basically an article on interpretation in which
   the concept of the words and music is the basis
   for deciding upon the type of tone, dynamics, and
   tempo.

289. Otto, Richard. "Singing Is Big Business at this Con-
necticut High School," School Musician, 21:20,
November, 1949.
   A brief report of the activities of a choir and

its rehearsal procedure.

290. Owen, B. J. "Some Fundamentals of Better Diction, "
Choral and Organ Guide, 13:36 ff., March, 1960.
A few points on final consonants and vowel
modification.

291. Page, Ralph. "Group and Individual Singing, " School
Music, 31:5 ff., May, 1931.
Pros and cons of solo and choral singing are
given with an interesting presentation of the Italian
(freedom, natural, bright) and French (relaxes soft
palate, covered, muffled) methods of studio and
choral teaching.

292. Parthun, P. "Choral Singers and Inertia, " Music
Journal, 24:54-55, November, 1966.
Attention to the psychological needs of the singer (goals, status, achievement, identity, experience, approval, and participation) will help solve
the problem of inertia in choral singing.

293. Paul, D. "It Must Be the Weather, " Music Journal,
13:62-63, January, 1955.
A report of an experiment on the relationship
between hearing acuity and atmospheric conditions
showing that inaccuracy of pitch in singing may be
caused by the weather.

294. "Peter Wilhousky Advises Singers, " Choir Guide, 1:3,
April, 1948.
In an interview with Wilhousky, the value of
choir experience is considered. The reasons why
singers are rejected in tryouts for chorus positions
on the Toscanini broadcasts are discussed.

295. Peterson, Paul W. Natural Singing and Expressive
Conducting. Winston-Salem, North Carolina: J.
F. Blair, 1955 (rev. ed. 1966).
Three main sections of this fine book are:
fundamental techniques of singing, advanced tech-
niques for the soloists and expressive conducting.

296. _____. "Problems of Choral Blend, " National As-
sociation of Teachers of Singing Bulletin, " 8:2,
May, 1952.
Pure language sounds, trained-untrained voices,

varying speech habits, and range are considered as
factors in choral blend.

297. _____. "Tone Up Your Choir," Journal of Church
      Music, 2:9-11, September, 1960.
          To achieve an effective choral tone, singers
      must be made aware of three major areas of vocal
      activity: breathing, diction and resonance.

298. Peterson, R. J. "The Unaccompanied Choir--Its Re-
      lationship to Expressive Speech," Music Educators
      National Conference Yearbook. Vol. 30. Chicago,
      1937, pp. 278-281.
          A sincere desire to express through songs will
      give the choir important guidelines to their approach
      to tone, dynamics, diction, and intonation.

299. Phillips, C. H. Psychology and the Choir Trainer.
      London: Dent, 1936.
          The role of psychology is illustrated with prac-
      tical methods for rehearsal and performance.

300. Pierce, Edwin H. "The Final S," Etude, 50:880-881,
      December, 1932.
          The problem of precision in placing the final S
      is solved by placing it on a specific beat of the
      measure.

301. _____. "Problems of Unaccompanied Choral Sing-
      ing and How to Meet Them," New Music Review,
      29:894-896, October, 1930.
          The problems discussed include the development
      of low basses, achieving the beauty of just intona-
      tion, and the vibrato of solo voices in relation to
      ensemble blend.

302. Pierce, John W. "A Joyful Noise: Voice Registra-
      tion," Organ Institute Quarterly, 5:12, Winter,
      1955.
          A discussion of voice registers and a few
      specific suggestions for the choir director.

303. Pitts, Carol. "As Heard by the Adjudicator," Edu-
      cational Music Magazine, 18:13 ff., January, 1939.
          From her experience as an adjudicator, the
      writer makes pertinent observations concerning in-
      tonation, tone, amount of tone, color, phrasing,

rhythm, tempo, and interpretation.

304. _____. "Diction," Etude, 62:510 ff., September,
1944.
Most faults in diction consist of: (1) complete
omission of sounds, (2) careless or partial utterance of sounds, and (3) faulty linking or liaison
of sound.

305. _____. "Enunciation ... How This Choir Problem
May Be Solved by the Alert Director," Educational
Music Magazine, 14:18, January, 1935.
Faults in diction may be divided into two classes:
sounds which are omitted entirely, and sounds
which are linked over to a sound or syllable to
which they do not belong.

306. _____. "Evaluating Choral Performance," Educational Music Magazine, 14:24, March, 1935.
The points discussed are tone, breath support,
intonation, correct tempos, diction and interpretation.

307. _____. "How to Keep in Tune," Supervisors Service Bulletin, 13:16 ff., January, 1934.
The common trouble spots of scales, chords and
melodic phrases are listed with attention then focused upon tone production.

308. _____. "In Search of Tone," Educational Music
Magazine, 23:12-13 ff., November, 1943.
Rehearsal procedures for achieving good choral
breathing, blend, and intonation.

309. _____. "Intonation," Etude, 62:90, February, 1944.
Achieve "oneness" of tone in quality, pitch, and
color, and then give attention to such factors as
breathing, hearing, free tone quality, and blending
the registers.

310. _____. "Planning the Year's Work," Supervisors
Service Bulletin, 13:20, September, 1933.
A few points for the beginning of the year, in-
cluding "keeping the pitch."

311. _____. "The Secret of Tone in Choral Work,"
Etude, 62:270, May, 1944.

A detailed description of breathing and vowel
formations with many techniques for teaching.

312. _____. "Securing Correct Intonation in the Training of A Cappella Choirs," Music Supervisors National Conference Yearbook. Vol. 25. Chicago,
1932, pp. 138-139.
A discussion of the tuning of intervals, chords,
and chord progressions.

313. _____. "Tone, the Glory of a Fine Chorus,"
Etude, 62:330, June, 1944.
Emphasis is placed upon extending the range
through blending of the registers and a release of
the upper tones.

314. _____. "Spring Festival Preparation," Supervisors
Service Bulletin, 13:22 ff., March, 1934.
Program building and posture of the singers are
discussed.

315. Plott, Donald. "Choral Technics (For Small Choirs-
Diction)," Music Ministry, 8:39 ff., November,
1966.
Improve diction through attention to pure vowels,
careful pronunciation and natural consonants.

316. _____. "Choral Technics (Vocal Production),"
Music Ministry, 8:39, October, 1966.
Good singing should emphasize the open throat,
breathing and forward resonance.

317. Remington, Emily. "Psychological Flatting," Journal
of Church Music, 9:5 ff., July, 1967.
Special emphasis is placed upon the listener's
response to the text and mood of the music being
sung.

318. Rhea, Raymond. "Voice Classification--Senior High,"
Music Education in Action. Archie Jones, editor.
Boston: Allyn and Bacon, 1960, pp. 168-169.
The need for continued testing and classifica-
tions of young voices and the basic methods for
teaching choral tone.

319. Rice, William. "Choral Technics," Music Ministry,
4:35-36, July, 1963.

A discussion of exercise patterns and anthems which may be used as choral warm-ups.

320. _____. "If Your Choir in Focus?" Music Ministry, 5:10-11, May, 1964.
A review of key points (e.g., blend, diction, interpretation, balance) which make an excellent performance.

321. _____. "Young Singers: Handle with Care," Music Educators Journal, 49:75-76, June, 1963.
A description of some outstanding characteristics of high school voices and guidelines for their proper care.

322. Richards, James E. "The Ubiquitous Phonetic Antithesis!" Music Education in Action. Archie Jones, editor. Boston: Allyn and Bacon, 1960, pp. 161-167.
Vowels and consonants are discussed with basic rules for execution. Vowel modification as the pitch ascends is presented in chart form.

323. Rieder, Kathryn. "'Balancing' Choral/Vocal Parts," Choral and Organ Guide, 22:11-12, December, 1969.
The balance of choral parts may be achieved through the careful selection of voices and exercises to develop listening habits.

324. _____. "The Ambitious Choir," Music Ministry, 6:12-13, July, 1965.
Through planning an ambitious program with high standards a choir can produce musically satisfying results.

325. _____. "Streamlining Choir Rehearsal, Etude, 62: 449 ff., August, 1944.
Helpful hints including length of rehearsals, warm ups, developing a listening attitude and personnel relations.

326. Risinger, M. D. "Vocal Instruction and Ensembles in the Senior High School," Music in the Senior High School. Washington, D.C.: Music Educators National Conference, 1959, pp. 33-43.
The committee on vocal instruction and ensem-

bles in the senior high school presents the broad
objectives and guiding principles of the vocal program.

327. Roberts, D. "When the Choir Sings Out of Tune,"
      Etude, 54:48, January, 1936.
          Good intonation depends on three factors: men-
      tal, physical, and intellectual.

328. Rodby, W. A. "The Choral Folio," School Musician,
      24:21, September, 1952.
          In this first column of the monthly series, the
      author discusses girls' glee clubs and the first
      rehearsal of a school year.

329. _____ . "The Choral Folio," School Musician, 24:
      18 ff., March, 1953.
          A discussion of the "scourge of the choral
      world," intonation.

330. _____ . "The Choral Folio," School Musician, 24:
      14 ff., April, 1953.
          A continuation of the previous month's discus-
      sion of intonation with emphasis upon solving the
      program through free, unconstricted tone produc-
      tion.

331. _____ . "The Choral Folio," School Musician, 25:
      26, September, 1953.
          In this issue, the author discusses vocal exer-
      cises for the choir and gives three short exam-
      ples.

332. _____ . "The Choral Folio," School Musician, 25:
      24, November, 1953.
          A discussion of vocal exercises with two exam-
      ples given.

333. _____ . "The Choral Folio," School Musician, 26:30,
      September, 1954.
          Voice testing, its problems, and the qualities of
      voices.

334. _____ . "The Choral Folio," School Musician, 27:
      34, September, 1955.
          The arrangement of voices in the choir and its
      effect upon tone quality.

335.   _____. "The Choral Folio," School Musician, 31:
             42 ff., September, 1959.
             There is wide disagreement as to what is good
             choral tone; however, whatever the characteristics
             of the tone, it must be uniform.

336.   _____. "Concepts of Presence in Choral Tone--A
             Challenge," School Musician, 39:46 ff., March,
             1968.
             An excellent discussion of the quality of
             presence in choral sound and how it may be
             achieved. Also appears in November, 1969, issue
             of Choral Journal.

337.   _____. "Techniques of Norman Luboff," School
             Musician, 39:44-47, December, 1967.
             Rodby presents a few ideas presented by Luboff
             in a Chicago workshop.

338.   _____. "Techniques that Really Work," School
             Musician, 35:58-59, May, 1964.
             The author presents techniques used by Daniel
             Tkach of Franklin Park, Illinois.

339.   _____. "The Windup," School Musician, 34:36-37,
             June, 1963.
             Rodby describes a technique of siren hums for
             curing chesty quality and creating a head tone of
             beauty and warmth.

340.   Rosborough, J. M. "A Cappella Singing vs. Accom-
             panied Singing," Music Teachers National Associa-
             tion Proceedings for 1933. Vol. 28. Oberlin,
             1934.
             The values of accompanied and a cappella singing
             are considered with the emphasis placed on the lat-
             ter.

341.   Rossel, Deuton. "Musical Melange," Educational
             Music Magazine, 16:11, January, 1937.
             A medley of thoughts and suggestions for the
             chorus, glee club and choir.

342.   "Round Table for Choral Directors," Educational Music
             Magazine, 16:38, September, 1936.
             The questions and answers were compiled from
             discussions during sessions of the 1936 National

Summer Conference.

343. Rowlands, Leo. <u>Guide Book for Catholic Church</u>
<u>Choirmasters.</u> Boston: McLaughlin and Reilly,
1938.
Discussions of conducting and voice production
are included with procedures for singing various
services.

344. Rowles, W. L. "A Cappella Singing in High School,"
<u>School Music</u>, 35:4 ff., January, 1935.
Tone quality, intonation, diction and interpretation are the major topics discussed.

345. Sanderson, Wendell. "In Search of Tenors," <u>Educa-</u>
<u>tional Music Magazine</u>, 15:27, November, 1935.
An understanding of the vocal characteristics
of changing voices, proper training in <u>mezzo-voce</u>
tone, and eliminating the "necktie" sound are the
points of emphasis.

346. Sateren, Leland. <u>Criteria for Judging Choral Music</u>
<u>and those Straight-Tone Choirs.</u> Minneapolis:
Augsbury, 1963.
Good unisons which are a result of uniformity
of pitch, color and dynamics have been confused
with straight tones. The tone is not straight;
however, excessive vibrato is the enemy of unisons.

347. _____. <u>The Good Choir.</u> Minneapolis: Augsbury,
1963.
A brief discussion of the elements which mark
excellence in choral performance.

348. Scarmolin, A. Louis. <u>The Chorister's Daily Dozen.</u>
New York: Pro Art Publications, 1951.
Twenty pages of vocal exercises with brief
guidelines for breathing, tone production and diction.

349. Schuetz, Warren. "A Small School Can Support a
Madrigal Group," <u>Music Educators Journal</u>, 41:58
ff., 1954.
The madrigal group is discussed with emphasis
placed upon the manner of performance.

350. Scott, Charles Kennedy. <u>Madrigal Singing.</u> London:

Oxford University Press, 1931.
Polyphonic choral techniques are discussed with
a few comments on voice production.

351. _____. Word and Tone. 2 vols. London: J. M.
        Dent and Sons, 1933.
        Volume one is addressed to theoretical aspects
        of vocal development. Volume two is concerned
        with practical voice exercises.

352. Seitz, Harry. "Problems of the Choral Singer and
        Conductor," National Association of Teachers of
        Singing Bulletin, 8:12 ff., May, 1952.
        A discussion of music reading, intonation,
        balance of parts, and ensemble.

353. Shaw, Robert. "Choral Art for America," Etude,
        63:564 ff., October, 1945.
        This excellent article describes the basic opera-
        tion of the Collegiate Chorale with Shaw's empha-
        sis upon "the qualities that make a choir success-
        ful and unique," namely, clarity of enunciation,
        vitality of rhythm, and variety of tone color. Ex-
        cerpts from his weekly letters to the singers are
        included.

354. Shields, I. "Special Choral Techniques," Music Edu-
        cators National Conference Yearbook. Vol. 32.
        Chicago, 1930-40, pp. 348-352.
        Relaxation exercises, freedom of physical move-
        ment, and appeal to the imagination are some of
        the techniques discussed.

355. Short, Eleanor. "Rehearsal Routine for A Cappella
        Choir," Music Educators National Conference Year-
        book. Vol. 32. Chicago, 1939-40, pp. 359-360.

356. Simon, William. Warm Up and Sing. New York:
        Carl Fischer, Inc., 1956.
        Twelve pages of warm-up exercises with a few
        comments.

357. "Singing and Playing Intonation," School Musician, 22:
        17, June, 1951.
        Good ensemble intonation depends mainly on
        three factors: (1) correct individual intonation,
        (2) proper dynamic balance, (3) uniformity of tone

balance.

358. Smallman, John and Wilcox, E. H. The Art of A
      Cappella Singing. Philadelphia: Oliver Ditson Com-
      pany, 1933.
          A discussion of choral technique and interpreta-
      tion illustrated through sixteen compositions.

359. Smith, Gregg. "Choraliasis in America," Music Jour-
      nal, 22:32-33 ff., September, 1964.
          A comprehensive description of the author's
      philosophy of choral music with attention to the
      major problems and weaknesses of the profession.

360. Spouse, A. "Voice Training Classes as a Basis for
      High School Choirs," Music Educators National
      Conference Yearbook. Vol. 27. Chicago, 1934, pp.
      149-151.
          The newer choral trend, with its demands for
      greater vocal ability makes formal voice training
      in high schools a necessity.

361. Staples, H. J. Choirmaster and Organist. London:
      The Epworth Press, 1939.
          A book of basic procedures in two parts: part
      one discusses the choirmaster, part two, the or-
      ganist. The choirmaster section included discus-
      sion of rehearsals, pitch, time and rhythm, tone,
      expression, enunciation, choir management, reper-
      tory and secular work.

362. Steck, G. H. "An Adventure in Choral Conducting,"
      School Musician, 11:8 ff., March, 1940.
          The author describes the various "mixed-up"
      standing arrangements which he uses with his choir
      and the advantages of such arrangements.

363. _____. "What Do Judges Expect from Singers?"
      Educational Music Magazine, 22:29 ff., September,
      1942.
          Judges expect evidence of the culmination of the
      year's work with essential attributes of intellectual
      and emotional capacity, vocal and dynamic range,
      and scope of tone quality and color.

364. Steckel, Edwin. "Improving the Boys' Glee Club,"
      Educational Music Magazine, 14:18-19, November,

1934.
Voice classes are recommended for high school
students and procedures for posture, tone quality,
and range are given.

365. Stewart, Albert. "Concerning Women's Choruses,"
      Music Journal, 13:21, October, 1955.
      A few helpful suggestions concerning the major
      weaknesses of women's choruses.

366. Stoessel, Albert. "Problems in Choral Singing,"
      Etude, 61:440 ff., July, 1943.
      A brief historical background of choral singing
      in America leading to practical suggestions con-
      cerning the selection of singers and the type of
      music to be performed.

367. Stone, J. B. "A Glimpse into a Rehearsal Conducted
      by Robert Shaw with the University of Kansas
      Chorale," American Music Teacher, 5:13, January,
      1956.
      A student MTNA member describes a few fea-
      tures of the rehearsal of Bach's St. John Passion,
      conducted by Robert Shaw.

368. Stone, Leonard. Belwin Chorus Builder, Volume I.
      Rockville Centre: Belwin, 1961.
      Basic techniques for developing rhythm, tone,
      pitch, diction, dynamics and phrasing.

369. _____. Belwin Chorus Builder, Volume II. Rock-
      ville Centre: Belwin, 1962.
      A more advanced version of volume one plus
      discussions of harmony, balance and blend.

370. Strickler, David. "Choral Technics (Don't Say It:
      Sing It!)," Music Ministry, 6:37, March, 1965.
      In communicating the illusive concepts of the
      choral art, don't talk, demonstrate by example.

371. Strickling, George F. "Building a High School Choir,"
      Etude, 64:258 ff., May, 1946.
      The basic organization and philosophy of the
      Cleveland Heights High School Choir are presented
      by its founder and director.

372. _____. "Diction - Diction - Diction," Etude, 64:

318 ff., June, 1946.
Fine diction makes for fine singing. A summary
of key points and pitfalls is given.

373. _____. "Ship or Sheep?" Educational Music Magazine, 31:25 ff., September, 1951.
Emphasize the consonants and do not distort the
normal pronunciation of the word. Many problem
words are used as illustrations.

374. Sunderman, Lloyd F. "Are There Secrets to Choral
Success?" Educational Music Magazine, 31:21 ff.,
September, 1951.
If there are secrets to choral success, and
there are, then very few directors pursue them
with the necessary idealism.

375. _____. "Choir Technics for Success," Educational
Music Magazine, 26:29 ff., September, 1946.
Testing and classifying voices, breathing and
attack, and diction are the three main topics discussed.

376. _____. Some Techniques for Choral Success.
Rockville Centre, L.I., New York: Belwin, Inc.,
1952.
Chapters two and three are "Singing and Speaking" and "Tone Production." The remainder of the
book is concerned with organization, conducting,
and rehearsal techniques.

377. Sur and Schuller. Music Education for Teen Agers.
New York: Harper and Brothers, 1958.
The many activities of the high school music
programs are presented.

378. Swan, Howard. "The Lost Art of Inspiration," Choral
Journal, 9:5-9, January, 1969.
A challenging presentation of our heritage of
choral practice, our present opportunities, and
inspiring guidelines for personal growth.

379. _____. "Style, Performance Practice and Choral
Tone," Choral Journal, 6:12-13, July, 1966.
As we become aware of style and performance
practice we will be able to make better choices
concerning repertoire and the type of tone used by

our singers.

380.   Swarm, Paul. Guideposts for the Church Musician.
       Decatur, Illinois: Church Music Foundation, 1955.
       A practical guide for the organist and choir di-
       rector including a short chapter on training the
       choir.

381.   Swift, F. F. Fundamentals of Conducting. Rockville
       Centre, New York: Belwin, 1961.
       A brief coverage of many aspects of conducting,
       both choral and instrumental.

382.   _____. "Let's Let Our Choirs Sing, " School Mu-
       sician, 23:19-20, September, 1951.
       A discussion of the proper role of techniques
       and exercises in the choral rehearsal with a list
       of fundamental guidelines for the inexperienced
       teacher.

383.   _____. "Songs Without Words, " School Musician,
       21:11, January, 1950.
       The "Christmas choral season" is the point of
       departure for some ideas to improve diction.

384.   _____. "Voice Classification, " School Musician,
       20:15 ff., December, 1948.
       A few points concerning voice classification.

385.   _____. "On Intonation, " School Musician, 20:20,
       March, 1949.
       A list and discussion of causes of flatting in
       choirs.

386.   _____. "Wild Pitch, " School Musician, 22:23,
       1950.
       A brief article on intonation with some advice
       for making improvements.

387.   Sydnor, James. "Choral Technics (Choir Words
       Understood), " Music Ministry, 6:31, February,
       1965.
       A discussion of the vowel, its duration, color
       and correctness.

388.   _____. "Choral Technics (Choral Craftsmanship), "
       Music Ministry, 6:31, October, 1964.

A brief presentation of the choral craft: pitch, rhythm, tone quality and diction.

389.   . The Training of Church Choirs. Nashville: Abingdon Press, 1963.
The author discusses the choir, the director, the literature and emphasizes rehearsal procedures and techniques.

390. Tallman, Harold. "Creating a Balance through 'Tonal Consciousness'," Supervisors Service Bulletin, 13: 22, November, 1933.
Listening skills, and the development of low bass and high tenor range are the key points of this discussion.

391. Thomas, Hugh. "Choral Technics (The Choral Instrument)," Music Ministry, 9:40, June, 1968.
Improve choral singing by elimination of the prejudiced and habitual approaches to diction.

392.   . "Choral Technics (Rehearsal)," Music Ministry, 9:40, May, 1960.
Attention to the key of the music and acoustics as deterrants to good choral intonation and sound.

393. Thomas, Kurt. "The Choral Rehearsal," American Choral Review, 5:2-5, No. 4, 1963.
Translated from Handbucher der Musiklehre, this article discusses basic rehearsal problems and procedures.

394.   . "The Formation of a Chorus," American Choral Review, 9:4-5, No. 1, 1966.
Translated from Lehrbuch der Chorleitung, the emphasis is upon the quality and range of choral voices.

395.   . "Problems of Intonation," American Choral Review, 10:121-124, No. 3, 1968.
A short discussion of the many causes of poor intonation as translated from Lehrbuch der Chorleitung.

396. Titus, P. "Neglected Consonants in Choral Art," Etude, 54:799, December, 1936.
A short article asking for the clear and simul-

taneous enunciation of consonants.

397. Tkach, Peter. Vocal Artistry. Park Ridge, Illinois:
      Neil A. Kjos Music Co., 1950.
      One hundred and thirty-two vocalises, drills and
      songs emphasizing rhythmic development and en-
      semble technics. Student book and teacher's manu-
      al.

398. _____. Vocal Technic. Park Ridge, Illinois: Neil
      A. Kjos Music Co., 1948.
      A fundamental course in voice and sightsinging
      for individual or ensemble singing. Student book
      and teacher's manual.

399. Treggor, P. "Can Warm-Ups for Choirs Build Good,
      Dependable Tone?" Diapason, 47:8, August, 1956.
      Breathing, pitch and tone quality exercises are
      discussed. The choral conductor should not at-
      tempt to give group voice lessons under the guise
      of warm-up exercises.

400. Tritchler, William. "Choral Music in Industry, "
      Music Journal, 5:25, January, 1947.
      A description of the activities in the recreational
      program of the Goodyear Tire and Rubber Company.

401. Ullemeyer, Grace. "'I Resolve' ... Says the Glee
      Club Director, " Educational Music Magazine, 14:
      22, January, 1935.
      The new year brings resolutions for the director
      and the ensemble.

402. Urang, Gunnar. Church Music ... for the Glory of
      God. Moline, Illinois: Christian Service Founda-
      tion, 1956.
      Worship in music, congregational singing, music
      in Christian education, the choir, "special" music,
      the place of the pastor, and studies in church music
      are the seven parts of this book.

403. Vail, J. S. "Dicshun, " Educational Music Magazine,
      32:22-24, March, 1953.
      This discussion of diction includes pictures of
      correct and incorrect mouth formations, and ad-
      vice ranging from special manipulations to basic
      principles.

404.   Van Bodegraven, Paul and Wilson, Harry R.   School
       Music Conductor.   Chicago: Hall and McCreary,
       1942.
            The problems and practices in choral and in-
       strumental conducting including one chapter on the
       choral rehearsal.

405.   Vandre, Carol (Richard Scott).   Sevenfold Choral
       Method.   Milwaukee: Handy-Folio Music Co., 1960.
            Exercises, rounds, and songs are given with
       accompanying instructions.

406.   _____.   The Well Trained Choir.   Milwaukee:
       Handy-Folio Music Co., 1958.
            Twenty pages of very basic drills and comment.

407.   Veld, Henry, "Choral Conducting," Music Teachers
       National Association Proceedings for 1934.   Vol.
       29.   Oberlin, 1935, pp. 46-56.
            A fine discussion of the a cappella choir, its
       development, philosophy, procedures, and conductor.

408.   _____.   "Effects of Choral Singing on the Solo
       Voice," Music Teachers National Association Pro-
       ceedings for 1948.   Vol. 43.   Pittsburgh, 1949,
       pp. 286-291.
            The qualities of fine choral singing are listed
       and followed by the values to the individual voice
       student of participating in such ensembles.

409.   _____.   "Good Choral Blend Relies Upon Proper
       Vocal Technique," Diapason, 47:16, October, 1956.
            Vocal blend will result from adherences to
       basic principles involving (1) the preparation (pos-
       ture, breathing, mental), (2) the attack, and (3)
       the vessel (clear mental concept of the phonetic
       sound).

410.   _____.   "Some Practical Thoughts on Choral
       Singing," Music Teachers National Association Pro-
       ceedings for 1936.   Vol. 31.   Oberlin, 1937, pp.
       180-181.
            A brief statement stressing the need for daily
       application of a method and correct principles to
       achieve better standards of choral singing.

411.   Vennard, William.   "Good Choral Tone," Music Edu-

cation in Action. Archie Jones, editor. Boston:
Allyn and Bacon, 1960, pp. 156-158.
   A concise statement of principles of choral tone
and exercises for its development.

412.   Votow, L. "Choral Intonation," Music Supervisors
          Journal, 17:50, October, 1931.
          Causes of poor choral intonation.

413.   Walls, Robert. "Appreciation through Performance,"
          Educational Music Magazine, 17:13, March, 1938.
          Singers should express the musical idea through
word, gesture, and a sympathetic tone quality
which grows out of the creative imagination of an
inspired group.

414.   Ward, A. E. Music Education for High Schools. New
          York: The American Book Co., 1941.
          The secondary school music program is dis-
cussed with chapters on general chorus singing, the
glee clubs, and choirs.

415.   Waring, Fred. "Capitalizing Your Musical Ability,"
          Etude, 66:21 ff., April, 1948.
          The operation of Waring's Shawnee-on-Delaware
is the essence of this article with emphasis upon
the operation of Shawnee Music Workshops.

416.   _____. "Choral Singing Is Growing Up," Education-
          al Music Magazine, 23:8-9, March, 1944.
          The author traces the development of his group
from the Penn State campus to its radio and film
successes. His basic philosophy of the "the song's
the thing" and the use of "tone-syllables" are explained.

417.   _____. "The Music America Wants," Etude, 63:
          65 ff., February, 1945.
          The history of Waring's organization and key
points of his musical-business philosophy.

418.   _____. "Radio: A Teacher of Music," Music Edu-
          cators Journal, 30:22 ff., February, 1944.
          Radio has made signification contributions to
teaching, namely in the areas of (1) musical effects made possible by new uses of voices and instruments, (2) choral techniques, and (3) program

building.

419. _____. "The Song Is the Thing," <u>Music Publishers</u>
Journal, 1:5, July, 1943.
The author suggests that through sincerity of
purpose and a tremendous desire to "put over the
song" his group has been successful with the radio
audience.

420. _____. <u>Tone Syllables</u>. Delaware Water Gap.
Pennsylvania: Shawnee Press, Inc., 1945.
An eight-page booklet explaining the tone syllable
method of diction.

421. _____. "The 'Vochestra'--A New Musical Combination," <u>Etude</u>, 63:125 ff., March, 1945.
A discussion of tonal balance and color as they
are employed in combinations of voices and instruments.

422. Werder, Richard, editor. <u>Specialized Activities in</u>
<u>Music Education</u>. Washington: Catholic University
of America Press, 1956.
The report of the 1955 summer music education
workshop at the Catholic University of America.

423. Wetzler, Robert. "Build a Better Choir," <u>Journal of</u>
<u>Church Music</u>, 3:2, November, 1961.
The author praises the midwestern choral tradition started by F. M. Christiansen and carried on
by the St. Olaf, Concordia, and Augsburg College
Choirs. He discusses the "principles involved in
building choirs of this tradition."

424. Whaley, J. C. "Is Your Chorus Ready for the Contest?" <u>Music Educators Journal</u>, 38:26-28, February, 1952.
A summary of some of the most common errors
made by choral groups and some helpful techniques.

425. Whikehart, Lewis. "Choral Technics," <u>Music Ministry</u>,
9:39, November, 1967.
A description of chorister "types" and suggestions for blending the various qualities.

426. White, Arnott J. "The Collegiate Chorale--to Democ-
racy through Singing," <u>Music Publishers Journal</u>,

1:6, May, 1943.
The story of Robert Shaw and his singers in the
Collegiate Chorale as told by one of the members
of the chorale.

427. Whittlesey, F. L. A Comprehensive Program of
      Church Music. Philadelphia: Westminster Press,
      1957.
      Part one of this book is devoted to discussions
      of the various church choirs. Part two is entitled
      music and worship. The consideration of two ap-
      proaches to the teaching of voice production, name-
      ly, physical and phonetic, is of special interest.

428. Widoe, R. "Amateur vs. Professional Standards in
      Choral Singing," Music Journal, 13:19 ff., Septem-
      ber, 1955.
      A strong statement against "technique happy"
      choralists who become obsessed with problems of
      intonation, blend, and diction, but who do not pro-
      ject the real expressive quality of music.

429. Wilcox, John C. "'Straight Tone' in Singing," Music
      Educators Journal, 32:62-63, November, 1943.
      A statement by the Chicago Singing Teachers
      Guild expresses their firm disapproval of the use
      of "straight tones" and states their conviction that
      the "straight tone" is not necessary to secure a
      perfect blend of unison voices.

430. Wilhousky, Peter. "Choral Conducting," Music Edu-
      cators National Conference Yearbook, Vol. 30.
      Chicago, 1937, pp. 286-288.
      Observations concerning the training of the
      choral conductor with attention given to such
      factors as inspiration, dynamics, tone, diction,
      rhythm, balance of parts, and baton technique.

431. _____. "Choral Problems and Choral Clinics,"
      Etude, 72:9 ff., September, 1954.
      The author tells how he works with groups in
      choral clinics: the problems to be solved, and
      basic procedures for solving them.

432. _____. "The Professional Chorister," Music Jour-
      nal, 5:8 ff., January, 1947.
      The demands which are made of the professional

chorister.

433. Williams, Julian. "Success with the Volunteer Choir,"
     Educational Music Magazine, 16:52, January, 1937.
          Some problems and helpful suggestions pertain-
     ing to the volunteer church choir are discussed.

434. Williamson, John F. "Balance the Voices," Etude,
     68:23 ff., May, 1950.
          Each singer must desire to create a choral
     structure that is architecturally beautiful. The
     role of each section is explained.

435. _____. "The Conductor's Magic," Etude, 69:23 ff.,
     April, 1951.
          Among the points of conducting technique dis-
     cussed in this article, the author states that "mood
     makes for correct breathing and correct breathing
     gives us the pace" of the music.

436. _____. "Correct Breathing for Singers," Etude,
     69:18 ff., February, 1951.
          Elaborate and complex theories are not neces-
     sary, but there is a need for a basic understand-
     ing of the use and importance of oxygen and the
     manner in which sound vibrations are set in motion,
     but not carried on the breath.

437. _____. "Correct Breathing for Singers," Etude, 69:
     22 ff., March, 1951.
          The secret of correct normal breathing lies in
     good posture and breathing for the mood which the
     singers expect to create.

438. _____. "Essentials of the Choral Conductor's Tech-
     nique," Supervisors Service Bulletin, 10:3, March,
     1931.
          Emphasis is placed upon an expressive approach
     to vowel colors, breathing and consonants.

439. _____. "Good Singing Requires Good Diction,"
     Etude, 69:23 ff., September, 1951.
          A basic approach to good diction is presented:
     be aware of the sounds within the words and make
     each phrase a legato line in which every sound is
     present in its relative value.

440. _____. "How to Classify Voices," Etude, 68:23 ff.,
June, 1950.
We can only classify voices accurately, (1) when
we decide whether the quality is absolutely natural
or affected; (2) when we concede that the range in
most voices is rather wide and does not tell us
too much about classification; and (3) when we
learn to recognize the lift in the voice.

441. _____. "The Importance of Vowel Coloring," Etude,
69:23 ff., October, 1951.
The choir must become sensitive to the many
color shadings of vowels if correct pronunciation
is to be achieved and the proper mood established.

442. _____. "Keep Your Choir Up to Pitch," Etude, 68:
14 ff., December, 1950.
Singing in tune is the result of knowing and
obeying fundamental laws of sound. Among them
are the need of oxygen, correct posture, memory
of intervals, and untempered tuning.

443. _____. "Make Friends with Acoustics; They Can
Make or Break Fine Choral Tone," Etude, 68:22,
November, 1950.
The author explains the acoustical laws which
support the balance of the Westminster Choir.
"When frequency doubles, energy squares." "When
amplitude doubles, energy squares."

444. _____. "Planning a Choir Rehearsal," Etude, 69:
18 ff., May, 1951.
For best results, each step of the rehearsal
should be carefully planned in advance.

445. _____. "Rhythm Makes the Music Go," Etude, 69:
18 ff., January, 1951.
The most difficult task the choir director faces
is that of making his choir sing in correct time
and yet keep the music moving forward in phrase
patterns. Vigorous tapping of the rhythms is ad-
vocated.

446. _____. "The Saga of the Westminster Choir,"
Etude, 61:501 ff., August, 1943.
The history, philosophy and successes of the
Westminster Choir presented by its founder and

conductor.

447.   . "The Technique of Choral Procedure,"
Music Supervisors National Conference Yearbook.
Vol. 24. Chicago, 1931, pp. 167-171.
An analysis of the vocal problems of the North
Central High School Chorus. The author stresses
breath control through emotional control, tone
production based upon vowel color, the importance
of consonants and their problems, and the fallacy
of the wide-open mouth.

448.   . "Training of the Individual Voice through
Choral Singing," Music Teachers National Association Proceedings for 1938. Vol. 33. Oberlin,
1939, pp. 52-59.
Breathing, tone, diction, rhythm, and interpretation are found, not through imposing shapes and
techniques, but as an outgrowth of creating the
mood of music.

449. Wilson, Harry R. "Artistic Choral Singing," Educational Music Magazine, 33:14-15 ff., November,
1953.
The author discusses the need for more emphasis upon style in choral singing attained through the
technique of appropriate diction (legato, marcato,
staccato), and good choral tone.

450.   . Artistic Choral Singing. New York: G.
Schirmer, Inc., 1959.
A complete coverage of choral teaching concepts
and procedures including many musical examples.

451.   , edited, arranged, and composed by. A
Choral Digest. New York: Paul Pioneer Music
Corp., 1953.
A collection of sacred and secular compositions
from early choral music to the present. Suggestions for the development of good choral tone are
included.

452.   . Choral Program Series, Guide for Choral
Conductors. New York: Silver Burdette Company,
1950.
Part one of this guide discusses how to conduct,
how to develop voices, and how to build programs.

Part two contains interpretative suggestions for the
Choral Program Series.

453. _____. "The Connection of Vowels." Choral and
Organ Guide, 5:18-20 ff., November, 1952.
The emphasis in this article is upon the altering
of vowels for high tones. Procedures for female
and male voices are given and "pure" vowels and
diphthongs are discussed.

454. _____. "Establishing the Resonance," Choral and
Organ Guide, 5:17 ff., February, 1952; 5:13 ff.,
March, 1952.
Part one covers posture and free vocal produc-
tion. Part two gives exercises for developing the
singing resonance.

455. _____. "The Formation of Vowels," Choral and
Organ Guide, 5:20 ff., October, 1952.
Procedures and pictures for the formation of
correct vowels.

456. _____. "How to Develop Choir Voices," Choir
Guide, 4:16-18 ff., May, 1951; 4:10-14 ff., June,
1951.
The May article includes posture, the singing
tone, and vowels. The June article discusses diction, breathing, flexibility, developing high notes,
flatting and the vibrato or tremolo.

457. _____. "How to Rehearse," Choir Guide, 4:18-20,
April, 1951.
This article discusses when and how long to rehearse, rehearsal procedures, and plans for learning the music.

458. _____. Music in the High School. New York:
Silver Burdett Company, 1941.
Three chapters are of special interest: the
general chorus, selected groups, and the voice
class.

459. _____. "What!--Another Voice Book?" Choir
Guide, 4:31-34, December, 1951.
The first of a series of articles presenting the
author's "latest thoughts on voice production."

460. _____. "What Is Wrong with the Singing in our
      Schools?" The Music Journal, 5:7 ff., January,
      1947.
            An attempt to correct some of the thin, breathy,
      devitalized singing in our schools by suggesting
      procedures for developing good full-bodied vigorous
      tone.

461. _____, and Lyall, Jack Lawrence. Building A
      Church Choir. Minneapolis: Hall and McCreary
      Company, 1957.
            Specific procedures for organizing and training
      the church choir.

462. Winslow, Robert. "Cultivating the Male Voice,"
      Educational Music Magazine, 25:24-25 ff., Novem-
      ber, 1945.
            The author deals with the male voice in four
      stages: pre-school, child voice, adolescent voice,
      and the changed voice. The latter section empha-
      sizes the mezzo-voce tone and the use of "cover."

463. _____. "Male Vocal Problems in the Secondary
      School," Music Educators Journal, 32:58 ff.,
      March, 1946.
            Tone quality, range, and intonation are discussed
      with specific procedures recommended.

464. Wodell, F. W. "Taking Some Bunk Out of Vocal
      Teaching in the Public Schools," Music Supervisors
      National Conference Yearbook. Vol. 24. Chicago,
      1931, pp. 92-98.
            The author criticizes some of the extreme prac-
      tice in vocal teaching and emphasizes the value of
      qualified teachers.

465. Woodgate, L. The Choral Conductor. London:
      Ascherburg, Hopwood and Crew, 1949.
            Diction and intonation are the aspect of choral
      technique emphasized in this book on conducting.

466. _____. Chorus Master. London: Ascherberg, 1944.
            The choral techniques of an English conductor
      of oratorio societies.

467. Woods, Glen. Ensemble Intonation. Chicago: Music
      Products Corp., 1937.

A fifty-eight page book of exercises and songs to improve the intonation, tone, and "unisonality" of ensembles.

468.   . "On Voice Range," Educational Music Magazine, 20:48-49, March, 1941.
Test the voices, balance the parts, and develop the tone and range of the singers through vocal exercises.

469. Wright, E. Basic Choirtraining. Croydon: Royal School of Church Music, 1956.
Section headings include breathing, tone production, stance, vowels, blend, balance, unaccompanied practices, rhythm and phrasing, and expression.

470. Wyatt, Larry. "Blend in Choral Sound," Choral Journal, 8:15-18, September, 1967.
A report of research concerning the role and importance of vowels in the blend of choral tone.

471.   . "Factors Related to Choral Blend," Choral Journal, 8:22-23, March, 1968.
The results of a questionnaire sent to over 100 well known choral conductors.

472.   . "Factors Related to Choral Blend - Tone Quality, Vibrato, Intonation," Choral Journal, 8: 7-9, November, 1967.
Statements by choral writers concerning factors related to blend.

473. Young, P. M. A Handbook of Choral Technique. London: D. Dobson, 1953.
Choral techniques of the English choral societies are illustrated by referring to excerpts in oratorio literature.

474. Young, Ruth. "Sing Unto the Lord," Journal of Church Music, 2:6-8, June, 1960.
Some simple suggestions for the improvement of choral tone.

475. Zimmerman, Alex. "Vocal Music in the School," Music in American Education. Chicago: Music Educators National Conference, 1955, pp. 205-208.

Statements of basic vocal principles as reported by the Music Educators National Conference committee on vocal music in the high school.

INDEX